D0248579

CHURCH FURNISHING & DECORATION
in England & Wales

Gerald Randall

B T Batsford Ltd London

To those incumbents who lock their churches
    and hide the key,
thus proclaiming that God is not at home to visitors,
    this volume is dedicated
in the hope that it may help to persuade them to change their minds.

First published 1980
© Gerald Randall 1980

Filmset in Monophoto Ehrhardt by
Servis Filmsetting Ltd, Manchester

Printed by
The Anchor Press Ltd, Tiptree, Essex
for the Publishers B.T. Batsford Ltd
4 Fitzhardinge Street,
London W1H 0AH

ISBN 0 7134 3382 5

Contents

List of Illustrations

Acknowledgments

The following are the owners of the copyright of the illustrations, and have kindly permitted their use:
Architect and Building News 44
James Austin 154, 184
G. Barnes 129, 254
G. Barnes/National Monuments Record 80
Barton Photographers, Axbridge 153
British Museum 253
J.R. Cordrey and St Peters, Ravenshead 11
Country Life 179
Courtauld Institute of Art 14, 136, 141, 164, 173, 218, 244, 263
Christopher Dalton 7, 155
Dean and Chapter of Chichester: 161; with Colin Westwood; Hare & Potter and Geoffrey Clarke: 81
The Duke of Bedford 226
English Counties Periodicals Ltd 158
Fine Art Engravers Ltd 175
Fisk Moore Studios, Canterbury 180
Leonard and Marjorie Gayton 40, 61, 115, 183
S.A. Jeavons 75
G. Kelsey 255
A.F. Kersting 1, 3, 19, 39, 41, 45, 51, 60, 71, 82, 89, 94, 101, 128, 133, 138, 142, 159, 160, 168, 169, 172, 186, 194, 205, 206, 209, 212, 215, 216, 221, 222, 224, 225, 236, 237, 245, 246, 256, 261
W. Maitland/National Monuments Record 38
Eric de Maré 46, 217
Eric G. Meadows 35
Metropolitan Museum of Art, New York 143
Philip Mockridge 109
Henry Moore OM 247

National Monuments Record 4, 8, 17, 42, 49, 66, 85, 98, 102, 149, 151, 162, 171, 174, 177, 182, 185, 187, 208, 226, 230, 233, 234, 235, 252, 254
Sydney W. Newbery 20, 250
Oxford City Library 185
Penguin Books (photo Walter Scott) 195
Herbert Pickwell 106
RCAHM (Wales) 157
Rushworth and Dreaper (photo Stewart Bale) 251
Salisbury Times and Journal series 196
School of Fine Arts, University of East Anglia 68, 188
Walter Scott 148
The late Edwin Smith 6, 9, 10, 25, 37, 47, 48, 59, 62, 67, 90, 170, 262
E.S. Taylor 50, 78, 91, 165, 229
Stanley Travers and Partners 260
P.D. Turner 152, 181, 213, 239
Victoria and Albert Museum 198, 241, 242, 243
Reece Winstone 63, 99, 130, 203
G. Bernard Wood 72
Laurence Whistler 193

The following photographs are from the publishers' collection: 2, 5, 12, 13, 15, 16, 18, 21, 22, 23, 24, 26, 27, 28, 29, 30, 31, 32, 33, 34, 36, 43, 52, 53, 54, 55, 56, 57, 58, 64, 65, 69, 70, 73, 74, 76, 77, 79, 83, 84, 86, 87, 88, 92, 93, 95, 96, 97, 100, 101, 103, 104, 105, 107, 108, 110, 111, 112, 113, 114, 116, 117, 118, 119, 120, 121, 122, 123, 124, 125, 126, 127, 131, 132, 134, 135, 136, 137, 139, 140, 144, 145, 146, 147, 150, 156, 163, 166, 167, 176, 178, 197, 199, 200, 201, 202, 204, 207, 210, 211, 214, 219, 220, 223, 227, 228, 231, 232, 238, 248, 249, 257, 258, 259

Preface

A year or two ago I was asked to take some evening classes on English Church Furniture, and when I drew up a booklist for students it was brought home to me that there was no up-to-date general historical introduction to the subject. This book is an attempt to fill the gap. Although it has been written partly with students in mind, it is designed just as much for the increasing number of people who are interested in the history of their local church and the even larger number of people for whom looking round churches is a natural part of a holiday or a Sunday afternoon drive.

I have not, alas, been able to see everything mentioned in the book, but I have worked from a first-hand knowledge of over a thousand of the more interesting churches, kept fresh in my memory by piles of guidebooks and several thousand slides. I have also had full access to the publishers' unique photographic archives, so that in most cases an article has been described with a picture of it in front of me.

The photographs used as illustrations span a period of more than half a century. Some of the oldest, and even a few of the more recent, show arrangements which have since been altered. They have been chosen deliberately. For example, Plates 42 and 157 show the original settings of the pieces concerned, while Plate 223 shows an important work now unfortunately destroyed. Conversely, other photographs have been taken specially for this book, in some cases, such as Plates 68 and 109, showing the effect of recent restoration work which has brought to light previously invisible details of painting.

It is difficult to be consistent about county names. Existing literature generally uses the historic counties, and some of the new administrative units bear little relation to anything outside the structure of local government. When the G.P.O. and the M.C.C. admit the death of Middlesex, when a native of Hull no longer considers himself to be a Yorkshireman, and Mancunians and Liverpudlians no longer feel Lancastrian, then the time will have come to abandon the old boundaries, even in a historical context. But since new road maps use the new boundaries, new county names, where applicable, are given in brackets in the index. The problem is slightly different in Wales, where the new regions have historic justification and may well come to command more loyalty than the old counties. Old counties have still been used, though, mainly because some of the regions are so large that it is difficult to locate a small village within them. I have preferred the Welsh 'Gwent' to the English 'Monmouthshire' because that county is now officially part of Wales, not of England.

Among the many who have helped me, I should like particularly to thank the Editor, Sam Carr, without whose support this book would not have been written; Ian Chilvers, sometime Picture Editor of Batsford, who was wonderfully patient with my changing ideas, and untiring in his search for the right photograph; and the photographers who made special journeys to take some of them. I am also grateful to Ian Chilvers, John Newman, and Benedict Read for reading part or all of the text, making useful suggestions, correcting errors,

and helping to compile the bibliography. Pauline Plummer generously discussed with me recent restorations of medieval paintings on wood, of which her own splendid work at Ranworth and Burnham Norton is illustrated. Needless to say, such errors as may remain are entirely my own responsibility.

Finally I must thank all those incumbents who, in days of thefts and vandalism, still have the faith and courage to leave their churches open, or to say where the key may be obtained. As keepers of a church key ourselves, my wife and I have found the inconveniences so minor that it is difficult to accept that any parish would be unable to make adequate arrangements. It can be bitterly disappointing to travel a long way to see a particular church, only to be unable to get in, and it is seldom possible to make arrangements in advance when one is on tour and last-minute decisions have to be made in the light of time available and weather conditions. I would also ask a small minority of incumbents to reconsider their prejudices against amateur photographers. Pirated postcards are rarely likely to be commercial enough to tempt the fly boys, whereas both amateur and professional art and architectural historians need a permanent photographic record. Few such, I venture to suggest, will fail to express their gratitude through the freewill offertory box.

Chapter 1

Introduction

In any historical survey of the contents of churches in England and Wales, the Reformation is a watershed, for while more medieval fabrics remain here than in any other country, the Reformation fundamentally changed the way people practised their religion and the accoutrements they needed for it. Much of what had previously been most deeply venerated and most dearly treasured was cast out, mutilated or destroyed as encouraging idolatry and superstition. There had been periods of destruction before, but they were usually due to accidents of warfare, not to theological conviction armed with political power, and their effects tended to be local or regional rather than national.

Even when the Norman conquerors rebuilt and re-equipped first the cathedral and abbey churches, then most of the parish churches within little more than a century of their arrival, they always sought to replace, bigger and better, what they felt to have been the inadequate efforts of their subjects, whom Paul of Caen, first Norman abbot of St Albans, had described as 'rudes et idiotas'. Doubtless much high-quality work was lost, for the Anglo-Saxons bred fine artists and craftsmen, as small quantities of surviving manuscripts, ivories, metalwork and stone carvings show. But in some respects at least the change was for the better, as greater wealth became available, and new styles and techniques were imported from the Continent sooner and with greater conviction than would otherwise have been the case. The decline in sculptural sensitivity from Saxon empathy to Romanesque impassivity was perhaps inevitable anyway, and English craftsmen seem to have shown little reluctance to adapt to new ways, especially as the scale of the works must have increased their prosperity. By the early twelfth century so well had the new lessons been learned that while men trained in the old tradition were still producing such masterworks as the Lazarus panels at Chichester, the master mason at Durham – and whether he was English or Norman matters little – was capable of revolutionary, large-scale technical innovation.

The Reformation was quite a different matter. Within the space of 17 years between 1536 and 1553, all the monasteries were dissolved and their churches pillaged, chantries were dissolved, shrines were robbed, and virtually all images destroyed or decapitated, especially the Great Rood, previously the dominant feature of every nave, which vanished everwhere practically without trace. Many altars were ejected and their plate melted down; paintings of all sorts were lime-washed, and most rood-lofts were dismantled together with many screens. Most Easter sepulchres disappeared, and even some fonts and tombs were destroyed. Much if not most coloured glass was smashed. Moreover, a great deal which managed to escape this ferocious onslaught fell to the Puritans a century later. Replacements in the later sixteenth century were meagre. Wooden communion tables replaced the stone altars, more benches appeared in some naves, new tombs were made, a few pulpits, fewer fonts, and an occasional set of altar rails. Sometimes wall-texts replaced the medieval figure paintings, but there was very little else till after 1600. In architecture too, the emphasis had swung to building the great houses of the new families of consequence, and, towards the end of the century, to the houses and cottages of the less well-to-do; the number of surviving Elizabethan churches can be counted on one's fingers.

Consequently not one medieval church interior now looks remotely as it did in its heyday. While for every generation after 1580 there are ensembles complete enough to be readily evocative of their period, to visualize what a medieval church looked like in its prime we have to piece together evidence from a large number of different places, and even then the jigsaw is incomplete. However, there are still a few pre-Reformation buildings where enough has survived to give the informed imagination a fair start.

The chancel of Hawton, Nottinghamshire, was built and sumptuously fitted out at the expense of Sir Robert de Compton about 1320–30. On the north side are Sir Robert's tomb, a vestry doorway, and the richest Easter sepulchre in England (166); on the south, a double piscina and triple sedilia, all lushly carved. At Heckington, Lincolnshire, there is a very similar set of chancel fittings paid for by Richard de

Potesgrave the Rector, at about the same time. In both places the stonework has completely lost its painting and gilding, and the wall-painting, glass and altar furniture also have to be supplied mentally. These chancels are, indeed, little more than the beautiful ghosts of what they once were, and the same is true of almost all the medieval stonework and much of the woodwork that we possess.

The choir of St David's Cathedral was furnished in the fourteenth and fifteenth centuries. The pulpitum was the gift of Bishop Gower, who died in 1347 and was buried in it. He also gave the bishop's throne, though this was remodelled in the succeeding century when the choir stalls with their excellent misericords were put in. There is a peculiarly enclosed feeling because the eastern end is also screened off, to divide choir from presbytery, and this screen, too, is medieval, though it was apparently not made for its present position.

Bovey Tracey, Devon, has a wealth of fifteenth-century fittings, some of them given by Lady Margaret Beaufort, mother of Henry VII, though it is not certain which. The rood screen sometimes attributed to her generosity has also been dated 1427, 14 years before she was born, and the stone pulpit is very similar in style. The font, the parclose screens, and the stalls with their misericords could all be later, and the brass eagle lectern certainly is, but even if the separate items were donated over a period of half a century, this is an unusual wealth to find in a single parish church, and, as a bonus, screens and pulpit are painted.

South-western churches in general at this time had very heavy, florid carving in both wood and stone, perhaps a reflection of the lushness of the countryside, and a deliberate contrast to the austere exteriors dictated by the intractable nature of the granite moorstone from which many of them were built. Clerestories were rare, and the low buildings were complemented by the stress on horizontals effected by the screens running right across the width of the churches, and the flat-topped benches.

East Anglian churches, on the other hand, were high and airy in the late middle ages, and their furnishings are lighter and more delicate with a greater vertical emphasis. So screens are tall, and rarely run right across a church, while bench ends have poppy-heads, and font covers are soaring spires.

Salle, Norfolk, was rebuilt entirely in the fifteenth century on a massive scale for a village church, and many original furnishings remain, including the seven sacrament font, its tall cover (and the pulley fixed to the tower balcony which raised the cover when the font was in use), most of the pulpit, various screens,

the stalls with their misericords, some benches, five doors, and some fragments of the glass. Doubtless some of the brasses commemorate people who helped to provide them.

Fairford, Gloucestershire, was rebuilt about 1500 by John Tame and his son Sir Edmund. Miraculously the complete set of original glass survives. There are also screens and stalls, a little wall-painting, two doors, one with its original lock and key, and the sedilia. Apart from the slightly earlier font, the medieval work is contemporary with the architecture, so that this is perhaps the oldest church in England to give a reasonably clear impression of what its original designer intended.

The glass at Fairford hints at the coming of the Renaissance. Its influence was hardly felt here until about 1500, but, after a very hesitant start, by 1550 it was rapidly replacing gothic as the national style, and although gothic survived in church furnishings until about 1680, and was revived as early as about 1750, from 1550 till about 1840 what can loosely be described as classical fittings predominated. The first datable truly renaissance feature in an English church is Torrigiani's tomb of Lady Margaret Beaufort, 1511, in Westminster Abbey, immediately followed by his monuments to Henry VII and Elizabeth of York. Other pure pieces include the terracotta tombs in East Anglia, of about 1525–30, also by Italian craftsmen, the screen and stalls at King's College Chapel, Cambridge, of about 1535, again by Italian or French designers, and the Tarrant Hinton Easter sepulchre, which does not look like English work either, and may be as early as about 1525.

But by the 1530s, benches in the West Country undoubtedly by English craftsmen were made with renaissance medallions, and an English renaissance pulpit appears at Catton, near Norwich. By the 1540s there are tombs at Framlingham, Suffolk, and Dean Salkeld's screen in Carlisle Cathedral *(118)*.

However, the volume of such work is small, and much of what was made has subsequently been thrown out. For this reason the humble village interior at Brooke, Rutland, is a precious survival. Here most of the church was rebuilt on conservative lines in 1579, and architecture and furnishings are all of a piece. The seating in nave and chancel, both box pews and benches, the screens across the width of the church, the north door with its massive iron hinges, the font cover and the reading desk all belong to the original work, while the communion table and rails, the tower screen, the pulpit, and a few of the box pews are only a generation later and completely in harmony with the rest.

In the reigns of James I and Charles I, Elizabeth I's Anglican settlement came of age, and in spite of the unrest of the times, large quantities of church furniture were once again being made, on a scale not to be repeated until Victorian times two centuries later. The most notable characteristic of this work is that nearly all of it was made of timber, and the most familiar ornament consists of blank arches set in wainscot panels.

Croscombe, Somerset, was ambitiously refurnished about 1616, the date on the pulpit. Apart from this there is a grand chancel screen, parclose screens, readers' desks and box pews. The chancel roof was renewed in 1664 in the same style *(2)*.

Ten years later, in 1626, the chancel of Passenham, Northamptonshire, was rebuilt and re-equipped by Sir Robert Banastre. The stalls, which are dated 1628, are a hybrid composition with careful gothic detail on the fronts and carved misericord seats, while the backs have an entablature supported by coupled Ionic columns with shell-headed niches between. Above are wall-paintings discovered in the 1950s and since painstakingly restored, containing figures of prophets and evangelists with Joseph of Arimathea and Nicodemus, also in shell-headed surrounds. Originally the chancel was divided from the nave by an Ionic screen, but in the mid-eighteenth century this was swept away, and much of the structure used to support a new west gallery, whose front bears a list of benefactors of the church. The box pews were also put in then, but the pulpit with its tester belongs to the Jacobean work.

Jacobean furnishings go well with medieval architecture, and one of the most unforgettable churches in the country is Abbey Dore, Herefordshire, where the elegant thirteenth-century Cistercian chancel was restored to use by Lord Scudamore in 1633–4 *(120)*. Screen, stalls, benches, pulpit, communion rail, west gallery and poor box all remain.

These are High Anglican interiors. Puritan arrangements were quite different. What they liked was a pulpit in the middle of one wall, such as one finds at Bramhope Chapel, West Riding, and seats facing inwards college-chapel-wise. Inward-facing seats were not a Puritan monopoly, however, and Nicholas Ferrar used them at Little Gidding, but seats for communicants round the table certainly were. With one exception the last few of these arrangements disappeared in the nineteenth century, the unique survival being at Deerhurst, Gloucestershire, *(148)*.

Gothic lasted longer in church architecture than in furnishings, and the gothic survival churches at Staunton Harold, Leicestershire, begun in defiance of the régime in 1653, and at St Ninian, Brougham,

Westmorland, of the 1660s, both of which retain most of their original fittings, are furnished in the Jacobean style.

For Jacobean, like Elizabethan before it, is indeed descriptive of a style rather than a reign or a period. It was defined during the reign of James I, but there is very little development during the reign of his son, and isolated Jacobean pieces were still being made in the early eighteenth century. There is in fact a constant overlap of styles, even discounting conscious revival, which makes the dating of pieces for which there is only stylistic evidence a very hazardous affair.

There was a conscious revival of gothic, in conjunction with renaissance forms, in the diocese of Durham under the inspiration and patronage of Bishop Cosin. Some of this handsome work is in Durham Cathedral, including the glorious stalls and font canopy *(39)* and other fine collections are at Brancepeth *(74)*, where he was incumbent before the Civil War, Bishop Auckland Castle Chapel *(131)*, Egglescliffe, Haughton-le-Skerne and Sedgefield.

But this mixed style, which seems to look back to gothic and forward to the baroque at the same time, and which has given the north of England some of its finest interiors, was a local and transient phenomenon. Generally speaking the late Stuart period was the age first of Wren and then of Hawksmoor, and of the outstandingly gifted craftsmen they used to equip their churches. As a result of the Great Fire of London, most of this work is there. Taken generally it is the most assured since the middle ages, and of more consistently high quality than any before or since.

A feature of about 1700 is the revival of wrought ironwork. Jean Tijou made his screens for St Paul's Cathedral about 1696 and his communion rail for St Andrew Undershaft in 1704, and the screen at Wrexham, possibly by Hugh Davies of Bersham was made about the same time. Another outstanding and apparently independent piece of the turn of the century is the communion rail at Lydiard Tregoze, Wiltshire *(150)*, but there is no doubt that Tijou inspired some of the best work of the next generation, like William Edney's gates and railings of 1710 at St Mary Redcliffe, Bristol, and Robert Bakewell's chancel screen of 1724 in Derby Cathedral *(127)*.

St Magnus the Martyr, Lower Thames Street, London, completed in essentials by 1676, though altered in the eighteenth and twentieth centuries is still a good late Stuart interior *(3)*. The best of the original fittings are the reredos, pulpit and west gallery, all of the highest quality, with fine work of Queen Anne's time in the communion rails, the sword rest and the organ. Outside London, Ingestre, Staffordshire, also built in 1676, and perhaps also by Wren, still looks much as it did when it was new, with furnishings well above average provincial quality *(75)*. But the finest of all, and perhaps one of the half dozen or so most beautiful church interiors of any age in Britain, is the Chapel of Trinity College, Oxford, c.1694 *(1)*. The sheer quality of every detail silences criticism. The scale is intimate, and the decoration, while sumptuous, is carefully contrived not to be overwhelming. Colour, for example, is more or less confined to the ceiling, and the over-riding impression is of polished wood, with the relative simplicity of the stalls separating the richly carved organ screen at the west from the equally elaborate reredos at the east. Grinling Gibbons's name is often associated with this work, and although there is no documentary proof, there can have been few other men, even at this time of great talent, capable of doing it. The upper walls and ceiling have delicate stucco decoration, and, in the centre of the ceiling, the one piece of bold colour allowed, the Ascension, by Pierre Berchet, flanked by two smaller panels.

Trinity College Chapel does not stand alone, however, for the Cambridge and, more particularly, the Oxford Colleges contain the best work of the late seventeenth century outside London. The restrained work at Oriel even belongs in part to the Commonwealth, and there is particularly fine work at University College, Oxford, done over a long period between 1641 and 1695, and at St Catherine's College, Cambridge c.1694–1704.

Most of the small quantity of baroque and rococo work in our churches is by foreign artists and craftsmen. Among them are some wonderful pieces, none better than the monuments made by Roubiliac, *(215, 216, 217)*, unrivalled in both inspiration and technique. The only two really baroque interiors in England, at Little Stanmore, Middlesex *(4)*, and at Great Witley, Worcestershire, are both connected with the Duke of Chandos, the patron of Handel. Little Stanmore was the parish church of the village in which Canons, the Duke's seat, lay, while on the demolition of Canons after the Duke's death about 1747, the glass and ceiling paintings from his private chapel were bought by Lord Foley and fitted into the church he had recently built next to Witley Court. Gibbs fitted the ceiling paintings in so cleverly – using papier mâché instead of stucco in the surrounds – that if their history were not documented, nobody would guess that they were not made for their present position *(177)*. Unfortunately Great Witley has Victorian seating and a Victorian font, while Little Stanmore has Victorian glass, and no Victorian could

have found himself sufficiently in sympathy with these settings to harmonise his work with them.

A little later, in 1763, West Wycombe church, Buckinghamshire, was reopened after being restored and partially rebuilt at the expense of Sir Francis Dashwood, probably by Nicholas Revett. The result was controversial and has remained so ever since. The *Royal Magazine* said that it was 'reckoned the most beautiful Country Church in England', while Charles Churchill, also commenting when it was new, (he died in 1764) called it

A temple built aloft in air
That serves for show and not for prayer.[1]

It is wonderful that the Victorians altered it so little, for to them it must have represented all that they regarded as pagan in Georgian taste – with some justification, for the nave was in fact modelled on the fifth-century Temple of the Sun at Palmyra. The pulpit-lectern *(89)* and the pair of reading desks *en suite* with it are mahogany thrones in the Chippendale style, and the font *(45)* has a unique charm to which few nineteenth-century minds would have been remotely susceptible, and which even the present generation has recently removed from the centre of the nave which was floored specially for it and relegated to within the altar rails of the presumably rarely used chancel. This chancel is thirteenth century in its bones, but the interior is all of c.1760, with a fine painted ceiling by Giovanni Borgnis, a beautiful communion rail, and the original communion table, reredos and stalls. Above the chancel arch is a huge Royal Arms of George III, and the nave ceiling has painted coffering, a technique also to be seen at Mereworth, Kent. Both nave and chancel have panelled marble floors.

It was about this time that the romantic strain in eighteenth century thought found expression in the first gothick churches. One's enjoyment of Shobdon, Herefordshire is tempered by the knowledge that an exceptionally fine Norman church was demolished to make way for it, but it is nevertheless a building of captivating charm *(7)*. The furnishings are gratifyingly complete, and virtually everything except the twelfth-century font dates from c.1753. The architect is not known for certain, though Henry Flitcroft has been suggested.

The gothick of Shobdon is in a delicate and playful vein, quite close in spirit to the rococo, and the same is true of Croome d'Abitot, Worcestershire, probably by Lancelot (Capability) Brown and Robert Adam. Not all Adam's interior is gothick, however, and the font *(44)*, still classical in style, is one of the most beautiful

1 Trinity College Chapel, Oxford, 1691–94

2 Left St Mary, Croscombe, Somerset: furnished c. 1616–64

3 Above St Magnus the Martyr, London Bridge: a Wren interior, c. 1675, restored 1924–5 by Martin Travers

4 Above left St Lawrence, Little Stanmore, Middlesex: 1715–20, decorated by Louis Laguerre and Antonio Bellucci
5 Above right St John, Chichester, Sussex: 1813, by James Elmes
6 Right St Cuthbert, Philbeach Gardens, Kensington: 1884–7, furnished by W. Bainbridge-Reynolds and Rev. E. Geldart

7 St John, Shobdon, Herefordshire: a gothick interior of 1752–6, possibly by Henry Flitcroft

8 Right Holy Innocents, Highnam, Gloucestershire: 1847–51, by Henry Woodyer; wall-painting by Thomas Gambier-Parry

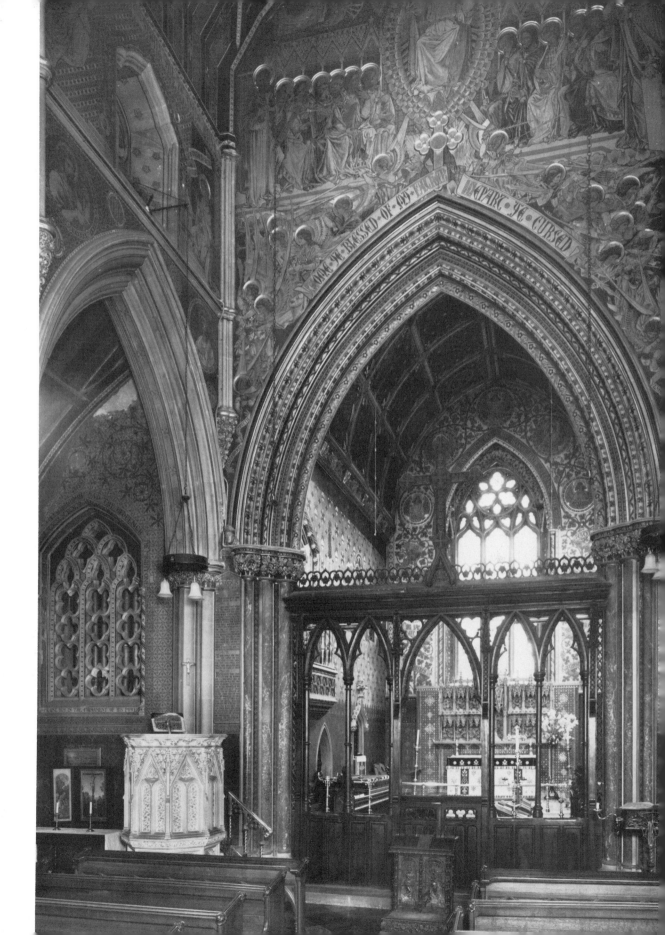

9 Left St Mary, Great Warley, Essex: 1904, screens, pulpit and lectern by William Reynolds-Stephens
10 Above Coventry Cathedral, Warwickshire: choir 1962, stalls and organ case by Sir Basil Spence; Tapestry by Graham Sutherland

11 St Peter, Ravenshead, Nottinghamshire: 1972 by Colin Shewring

of its age. The whole building, outside and in, survives virtually intact.

In 1782, George Richardson built a lovely little gothick church at Teigh, Rutland, for the fourth Earl of Harborough, and the following year a similar but rather larger one for the same patron nearby at Stapleford, Leicestershire. Both these churches retain most of their furnishings, and show admirably the restraint of which gothick was capable in sensitive hands. Both are seated college chapel-wise, the main difference being that while at Stapleford the west end has the Earl's gallery, at Teigh the pulpit, reading desk and clerk's pew are placed there in what must surely be a unique arrangement. The pulpit is backed by a *trompe l'oeil* painting of a simple arched window with plain glass and a tree visible through it, a design which must have been remarkably convincing before misguided Victorians filled the real windows with tracery.

A genuine low-church ensemble, as near as one can get to Puritan survival within the established church, exists at St John, Chichester, a strange octagonal building of 1813 *(5)*. Here there is none of the fancy ceiling painting or stucco work associated with the high Georgian arrangements we have been considering. Indeed, it looks much more like a Nonconformist church than an Anglican one, with galleries on cast-iron columns and pews all facing the high three-decker pulpit, which stands centrally, unequivocally the focus of attention, completely obscuring the communion table. The organ stands in the east gallery, above the pulpit.

But in the early years of the nineteenth century the emphasis was already changing. Georgian gothick was largely classical design in gothick dress. Now, clumsily at first, but with increasing assurance, architects were turning to a serious archaeological interpretation of medieval art both for their buildings and for their contents. But before gothic hardened into *the* Christian style, there was still room for experiment. When T.H. Wyatt and D. Brandon built St Mary and St Nicholas, Wilton, in the early 1840s they chose the Italian Romanesque style and furnished it as far as they could in marble and Cosmati work.

A contemporary experiment, completed in 1842, is the church at Wreay, Cumberland. It is remarkable on three counts: it is highly eclectic, it is by an amateur architect, and that amateur was a woman in a man's world, Sara Losh. It is moreover a very attractive church at a time when such were few and far between. Her ideas came from Early Christian and Lombardy Romanesque sources, but Wreay is no imitation; indeed in many ways it is a precursor of the Arts and Crafts movement of late Victorian and Edwardian times, much closer in spirit, say, to Great Warley, than to anything by Scott, Street or Butterfield. Her altar *(154)*, of green marble supported by two brass eagles, is placed so that the celebrant faces the congregation, a position familiar now, but almost unheard of then when north-end celebration was standard, and the eastward position an imminent Oxford Movement novelty. It was furnished with alabaster lotus-flower candlesticks. As a complete contrast to this sophistication, the pulpit is a hollowed-out tree trunk, and there are two lecterns, also using natural wood forms, one with an eagle, the other with a pelican. Some of the carving was done by Miss Losh herself, some by her cousin William, and more by a local man, William Hindson. Thus she avoided all the clichés of her age and produced a building which is as fresh today as when it was built, for it contradicts all our accepted notions of what early Victorian churches are like.

High Victorian ensembles have come in for heavy criticism from their own day to this, and even today there are many people who cannot enjoy the exuberance and self-confidence of these buildings at their best. Though they use a medieval vocabulary based on an increasingly sound knowledge of the middle ages, they are often exciting, vital, and original buildings. Quite a lot have survived fairly well intact, though all too many have been altered internally or even demolished.

High Victorianism is in large measure a product of the Oxford Movement, and the Tractarian conviction that a new age of faith had dawned was closely reflected in the churches built for them. It is no coincidence that the prophet of gothic was Augustus Pugin, a zealous catholic, and catholic revival meant a reintroduction of colour and imagery on a bold scale. Two churches which owe their existence to the Oxford Movement are All Saints, Margaret Street, London, and Highnam, Gloucestershire. All Saints, Margaret Street was designed by the youthful and self-confident William Butterfield. Its foundation stone was laid in 1847 by Dr Pusey, and it was completed a decade later. The interior is a *tour de force*. Even the *Ecclesiologist*, journal of the Cambridge Camden Society, under whose auspices the church was built, called it ugly, and certainly it is first and foremost a theological rather than an artistic statement. Virtually every inch of wall space is decorated, and in a bewildering variety of media: Painting, gilding and stained glass of course, but also tile mosaics, marble, and incised patterns filled with mastic. Even the piers are assertive. They are made of polished Aberdeen granite, an extraordinary choice for a London church.

Butterfield's former pupil Henry Woodyer, completed Holy Innocents, Highnam, Gloucestershire, in 1851 *(8, 41)*. As richly coloured as All Saints, Margaret Street, the means employed are less varied, and it is more attractive. The squire, Thomas Gambier-Parry, was an artist, and he did the wall-painting himself using his own new technique of spirit-based fresco. The glass, by the best makers of the time, Clayton and Bell, Hardman, O'Connor, and Wailes, is fully in keeping, and the overall effect is rich and mysterious, for one of the aims of the Oxford Movement was to restore the awe-inspiring numinosity which they understandably felt that churches had lost at the reformation.

No Victorian architect has come in for more vilification than Sir Gilbert Scott, largely because of his self-confident propensity for 'correcting' genuine medieval work. Scott was not, of course, the only offender, and it would be a pity if the quality of his best work should be obscured by recognition of his errors of judgement. Scott spent years of loving care on Lichfield Cathedral, a building of great beauty which had suffered grievously through the accidents of history. His chancel furnishings, fortunately, survived intact long enough for them once again to be appreciated and carefully restored. They are approached through a magnificent metalwork screen *(129)*, made, like so much of Scott's metalwork, by Francis Skidmore of Coventry. The stalls and throne, the reredos and statue-screen, and the pavement are all Scott's designs, and show his mastery of a variety of media – stone, wood, metal, and tiles. At Worcester Cathedral, where the choir is comparable, Scott also designed the beautiful west window, executed by Hardman.

Much Victorian work in older churches was at the expense of the furniture of the Stuart and Georgian periods. Apart from the usual generation gap which tends to make every age insensitive to the taste of its immediate predecessor, and which is perhaps a necessary prerequisite of development and change, there was a strong conviction that non-gothic fittings were ill-suited to gothic architecture. Thus while Wren's churches generally came through because they were all of a piece, Inigo Jones's screen of 1638 was torn out of Winchester Cathedral. Britton, a pioneer of the medievalizing movement, had described it as early as 1817 as 'an ugly piece of patchwork in a fine dress', and all that now remains of it in the cathedral is the pair of bronze statues of James I and Charles I by Hubert Le Sueur. The present screen is by Scott.

Victorian churchmen, moreover, their zeal fired by Evangelicals and Tractarians alike, and fuelled by Macaulay, deplored the corrupt, easy-going spiritual outlook of the Georgian church in whose tangible legacy they all too readily saw classical paganism. If they understood the necessity of lowering the ecclesiastical temperature in the eighteenth century after the turmoil of the seventeenth, they were unable to sympathise with those who kept it low once the religious peace that was the achievement of the Georgian divines came to be taken for granted. So, with much the same confidence in their own taste and moral rectitude that had inspired the Norman lords seven centuries earlier, they blithely replaced the mellow and old by the shiny and new.[2]

This means that even now, when Victorian furnishings in their turn are rather slowly beginning to mellow, it is easier to appreciate them in contemporary buildings. Ensembles as happy as Scott's choirs at Lichfield and Worcester are rare, and many an old church has been irrevocably spoilt by well-meaning Victorian interference.

But, in the right setting, there is a nobility about mature Victorian work which is both impressive and moving. One such church is Toddington, Gloucestershire, built between 1873 and 1879 by G.E. Street. Its furnishings are practically intact and are not so much memorable in themselves but in the way they form a perfect foil for a noble piece of architecture. Decoration is, rightly, very restrained.

Another architect of the later Victorian years capable of such restraint was G.F. Bodley. However, Bodley, though avoiding the polychromatic exuberance of Butterfield and Woodyer, nevertheless appreciated the contribution warm, rich colours could make, and he had a sharp eye for quality. Right from their youth and his own he employed the best artists and craftsmen of their day like C.E. Kempe, mostly known for his glass, though he worked in other media too, and Morris and Co. who, through Morris's association with the pre-Raphaelite brotherhood, were able to call upon the talents of such men as Sir Edward Burne-Jones, Ford Madox Brown, D.G. Rossetti and others. There is no better example of the co-operation of Bodley and the pre-Raphaelites than St Martin, Scarborough, completed in 1862, where the east wall painting is by Burne-Jones, with a Morris background, the ceiling painting by Morris and Philip Webb, the pulpit has designs by Rossetti, Brown, and Morris *(80)*, and the glass is by Morris, Rossetti, Brown and Burne-Jones. Later on, in 1889, Bodley himself contributed the reredos, rood screen and organ case.

St Cuthbert, Philbeach Gardens, Kensington, *(6)*, was furnished in 1887–8 by the young William Bainbridge-Reynolds, who worked in the new Arts and Crafts fashion. The work is exuberant in a High Victorian way, but the detail and the underlying spirit are different, and it is instructive to compare his metalwork with Scott's designs of a generation before. Bainbridge-Reynolds produced several screens, two sets of communion rails, sedilia and piscina – a characteristic piece of Anglo-catholic medievalism – the clock, the pulpit, the Royal Arms, some glass, and, finest of all, the iron and copper lectern.   Later Arts and Crafts work, especially where it was most closely attuned to its continental blood-brother, Art Nouveau, can be more self-conscious and whimsical than Bainbridge-Reynolds was, but very close to his spirit is the work by Henry Wilson at St Bartholomew, Brighton. Wilson also employed marble, at about the same time that the first of the marble panelling was being installed in Bentley's Westminster Cathedral. Wilson worked at Brighton between 1895 and 1910, and there is a typical turn-of-the-century contrast between the plain marble of the font, pulpit, and ciborium, and the elaborate metalwork of the high altar rails and the Lady altar and cross.

William Reynolds-Stephens, who furnished C.H. Townsend's new church at Great Warley, Essex, about 1904, also made effective use of the contrast between plain marble and elaborate metalwork. Like all sumptuous ensembles it takes a little getting used to, but the overall effect, from the reredos in the apse, via the organ case and screens to the pulpit and lectern and finally the font, is impressively rich. The rood screen is particularly remarkable *(9)*. The green marble base and the square, tapering columns, which take the place of mullions, have an elegant simplicity, but lead to exceptionally ornate upper parts with their angel figures and their vigorous foliage and flowers.

The appreciation of the natural beauty of coloured marble, which led Wilson and Reynolds-Stephens to leave its surfaces free from ornamental carving, was shared by Bodley, now nearing the end of his career, when he made the dark green font for Southwark Cathedral. But the most striking use of marble, and of mosaic work, in England is at Westminster Cathedral *(194)*. Here, although the design was conceived and begun at this period, the actual execution has already occupied over 70 years and is still far from complete, so that it is not, strictly speaking, a period piece.

At Westminster Cathedral there is a fine set of stalls in St. Andrew's Chapel by Ernest Gimson *(141)*, who also worked for E.S. Prior at St Andrew's, Roker, Sunderland *(90)*. Prior used the best artists of the old

and the new generation in this church, built in 1906–7; there is a Morris and Burne-Jones tapestry and a Morris carpet; the lectern, the altar cross *(262)* and the processional cross are by Gimson; the font is by Randall Wells, and the dedication plate by Eric Gill: names which span British craftsmanship from the 1850s to the 1930s. One might expect some discordance in the use of such varied talents, but there is none.

The period 1914 to c.1955 is difficult to write about. The notorious blind spot each generation has for the taste of its predecessor means that the churches of this period have yet to receive their due. Even so, the amount of good work done is meagre compared with many past times. There may be several reasons for this. One is certainly economic. The cumulative effect of two world wars, the depression of the 'thirties, and a marked decline in church attendance, did not make for ambitious schemes, and most new furniture was merely ordered from catalogues. Such money as was available tended to be spent on noble architecture rather than expensive fittings – one thinks of the Anglican cathedrals at Liverpool and Guildford. Moreover, it was an era of uncertainty in church art. Secular art had undergone a revolution inspired by men like Picasso and Braque, but such artists had not converted popular taste, and to have designed church fittings in uncompromisingly modern terms would have been unacceptable to the majority of clients. So artists and craftsmen strove to escape from Victorianism, and yet remain traditional, even gothic in spirit. Most of the large output of Sir Ninian Comper can be seen in this light: rich, meticulous work, able to fit into ancient fabrics with dignity, like his fine font cover at York Minster, and yet, one feels, pastiche. But if a work of art is allowed to state its own terms, and not to be thought of in terms of mainstream evolution if it happens to lie outside it, a church like St Mary, Wellingborough, Northamptonshire, designed and furnished by Comper, between 1908 and 1931, using gothic and classical forms, may come to be regarded as one of the best works of its period. Gothic, indeed, was still used as late as 1949 in the screen at Turkdean, Gloucestershire, by Peter Falconer.

Although there were precursors, such as Crownhill, Plymouth, of the 1950s, the challenge and opportunity given by the rebuilding of Coventry Cathedral in the early 1960s and its successful use of untraditional forms in its furnishings gave a tremendous impetus to new developments *(10, 128, 245)*. Coventry is too well-known to need description, but in his use of artists of international reputation and his recovery of the sense of grand scale in furnishings, Sir Basil Spence did far more than design a fine cathedral.

What had been scorned in prospect by a generation that still expected its cathedrals to be gothic, was discovered in practice to have a beauty and symbolism which the public could enjoy and understand, and nothing was more successful than the purely abstract glass of John Piper's great baptistry window. Perhaps it could have been done nowhere else. The rise of the cathedral, phoenix-like, from the ashes of war stirred at the same time a deep sense of patriotism and a new sense of international understanding and longing for peace. From the day it was opened it became a place of pilgrimage.

The acceptance of a truly modern idiom, of abstraction alongside representational art, has been the hallmark of the late 1960s and 1970s. Budgets have still been tight, and the decline in church attendance has continued. But, in spite of lack of funds, some very effective interiors have been designed. The two new Roman Catholic cathedrals at Liverpool *(158)*, and Clifton *(50)* use architecture and furnishing to give a sense of tranquility usually only found in buildings of a venerable age. At Liverpool the light diffused through Piper's tremendous expanse of glass is richly coloured and reflects from white plane surfaces. At Clifton, though the basic plan of the building is similar, with a central high altar, the effect is totally different because concealed white light is used, and the colours in the furnishings are quietly harmonious.

If these two cathedrals were built on a shoe-string, there has been far less available for parish churches. There can be no new Ludlow, or Ingestre or West Wycombe or Highnam today. Instead architects try to provide something suitable for current liturgical practice, in line with modern theology, as symbolic as funds permit, and contemporary in idiom. St Peter, Ravenshead, Nottinghamshire *(11)*, and Churchill College Chapel, Cambridge are good examples: simple, practical, not expensively finished, but furnished with dignity and feeling.

But today's problem does not lie in new churches: it lies in the continuing dwindling of congregations and of revenues which together mean that many churches seem to have come to the end of their useful lives as places of worship. Only the realization that in the deepest sense they and their contents are part of the spiritual and cultural heritage of us all, irrespective of church membership or religious belief, can prevent a new era of destruction as far-reaching in its consequences as the Reformation. 469 years separate the landing of St Augustine in 597 from the Norman Conquest in 1066; 470 years separate the Norman Conquest from the beginning of the Dissolution of the Monasteries in 1536. Another 470 years take us to the year 2006. Hopefully when we reach that date, we shall not be struck by the coincidence, but, if present trends continue it seems sadly likely that we shall.

Chapter 2
The Porch

The porch has come down in the world. In the middle ages it was often the most spectacular feature of the church, and such expenditure would never have been undertaken merely to protect the entrance doors and to provide a place where notices could be pinned and parishioners could gossip in the dry before and after service. Indeed, at that time it served important liturgical purposes. Among its ancestors was the early christian narthex, where catechumens were taught, and from where they were permitted to watch the first part of the mass. Traces of such an arrangement survive in the Saxon church at Brixworth, Northamptonshire.

Baptism naturally often took place in the narthex during the missionary period, but with the universal baptism of infants, fonts were placed inside the church. The ceremony, however, still began in the porch, where the priest received the child, breathed on it, and administered salt as a symbol of incorruptibility.

The wedding ceremony also took place there – as Chaucer's Wife of Bath says, 'Husbondes at chirche dore have I had five' – and only when the contract had been made did the bridal couple, with their family and friends, enter the church for the nuptial mass. Apparently this custom survived in a Protestant form in some places until the Commonwealth, and at South Pool, Devon, there is even a medieval altar table in the porch itself.

Medieval penitents, who had been excluded from the church on Ash Wednesday, were received in the porch for absolution on Maundy Thursday, and the first part of the Churching of Women after childbirth took place there too. If the church possessed a portable shrine, as many did, it was borne round outside during the Palm Sunday procession, and was then held aloft in the porch while the congregation passed beneath it into the church. A boy was stationed in a gallery to represent an angel, and some of the galleries attached to the inside of porches, like those at Great Dunmow, Essex, Mildenhall, Suffolk, and Clapton-in-Gordano, Somerset, may have been built partly, at least, for this purpose. Others, which may well have been temporary structures, are revealed in

churchwardens' accounts, and by otherwise inexplicable staircases like the one at St Helen Auckland, Co. Durham.

On Holy Saturday all the lights and fires in the parish were extinguished to symbolize the end of the old dispensation. Then, in the porch, flint and steel were used to kindle a charcoal brazier, the New Fire, symbolising Christ the Light of the World, and from here first the church lights, including the Paschal Candle, were lit, and then domestic lanterns were taken home to relight the lamps and kindle the hearths and ovens. It has been suggested that the fireplace in the early sixteenth-century porch at Crostwick, Norfolk, was used for this purpose.

Porches also sometimes served as courtrooms for the trial of minor offenders, and as a place where business transactions were conducted. These last functions were perhaps one reason for the frequent construction of a room over the porch in the late middle ages, though these 'parvise' chambers, as they were called, also acted as schoolrooms, and as living quarters for the priest. At Mendlesham, Suffolk, the parvise became at some stage the parish armoury, and the armour is still to be seen there, while the exceptional porch at Cirencester, Gloucestershire was used first by the Abbey for secular administration, and then, until the eighteenth century, as the Town Hall.

It is not surprising in view of the various roles of the porch that the commonest items of medieval furniture found there are benches, usually of stone, running the length of the ground floor on either side. Many still exist, though, being plain, are seldom given a second glance. Many more have been replaced in more recent times by wooden ones.[3]

Parishes whose churches lacked porches were therefore at a disadvantage in the vagaries of the English climate. Until the late thirteenth century porches were rare,[4] and it is likely that before this time their liturgical functions took place in the doorway instead, a supposition which helps to explain the lavish ornamentation of many early medieval doorways, and perhaps for their frequent survival when churches were enlarged or rebuilt. Another possible substitute in early days was the ground floor of the tower, when there was one, and when it was accessible from outside.

Stoups were commonly placed in porches, or just inside the church door. They were filled with consecrated water into which parishioners dipped their fingers on entering the church and signed themselves with the cross. This clear reminder of baptism does not seem to have affected the design of stoups very much, for they generally resembled piscinas rather than fonts. However, at St Peter Mancroft, Norwich and at East Dereham, Norfolk, there are pairs of stoups either side of the porch entrance which are explicitly font-like in shape, though the ones at St Peter Mancroft are now entirely the work of the restorer. There is a similar stoup on the outside of the porch at Blythburgh, Suffolk, and, even more explicitly, when the thirteenth-century font at Crowland, Lincolnshire, was superseded in the fifteenth century, it was built into the tower arch as a stoup.

Other outstanding stoups can be seen at Toddington, Bedfordshire, in the porch, at St Endellion, Cornwall, and at Throwley, Kent, where it is right inside the church by a pier. One of the earliest must be the strange one at Kilpeck, Herefordshire *(13)*, which could well be older than the early twelfth-century church, and which has hands and feet like a little pot-bellied, decapitated statue. Many stoups have been destroyed since the Reformation, but every church entrance used to have one, and sometimes, especially in out-of-the-way places like Llandyfynan, Anglesey, they are still there.

Obviously people needed to know the times of services, and so scratch dials or more elaborate sundials were placed on the exterior of the church, more often than not on the south porch. In the case of scratch dials, of which traces quite frequently survive, the hour of mass is generally marked more heavily than the other divisions, and usually no attempt is made to indicate hours which are of no ecclesiastical importance.

Several Saxon sundials survive, of which the best are perhaps at Daglingworth, Gloucestershire, and Kirkdale, North Riding *(12)*. The latter dates from about 1060, and has an inscription which, translated, reads: 'Orm, Gamal's son, bought St Gregory's minster when it was all broken and fallen, and he has had it rebuilt from the ground for Christ and St Gregory, in the days of King Edward and Earl Tosti.' The sundial is signed: 'Hawarth wrought me, and Brand, priests.' At Bishopstone, Sussex, the sundial is simply inscribed 'Eadric', and is also Saxon work, though whether before or after the Conquest is impossible to say. The sundial at Clynnog Fawr, Caernarvonshire, of pre-Norman work, is only loosely datable to between about 900 and 1200.

It was doubtless a combination of conservatism and poverty which ensured that sundials did not go out as clocks came in. Church clocks (qv.) began to become

12 Left Kirkdale, Yorkshire: sundial,
c.1060

13 Above Kilpeck, Herefordshire: stoup,
Early twelfth century (?)

14 Right Staplehurst, Kent: south door.
Ironwork eleventh or twelfth century

15 Above left Eaton Bray, Bedfordshire: south door, ironwork mid-thirteenth century
16 Left Skipwith, Yorkshire: south door, ironwork thirteenth century
17 Above Harpley, Norfolk: south door, early fifteenth century

18 Right Stogumber, Somerset: closing ring of rood-stair door, c. 1500
19 Below left Durham Cathedral: north door-knocker, c. 1130–40
20 Below right Adel, Leeds: south door – closing ring c. 1160

relatively common in the seventeenth century, but many parishes did not have one until well into the nineteenth. So Commonwealth sundials appear at Holy Trinity, Berwick-on-Tweed, and at Linchmere, Sussex, while a fine group were made by John Berry about 1760 for the Devon churches of Kentisbury, Marwood and Tawstock. A later Devon sundial at Tedburn St Mary bears the names of the vicar, Rev. G.T. Carwithen, and the wardens, Edward Osmond and John Francis. It is dated 1817. Later sundials were sometimes placed, like clocks, on towers rather than porches, as at Wimborne Minster, Dorset, or even free-standing in the churchyard as at Long Preston, West Riding, and, formerly, Trelleck, Gwent.

Burials sometimes took place in the porch. Indeed, in the seventh century, when burial in church was first permitted, the porch was the only sanctioned place, and one of the reasons for the multiplication of porticus in Saxon churches may have been to provide extra places of sepulture. St Augustine, King Ethelbert, and Queen Bertha were among the first in Britain to be accorded this honour, but the custom continued right up to the reformation, even though the rest of the church had long been permissible. A fourteenth-century rector's tomb is to be found in the west porch at Orpington, Kent, in accordance with his will of 1370, and the donor of the south porch at St Peter Hungate, Norwich, lies beneath it.

Gates to porches are not usually very interesting. They are normally wooden and more or less recent, or of wire mesh to keep birds out. However in the eighteenth century some attractive wrought-iron gates were made for porches at Peterborough Cathedral, Sherborne Abbey, and Finedon, Northamptonshire.

As well as all its other purposes, a porch protected a door, and although there are fewer interesting doors than interesting doorways, there are some fine pieces of work remaining. The south door of Stillingfleet, East Riding, is placed in an elaborate doorway of about 1160, but the door itself seems to be of an older type, with its curling ironwork and its representation of what looks like a Viking ship. Styles have remarkable powers of survival in conservative country districts, but the ironwork is nearer to the fashion of 1060 than of 1160, though very similar C-hinges are found on the early twelfth-century door at Old Woking, Surrey. A similar door at Staplehurst, Kent *(14)*, also has C-hinges, a ship, some strange sea creatures, a crescent moon, and some abstract designs. It is not exactly datable, but may well be eleventh rather than twelfth century. Among other doors undoubtedly not later than the twelfth century one

can pick out one to the cloister at Durham Cathedral, another at Worksop Priory, Nottinghamshire, both with scrolly ironwork, and the south door at Letton, Herefordshire, with spiky ironwork.

Ironwork, however, was never better than in the thirteenth century, as numerous doors demonstrate. The door to what is now the Albert Memorial Chapel, Windsor, signed by Gilebertus, is one of the best. In similar scrolly style are the doors at Eaton Bray *(15)* and Leighton Buzzard, Bedfordshire, often ascribed to that Thomas of Leighton who designed the grille for the tomb of Queen Eleanor in Westminster Abbey, and quite possibly by him or by one of his associates. More delicate, less robust scrolls lengthened into spirals are found about the same time on the west doors of Lichfield Cathedral. Kingston Lisle, Berkshire, has good iron hinges of about 1200, while Uffington, Berkshire, has ironwork which seems to be a development of the C-hinge type found at Stillingfleet and Staplehurst. At Skipwith, East Riding *(16)*, there is a different tradition of thirteenth-century ironwork, though a few of the motifs, like foliated crosses, are familiar. The effect is more like intersecting shields with bosses at the centre, one of which contains the sanctuary knocker.

Later in the middle ages, interest shifts from the ironwork to the woodwork of doors. Many are traceried in the style fashionable for windows at the time, among the best being the reticulated design at Brent Eleigh, Suffolk, and the almost contemporary early fourteenth-century door at Brent Pelham, Hertfordshire. Later in the century there is a delicately traceried door at Higham, Kent, and the following century produced the more elaborate door at Hazlewood Castle Chapel, West Riding.

Occasionally there is further elaboration. At Finchingfield, Essex, in addition to fourteenth-century tracery, there are a number of carved figures including a crucifix, a pelican, and a dove. The south door at Harpley, Norfolk *(17)*, has figures of saints, with a bull and an eagle, symbols of the evangelists Luke and John, on the wicket. Original wickets are not very common, but there are several of interest. At Humbleton, East Riding, the wicket is ogee-headed, and at Gedney, Lincolnshire, the wicket is inscribed 'in hope', and has a little contemporary French ivory crucifixion. On the inside is a lock inscribed 'John Pette auyseth beware before'. A further inscription is on the outside of the main door: *'Pax Christi sit huic domui et omnibus habitantibus in ea hic requies nostra'* – 'The peace of Christ be on this house and all who dwell in it. Here is out rest.' Ballflower decoration dates the door to the first half of the fourteenth century. Inscriptions on doors are not very common, though one or two commemorate donors, like those at Worsborough, West Riding, and Sco Ruston, Norfolk. Two shears on a batten of the late fifteenth-century north door at Littlebury, Essex, suggest that, like so much else in our churches, it was paid for out of the profits of the wool trade.

Several early closing rings and knockers survive, like the famous bronze lion on the north door of Durham Cathedral *(19)*, one of the outstanding pieces of twelfth-century metalwork in Europe. Handles and knockers were, indeed, often decorated with beasts: a twelfth-century cat at Dormington, Herefordshire; a lion's head and lizards on the thirteenth-century tower door at Boston; winged dragons of the fourteenth century at Iwade, Kent; and late medieval salamanders at Withersfield, Suffolk, and a lion's head at All Saints Pavement, York. At Adel, Leeds a twelfth-century monster swallows a man *(20)*, while at St Gregory, Norwich, a man is eaten by a late medieval lion. The ferocity of some of these creatures, and the obvious allusion to the jaws of hell at Adel and St Gregory, Norwich,[5] may have been intended to serve as a warning against sacrilege and the violation of sanctuary. What may be the oldest door in England, at Hadstock, Essex, from the church built by Canute about 1020, has an even grimmer warning. The door is relatively plain, with three long iron straps riveted to the oak, but fragments of human skin were found attached to it, a reminder of the terrible penalty for sacrilege of flaying.

Sometimes it is the surround of the closing ring which is ornamented, in the form of ironwork developed from the old scroll hinges. This occurs in several Norfolk churches, most notably at Tunstead, in the form of a foliated cross. Internal doors, too, are sometimes treated with great care. The rood-loft stair door at Stogumber, Somerset *(18)*, has carved tracery and a closing ring mounted on a circular plate pierced with an abstract pattern.

An unusual form of construction is the lattice-framed thirteenth-century door at Potterne, Wiltshire, but a commoner alternative to the types we have been considering is studding, which can be found, for example, in the fifteenth-century door at Plemshall, Cheshire, and in post-reformation doors at Chedzoy, Somerset, where the door was probably made during Mary Tudor's reign, and at Old St Chad, 1663, and St Mary, 1672, both in Shrewsbury. These three doors are panelled, and the Chedzoy example has lozenges in the panels.

In fact, disappointingly few post-Reformation doors are more than typical examples of good, honest local craftsmanship. At Clifton, Nottinghamshire, a door of 1632 is indeed still in the late medieval style, in total contrast to the almost contemporary south-west door of St Helen, Bishopsgate, London, with its beautiful Inigo Jones-style doorcase with fluted columns. There are also three fine doorcases of about 1680 at All Saints, Northampton, and even better is the west door of Beverley Minster with figures of the four evangelists and *putti* representing the four seasons. It was perhaps designed by Nicholas Hawksmoor, who acted as consultant architect there from 1716 to 1720.

Among more recent examples two may be singled out. First the door of bronze made in 1904 for St Mary Nottingham by Henry Wilson, and secondly the bronze-clad doors of the 1960s by William Mitchell at the Metropolitan Cathedral of Christ the King in Liverpool. The Liverpool doors bear symbols of the evangelists in a style as ferocious as the twelfth-century knockers at Durham and Adel. They seem to stand guard over the cathedral, and it is an extraordinary transformation to step between them, walk along a short passage, and then enter the glorious peace of the great space within.

Chapter 3
Fonts

Remarkably few fonts earlier than the twelfth century survive in Britain. The oldest may be the huge, primitive tub at Old Radnor, perhaps as early as the sixth or seventh century, and roughly carved out of a single gabbro boulder which may once have been a pre-Christian sacred stone *(21)*. Claims for a sixth century origin for the font at St Martin, Canterbury owe more to a wish to have the font in which St Augustine baptized King Ethelbert than to objective scholarship. Unusually made up of a number of small stones cemented together like bricks, in its present form it is probably twelfth century, though parts of it may be earlier.

The font at Deerhurst, Gloucestershire, elaborately carved with trumpet spirals and vine scrolls, is attributed to the ninth century, and the big plain font at Patricio, Brecknock, is dated by an inscription to around 1060. There is no means of telling when Roman altars like the ones at Haydon Bridge and Chollerton, Northumberland, were converted into Christian fonts, nor when parts of Saxon cross shafts, like the one at Melbury Bubb, Dorset, were adapted. Slader attributes the conversion at Dolton, Devon, to the Normans;[6] on the other hand, it is known that at Penmon Priory, Anglesey, it did not take place until the nineteenth century. The remaining early fonts are mostly plain, and it is possible that some plain fonts generally labelled Norman through lack of any detail may in fact be older.[7]

By contrast, the number of surviving Norman fonts is very great. They are common in most counties, and Devon and Cornwall, for example, each have over a hundred. The main reason for this sudden change is undoubtedly the great rebuilding of parish churches in the twelfth century. But, though it is easy to understand the desire of Norman landowners to replace what they regarded as the outworn relics of a schismatic church, it is difficult all the same to account for the almost total disappearance of a practical object in a hard-wearing material, which virtually every church must have possessed. Clearly churches with the best Norman fonts were replacing their old one by something superior, but this does not explain the disappearance of Saxon fonts in the many churches

where their Norman successors are plain, or primitively and naively carved. Nor was there any change in the baptismal rite to account for it, since the custom of baptizing infants by immersion in England persisted until the reformation, and the first Prayer Book of Edward VI in 1549 enjoins it. Even in 1604, the rubrics for private baptism included the option of immersion:

. . . the said lawful Minister shall dip it in water, or pour water upon it.[8]

So there has to be another reason for the destruction of Saxon fonts by the Normans, and it is impossible to be certain what it was. However it is worth recalling that many of their new stone churches replaced wooden ones, like the solitary survivor at Greensted, Essex. Did the same apply to fonts? Wooden fonts were uncanonical, since the hallowed water which normally stood in them for long periods at a time might tend to seep through. Doubtless the Saxons, using lead linings, could have reduced this risk to a minimum, and would have been unconcerned about papal disapproval: wooden fonts, indeed, were made occasionally even in the late middle ages, as the one at Marks Tey, Essex, shows, and there is another in Wales at Efenechtyd, Denbighshire.

There is no direct evidence for such wooden fonts, but one hint that there may be some truth in the suggestion is the popularity of the cable moulding round the rim and sometimes the base of twelfth-century stone ones.[9] Such ropes might well have been used to bind the timbers of wooden fonts securely together, and to have been translated to their successors merely as ornaments, preserving a memory of the original.

Twelfth-century fonts are usually large, and sometimes square or more often tub-shaped. They are frequently carved with rich but barbaric details without any coherent iconographical scheme, but a few are highly civilized and beautifully carved. It is worth remembering that they would originally have been painted. None is better than the one at Southrop, Gloucestershire *(25)*, with high relief sculptures of Moses, Synagogue and Ecclesia, and the virtues trampling on the vices, all in trefoiled arcaded niches. In the spandrels are little reliefs of churches, and above is a decoration of leaves and trails suggesting prototypes in studded metal.[10] There is a very similar font at Stanton Fitzwarren, Wiltshire, and others at Thorpe Salvin, West Riding, and Avington, Berkshire. The font at Brecon Cathedral, though it has no arcaded figures, has a variety of studded trails.

Inhabited arcades are also a feature of the best twelfth-century lead fonts. Perhaps the oldest is at Walton-on-the-Hill, Surrey, with seated figures no longer identifiable; at Frampton-on-Severn, Gloucestershire, and five other nearby fonts probably made from the same mould, such figures alternate with foliage scrolls reminiscent of the ironwork of the period.[11] The lead font at Brookland, Kent (27), showing the labours of the months and the signs of the zodiac, was made about 1200, quite possibly in France.

At Bridekirk, Cumberland, (26) there is a stone font with carvings of the baptism of Christ, dragons, monsters and foliage, and a runic inscription which is variously translated, but which is certainly the signature of the sculptor, Rickart, who depicts himself working on the east face.

Another excellent twelfth-century font with lively figure carvings is at Lenton, Nottingham (22) with four scenes of the resurrection, the tomb of Christ being represented by a building looking like a small domed Byzantine church, perhaps supposed to be Holy Sepulchre, Jerusalem. Another square font, at Burnham Deepdale, Norfolk, shows the labours of the months, while at West Haddon, Northamptonshire, the four faces depict the Nativity, the Baptism of Christ, the Entry into Jerusalem, and Christ in Glory between the symbols of St Matthew and St John.

The group of craftsmen who have been called the Herefordshire School produced four fine fonts with exceptionally crisp and vigorous carving at Castle Frome (24) and Eardisley, Herefordshire, Chaddesley Corbett, Worcestershire, and Stottesdon, Shropshire. But some of the most accomplished twelfth-century fonts contain no figure sculpture, merely foliage and abstract decoration. Included among them are the one at Bowness-on-Solway, Cumberland, and the groups centred on Fowey, Cornwall, and Aylesbury, Buckinghamshire, presumably the products of local workshops.

Cornwall and parts of South Wales have many fonts of vaguely capital shape with faces at the corners. The most sophisticated ones have five supports, one in the centre, and slimmer ones at each corner, which are given bases and sometimes even abaci, the faces forming the capitals. The best is at Bodmin (28), and there is another very good one at Roche. There is a naive but attractive variant far away at Anstey, Hertfordshire, where the faces at the corners belong to mermen whose forked tails form the decoration of the sides of the bowl.[12]

A few Tournai marble fonts were imported in the twelfth century, four of them in Hampshire, and all within easy reach of the coast or a navigable river. They are strongly carved, the best perhaps being those at Lincoln and Winchester cathedrals, and at East Meon, Hampshire. The East Meon font has scenes from the Adam and Eve story; the one at Winchester (23) depicts the life of St Nicholas, while at Lincoln there are monsters, probably from a bestiary.

Far more common are fonts made of English shelly limestones which will take a polish and are usually known as marble. Ifield and Rudgwick have twelfth-century fonts of Sussex marble, and the one at Harrietsham, Kent, is made of very similar stone from Bethersden. But the majority, both in the twelfth and the thirteenth centuries, were turned out by the Purbeck workshops in Dorset. These Purbeck fonts rarely show any originality. Almost all of them to begin with are square, with two shallow blank arches on each side, round-headed at first, and then, with the introduction of gothic architecture, pointed (41). It is difficult to understand their popularity unless they were designed to contain painted figures as a cheap substitute for fonts of the Southrop type which few parishes would have been able to afford. Their distribution makes it clear that waterborne transport was usual.

At Youlgreave, Derbyshire, (29), the font made about 1200 has a subsidiary bowl outside the main one which may have been used to cleanse the chrism, or baptismal oil, from the fingers of the sponsors. A similar secondary bowl was made in what was presumably a font, made of oak and found in a bog near Dinas Mawddwy, Merioneth, last century. A number of other fonts, some later, have projections of various sorts. The one at Sutton Bonnington, Nottinghamshire, has three, perhaps for book, salt and candle, and it has been suggested that the Bodmin type of font was contrived to provide similar rests, which may account for its persistence from the twelfth century till the end of the middle ages.

After such an abundance of twelfth-century fonts, it is not surprising that there are few of the thirteenth, and fewer still of more than local interest. Eaton Bray, Bedfordshire, has a font which could well be by the craftsmen based on the nearby Totternhoe quarry who made the beautiful north arcade. The font has five supports, like the Cornish ones, but instead of faces on the capitals of the corner columns, there is excellent stiff-leaf carving. Barnack, near Peterborough, home of a great quarry from Saxon times, has an interesting font on a centre support with a trefoiled arcade to support the outer parts of the bowl. It looks rather like an iced cake on a stand *(30)*.

A notable fashion in the fourteenth and fifteenth centuries was to carve tracery patterns in shallow relief on each panel of the bowl. These were often window designs, taken from pattern books. Sometimes, as at Rickinghall Inferior, Suffolk, the tracery is very like that used in the windows of the church. For those who like their medieval styles neatly parcelled, it must be confusing to find so many with a mixture of Decorated and Perpendicular patterns – one strand in the evidence that suggests that in many parts of England these two styles existed harmoniously side by side for half a century or more.

Traceried fonts probably evolved from the arcaded ones of earlier periods, and early examples, of about 1300, exist as far apart as Hockham, Norfolk, with geometrical tracery, St Columb Major, Cornwall, and Harringworth, Northamptonshire, the last of which looks as though it is transitional between the Purbeck and the full-blown window tracery types. Later on tracery became a predominantly eastern English fashion, though it was also popular in the midlands; the one at Brailes, Warwickshire is a good example *(31)*.[13]

In the later middle ages, eastern prosperity is as obvious in fonts as in architecture and carpentry. East Anglian fonts, like the one at Fritton, Norfolk *(32)*, are unmistakable with their lions, wild men or angels against the stem. They almost always contain one rectangular panel to each face with such motifs as the symbols of the evangelists, or of the Trinity, which since baptism was always in the threefold Name, is particularly appropriate. At least as common are the instruments of Christ's passion – nails, cross, lance, sponge, scourge, etc. – and other scenes are occasionally shown, such as the Pietà at Acle, Norfolk, and the baptism of Christ. Some of the best depict the seven sacraments of catholic christianity,[14] while the eighth face of the bowl contains an additional scene such as the crucifixion. The style of the carving varies considerably, and it is interesting to compare such seven sacrament fonts as those at Walsoken, Norfolk, *(33)*, East Dereham, Norfolk, and Cratfield, Suffolk. What is clear is that although the stone had to be imported from the great oolite quarries of the east midlands, the carving was done locally in East Anglia.

It will have become apparent that fonts were now usually octagonal. The custom seems to have begun with the Purbeck marblers *(41)*, who moved away from the square table-top type about the end of the twelfth century. All sorts of shapes were found for a while. The traditional square and round bowls continued, but by the thirteenth century there were occasional hexagons, a heptagon at Llanfaglan, Caernarvonshire, and a dodecagon at Marden, Herefordshire. The fifteenth century also reverted occasionally to unusual shapes, like the nonagon at Bigby, Lincolnshire, and the decagon at Foy, Herefordshire. The pentagon alone seems to have been studiously avoided, as always in ecclesiastical work, probably because of its magical connotations.

A few other late medieval fonts are worth noticing. Every county has interesting examples. One at Ware, Hertfordshire, made about 1400, has an unusual assembly of figures round the bowl: the Angel Gabriel, the Virgin Mary, and Saints Christopher, George, James, John the Baptist, Catherine and Margaret. In the north, Frosterley marble continued to be used. It is bluish if unpolished as at Ripon Cathedral, but black if polished as at Catterick, North Riding, and Newcastle Cathedral *(38)*. The fonts at Padstow and St Merryn, Cornwall were made by that fine craftsman known to us as the Master of St Endellion, who also made some tombs, and the stoup at St Endellion mentioned above (p. 32). At Chignal Smealy, Essex and Potter Heigham, Norfolk, the fonts are made of brick. At Potter Heigham traces of glazing remain, though it is not clear whether it was all glazed originally.

Covers were essential to medieval fonts, since the water remained in them for long periods at a time, and had to be protected both from dust and from superstitious abuse. The Council of Durham in 1220 ordered that fonts, chrism and holy oil were to be kept under lock and key 'on account of enchantments',[15] but very few early lids have survived, though staples often tell of their former existence. At Farcet, Huntingdonshire, and Wickenby, Lincolnshire, the iron bars which lay across the cover and were padlocked to the font still exist. Such covers were simply lifted off for baptism, but with the enthusiasm for elaborate carpentry characteristic of the late middle ages, many font covers became richly ornamented openwork spires. The most popular method of lifting them was by means of pulleys, which either raised the whole thing, as at Salle, Norfolk, or raised the lower part telescopically over the upper part as at Ufford, Suffolk. This cover, *(37)*, admired even by the puritan iconoclast William Dowsing, who spared it, is the most ornate, though there are several others nearly as good, like the one in Newcastle Cathedral *(38)*.[16] Strangely enough, West Country carpenters, whose skill was the equal of the East Anglians', did little in this direction, and fonts in general do not seem to have inspired much enthusiasm in the west in the late middle ages.

An alternative was to provide a cover with doors. This was a sixteenth-century fashion found, for example, at Rotherfield, Sedlescombe and Ticehurst, Sussex, all of Henry VIII's time. A similar, rather more elaborate contraption at Swimbridge, Devon, has a tester over it – a feature of one or two other Devon fonts, like Pilton – but the panels seem to be of different periods, and it is uncertain what its history is.

Three churches have beautiful medieval font canopies, within which priest and sponsors could stand during the baptism. Since this tended to obscure the view of others, it is directly opposed to the normal East Anglian habit at this time of raising the font on steps to make it more open to view. It is therefore surprising in some ways to find that two of the three are in East Anglia, but less surprising to find that they are elaborate pieces of carpentry. These, both made about 1500, are at Trunch *(34)*, Norfolk, and St Peter Mancroft, Norwich. The canopy at Trunch dominates the modest village church even more than the cover at Ufford. Both have traces of painting, though the whole of the upper part of the St Peter Mancroft Canopy is the work of a restorer.[17] The earliest and finest of them, however, is the stone creation at St Mary, Luton *(35)*, made about 1330 and shaped like a corona. A fourth fine canopy was made of wood in 1663 under Bishop Cosin's patronage for Durham Cathedral *(39)*.

The more extreme reformers sometimes destroyed fonts in the sixteenth century, and shortly after her accession, Elizabeth I had to issue an order that they should remain in place, and that baptism should be administered in them, not in basins. Puritans frequently chose to ignore this injunction, which had to be underlined frequently in visitation articles issued by bishops, and laid down in a canon of 1603. Another problem to the authorities at this time was the custom of making fonts in precious metals. Ironically the only one that seems to be in use today is

21 Old Radnor: font, possibly sixth, seventh or eighth century

22 Lenton, Nottingham: font, twelfth century

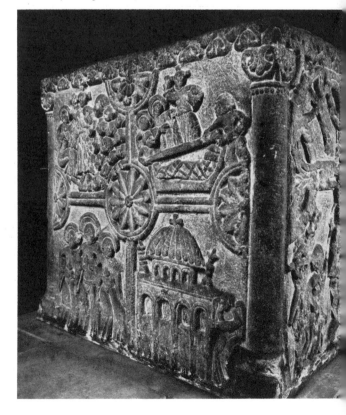

23 Above left Winchester Cathedral: font, Tournai marble, c. 1130–40

24 Above right Castle Frome, Herefordshire: font, c. 1170

25 Left Southrop, Gloucestershire: font, twelfth century, detail

26 Above right Bridekirk, Cumberland:
font, mid-twelfth century. Detail –
Rickart the sculptor

27 Right Brookland, Kent: lead font with
Signs of the Zodiac and Labours of the
Months, perhaps French, c. 1200

28 Left Bodmin, Cornwall: font, twelfth century

29 Below left Youlgreave, Derbyshire: font with projecting side-stoup, c. 1200

Opposite

30 Top left Barnack, Huntingdonshire: font, thirteenth century

31 Top right Brailes, Warwickshire: font, early fourteenth century

32 Right Fritton, Norfolk: font, late medieval

33 Far right Walsoken, Norfolk: seven sacrament font, 1544

34 Above left Trunch, Norfolk: font and canopy, c. 1500
35 Above right Luton, Bedfordshire: font and canopy, c. 1330–40
36 Left St Botolph, Cambridge: font case and cover, 1637

37 Left Ufford, Suffolk: font and telescopic cover, c. 1500

38 Above right Newcastle Cathedral: Frosterley marble font, fifteenth century; cover c. 1500

39 Opposite Durham Cathedral: font and canopy, c. 1663
40 Above left Marden, Kent: font and cover, 1662
41 Above right Knapton, Norfolk: Purbeck marble font, thirteenth century; cover, 1704

42 Above left Twickenham, Middlesex: font and cover, c. 1680, from All Hallows, Lombard Street, London

43 Left Beverley Minster, Yorkshire: Frosterley marble font, twelfth century; cover, 1713

44 Above right Croome d'Abitot, Worcestershire: wooden font, c. 1763, probably by Robert Adam

45 West Wycombe, Buckinghamshire: font, c.1760
46 Below Essendon, Hertfordshire: Wedgwood black basalt
ware font, 1780

47 Ottery St Mary, Devon: font and cover, 1850, by William Butterfield

48 Above left St Mary Abbots, Kensington: font and cover c.1872, by Sir G.G. Scott

49 Above right Highnam, Gloucestershire: font and cover c.1851, by Henry Woodyer

50 Below Clifton Cathedral, Bristol: Portland stone and Purbeck marble font, 1973, by Simon Verity

the royal font, made later to the order of Charles II.

Many of the fonts made between the Reformation and the Commonwealth are plain, but there is an alabaster one at Risley, Derbyshire, of the 1590s with strapwork decoration, and Canterbury Cathedral has one of 1639 made of black and white marble with a gadrooned and fluted bowl, and figures of the evangelists. There was further destruction of fonts by the Puritans, and it seems quite possible that new ones provided in the 1660s, like a few earlier ones, were deliberately reminiscent of their predecessors. Thus one may account for the Perpendicular style fonts at Over Compton, Dorset, 1620, Bray, Berkshire, 1647, Ashwellthorpe, Norfolk, 1660, Eglingham, Northumberland, 1663, and Alnham, Northumberland, 1664, and the Purbeck revival font at Swanage, Dorset, close to the quarries, of 1663.

Many other Restoration fonts were quite plain, with plain covers, like the one of 1662 at Marden, Kent *(40)*. More beautiful were the classical fonts made of marble with winged cherubs' heads round the bowl, and matching covers, clearly metropolitan work, like the one at Willen, Buckinghamshire, and the very similar one, made for All Hallows, Lombard Street, now at Twickenham *(42)*.

The objection to materials other than stone seems to have weakened over the years. A revival of the use of lead may have begun with the font at Down Hatherley, Gloucestershire, in the sixteenth century, and continues with those fonts, also in Gloucestershire, like Slimbridge, 1614, and Haresfield. Lead, of course, had been commonly used to line stone fonts, and so its employment was hallowed by custom, but at Little Gidding, Huntingdonshire, there is a fine brass baluster font on claw feet with a crown-like cover, installed about 1625 during the incumbency of Nicholas Ferrar.

More common is wood. Now that the water did not lie in the font for several months on end, the old objection of seepage lost its validity. So one finds them occasionally, as at Dymock, Gloucestershire, and St George's Windsor. More frequently in the seventeenth century, wood was used to encase and cover the font, as had been done in the sixteenth century. There is a fine example at Stanford-in-the-Vale, Berkshire, and another, dated 1637, at St Botolph, Cambridge *(36)*. Covers were sometimes elaborate, none more so than the tall gothic spire at Terrington St Clement in the Norfolk Fenland, where the bottom part opens to form a sort of triptych when the font is in use, painted with scriptural scenes including the baptism of Christ, and the four evangelists.

The arrival of the baluster font early in the seventeenth century witnesses the belated English decision to follow most of the rest of western Christendom and to baptize by affusion instead of immersion. By the eighteenth century most fonts reflect the changed custom, though by way of complete contrast there is an adult immersion font at Otley, Suffolk, perhaps used by Anabaptists during the Commonwealth, and provision was also made for the immersion of adults in a few other places like Cranbrook, Kent, 1725, and Llanbister, Radnorshire.

Gadrooning was a standard ornament for bowls of baluster fonts in the eighteenth century, and while marble remained the most usual material, a few of the most interesting fonts use other materials. At Essendon, Hertfordshire *(46)*, and Cardington, Bedfordshire, are fonts made respectively in 1780 and 1783 from black basalt ware by Wedgwood. They stand on fluted tapering square pillars, with swags on both pillars and bowls. The effect is reminiscent of the taste inspired by Robert Adam in his later years, but the only font which seems to have been designed by him – unless he was responsible for the tiny marble font, about a foot square, at Gunton, Norfolk – is the one at Croome d'Abitot, Worcestershire, dating from 1763 *(44)*. It is made of wood, with claw feet, and the ornamentation is in his more florid earlier idiom, closer to William Kent. There are winged cherubs' heads, and bold use of acanthus, as well as the swags and fluting used later in the Wedgwood fonts.

Another interesting eighteenth-century font is at Teigh, Rutland, made of mahogany about 1782, and originally fixed by a bracket to the corner of the communion rail. The sanctuary was not an uncommon place for a font at the time, but the fashion was short-lived, and a stone font was provided by the rector about 1830 in the body of the church. Recently the mahogany vase has been moved near to it.[18] But the most remarkable eighteenth-century font is the one at West Wycombe, Buckinghamshire *(45)*, put in about 1760. It has bold claw feet supporting a very slender column round which a snake is curled. A dove perches on one side, stretching up towards the tiny bowl round which four other doves stand as though round a bird-bath. It has attracted a good deal of censure, of course, for daring to be different, and as late as 1912, Dr Charles Wall described it as 'the worst possible substitute for a font'.

Covers for older fonts continued to be made in the eighteenth century, but most of them are noticeably lighter than their predecessors. Typical are the good country pieces at Long Stratton and Knapton, 1704, Norfolk *(41)*. Much less typical is the vast and florid masterpiece of 1713 in Beverley Minster *(43)*, which would look thoroughly at home in one of Hawksmoor's London churches.

Costs are interesting. Quite an ambitious locally made font at Moulton, Lincolnshire cost £7.3.0. in 1719, which gives an illuminating standard of comparison for the £350 charged by Francis Bird, one of the leading sculptors of his generation, in 1727 for the font in St Paul's. Even allowing for inflation, however, this seems modest enough compared with the £2000 paid in 1868 for the elaborate marble font at Ashley, Northamptonshire.

Although the Victorians had no intention of returning to immersion, they liked fonts in which this could have been done, and disapproved of balusters. Most Victorian fonts were of stone, and more or less gothic. The more enterprising designers sometimes looked overseas for inspiration. Sara Losh at Wreay looked to Byzantium, but to local Cumbrian alabaster for her material. Sir G.G. Scott at St Mary Abbots Kensington, 1872, looked to the Low Countries, especially for his openwork wrought iron cover *(48)*; Butterfield at Ottery St Mary, Devon, *(47)* seems to have looked to both. Yet in each case, though far from English precedents, the results are unmistakeably English, as is Woodyer's bold design at Highnam *(49)*. Completely different is the Doulton porcelain font in the Roman Catholic church of St Peter and St Edward, Buckingham Palace Road, London, an unusual choice of material, and, of course, superior to the foot-high earthenware ones at Asgarby and Biscathorpe, Lincolnshire. At Hawes, North Riding, an earthenware basin of 1822 is set into a marble bowl. Finally, for a contrast in nineteenth-century designs, Merton College Chapel, Oxford, has a green Siberian marble font of 1816, given by Tsar Alexander, and a Butterfield font of 1851.

There is a memorable Edwardian font at Great Warley by William Reynolds-Stephens, with a standing bronze angel either side of the bowl, and about the same time, Henry Wilson made the round alabaster font for Norton-sub-Hamdon, Somerset, ornamented with spiral-fluting, fish, and flowers.

With the exception of Sir Albert Richardson's pleasant font of 1937 at Southill, Bedfordshire, there is little else of significance until after the Second World War. Alan Dent's font at Llandaff Cathedral, 1952, is reminiscent of the style of Eric Gill, with scenes of the Fall and the Redemption, and from the lives of Saints Dyfrig and Teilo carved in low relief. Sir Basil Spence at Coventry Cathedral used an unhewn boulder from Bethlehem to great effect in the simple baptistry, and in another simple modern baptistry, in Liverpool Metropolitan Cathedral, the emphasis is on white, the colour of purity. The font itself is a completely plain drum of pure white marble from Skopje, made from the same block that was used for the high altar. At Clifton Cathedral the font by Simon Verity, 1973, *(50)* is made of Portland stone and Purbeck marble with a small pool alongside. As well as the traditional dove symbolism, he also uses fish, the Early Christian symbol for Christ so suitable, but so rarely used in this context. At Blackburn Cathedral, there is another plain new white font, this time egg-shaped to symbolise resurrection, and with a fine bronze cover by John Hayward depicting the baptism of Jesus. A more difficult task faced the designer of the new font at Passenham, Northamptonshire, where it had to be both contemporary, and in keeping with the seventeenth and eighteenth-century furnishings. The result is a modern wooden baluster, both attractive in itself and at home in its surroundings. Finally, one of Dean Hussey's last acts before he retired as Dean of Chichester, was to commission a new font for the cathedral from Henry Moore, not yet made at the time of writing (1979).

Chapter 4
Congregational Seating

Until the late middle ages congregations stood or knelt, though occasionally stone benches were provided along walls or round the bases of piers for the aged and infirm and for women with babies.[19] Probably such seats were originally much commoner: simple wooden benches along walls would have disappeared with the introduction of fixed seating, and even stone ones may have been hacked off to allow more space for pews. But they still exist in a number of places like Tintagel, Cornwall, Sundon, Bedfordshire, and Patrington, East Riding, along walls, and at Sutton Bonnington, Nottinghamshire, Clifton Hampden, Oxfordshire, Hunstanton and Snettisham, Norfolk, round piers. It may be significant though, that with the possible exception of Tintagel, none of these is earlier than the fourteenth century, by which time rows of benches were being introduced, so that it may have been an alternative rather than an earlier form, which still left the floor of the nave unencumbered for such functions as church ales. But in spite of this advantage, in the long run, rows of seats, transforming naves into auditoria, prevailed.

What are generally reckoned to be the earliest benches to survive are at Clapton-in-Gordano, Somerset, Dunsfold, Surrey (51), and two churches not far from Dunsfold over the Sussex border at Didling and Loxwood. They are simple, and generally attributed to the years around 1300, but in the absence of very definite features, dendrochronological confirmation would be welcome. Certainly most medieval seating was installed in the fifteenth and early sixteenth centuries, and in East Anglia and the south west in particular it was often ornately carved. The traditions are quite distinct. In the West Country, the bench ends are usually the only part to bear carved decoration, and are square-topped, while in East Anglia base plates and bench backs are often carved as well, and the ends have poppy-heads, often with supporting figures in front, or in front of and behind the finial. The term poppy-head is derived from the French 'poupée', a doll, and refers to the figure carving. By far the majority of English poppy-heads have simple fleur-de-lys finials. In other parts of the country, both flat-topped and poppy-headed benches

are found, usually without the same wealth of detail, though there are interesting ones at East Barning, Kent, and the ends of the pew fronts at Tideswell, Derbyshire, have figure carving (52).

Though the few dates we know are scarcely adequate evidence, it seems possible that the East Anglian style of benches did not survive the Reformation, which is surprising, unless in fact the process of seating churches was virtually complete by then. The survival of so many is probably due to the uncontroversial nature of the figure carving, like the thatcher at Ixworth Thorpe, Suffolk; and nobody seems to have objected very much to the lively carving of the Seven Deadly Sins in the Puritan-scoured church at Blythburgh, Suffolk. Instruments of the Passion, such as occur on the back panel of the back row of benches at Fressingfield, Suffolk, seem to have excited no anger either, and the whole set of benches in this church is a fine sight, as the oak has weathered to a pale silvery-gold, and the carving is still wonderfully crisp (53). Some East Anglian churches have even more ambitious ends, like those at Ufford and Dennington, Suffolk, and Wiggenhall St Germans and Wiggenhall St Mary the Virgin (54) in the Norfolk Marshland. But most are simpler, and the appealing rusticity of such sets as those at Ixworth Thorpe and at Ashmanhaugh, Norfolk, make a foil to the admirable professionalism of the Wiggenhall work, while the aisles in many East Anglian churches have elementary backless benches with plain fleur-de-lys finials.

In the West Country many churches still have virtually complete sets of benches, mostly put in during the sixteenth century. Thus in Cornwall Gorran has 53 carved ends, Launcells over 60 and Altarnun 79; while in Devon East Budleigh has 63[20] and High Bickington about 70. Dates are much more frequently known in the west, sometimes through carvings on the ends themselves, sometimes through churchwardens' accounts. They suggest a continuous process of providing seating as funds allowed, uninterrupted by the Reformation.[21] The subject matter of the carving changes of course, but by no means suddenly, as the effects of both Reformation and

Renaissance percolated slowly. The Instruments of the Passion are very popular in earlier sets, especially in Cornwall, as at Launcells *(57)*, but also elsewhere as at Curry Rivel, Somerset. On one end at Bishop's Hull, Somerset, *(55)*, Christ is shown stepping out of the tomb via the body of a sleeping soldier, a convention which M.D. Anderson has shown to be derived from the practice of actors in Mystery plays.[22] Other ends show biblical subjects too, like the beautiful Flight into Egypt at Hilfield, Dorset – though the date of these benches is a matter for conjecture, and they could well be post-Reformation – but secular ones were also common, like the windmill at Bishop's Lydeard, and the Marian ale-taster at Milverton, Somerset. At East Budleigh, one end bears fleecing shears, a dolphin, and a heraldic unicorn, presumably the gift of a wool merchant, and at Chedzoy, one end has an M commemorating Mary Tudor rather than the Virgin. About this time, and during Elizabeth's reign, a carver named Simon Werman worked in the Taunton area, identifiable by his signature on a bench end at Broomfield. Most of his decoration consists of fruit and foliage, including vine trails, a motif which had survived from Saxon times via the breastsummers of medieval screens.

The hesitant appearance of the Renaissance in the 1530s is illustrated by the bench ends at Barwick and Crowcombe, Somerset *(58)*, while contemporary ones like those at North Molton, Devon, are still entirely gothic. Linenfold is an ornament which straddles the change. Simon Werman used it at Trull, and there are good sixteenth-century examples at Barton-le-Clay, Bedfordshire, a complete set, and at other churches nearby.[23] It was popular also in the Midlands and the Severn Valley, and the best example of all is at Strensham, Worcestershire, where the benches are matched by wall-panelling, also with linenfold – and hatpegs.

The Midlands have many examples of plain buttressed bench ends, usually regarded as medieval, as some of them doubtless are, but there is no reason why such an inoffensive design should not have become traditional in conservative country districts long after the Reformation, just as the West Country type did. In the north, some bench ends have the particular regional brand of flamboyant tracery also to be found in stalls. There are some good ones at Drax, West Riding, while others at Drax, perhaps a little later, have renaissance motifs. As in the south west, the provision of seating can be proved to have gone on long into Elizabeth's reign, and in most cases replacement seems out of the question. Either an existing stock was being added to, or these were the first seats the church possessed.[24] Increasingly desirable in the late middle ages, seats were really made essential by the more auditory nature of the reformed services, and it is a commentary on the conditions of the age, both religious and economic, that it took so long to provide them.

Occasionally there was a revival of the old idea of wall-seating, and the Jacobean benches running along the aisle walls at Buckland, Gloucestershire *(63)*, installed in 1615, have hatpegs on the back wainscoting, and, unusually, testers between the windows. The tradition of benches continued well into the seventeenth century with examples like Easton-on-the-Hill, Northamptonshire, dated 1631, Upholland, Lancashire, 1635, Elwick, Co. Durham, 1665, Eye, Herefordshire, with dolphin panels, 1684, and Milden, Suffolk 1685. In remote villages like Llangelynin and Llanfaglan, Caenarvonshire, they were still made in the eighteenth century, with simple ends, and either plain backboards or none, perhaps reproducing their predecessors, and a reversion to plain benches occurred occasionally in the early nineteenth century, like the set at West Grinstead, Sussex, which still bear the names of the farms of their owners *(61)*.

Box-pews *(4, 5, 62, 79, 115)* grew out of benches by carrying up the height of the backs, and inserting doors to reduce draughts. Doors had already been inserted in some Somerset churches by the middle of Elizabeth I's reign, and the evolution, though influenced from abroad, was natural and gradual. These pews were generally made of plain wainscot oak, though walnut is used at Sprotbrough, West Riding. Later, when farms had their own pews, the family sitting with their employees, benches were sometimes set round three sides of a pew, the door facing the pulpit. Such an arrangement dating from 1742 can be seen at Thurning, Norfolk. Sometimes the height of the backs and doors was such that the family inside had complete privacy from everyone else except the parson, the clerk, and any occupants of an elevated squire's pew. Most of these high pews, familiarly named horse-boxes, which scandalized Victorian ecclesiologists, and whose snugness was allegedly made unnecessary by Victorian 'tortoise' stoves, the first form of heating for the general congregation most of our churches knew,[25] have been ejected, but they still survive in a few places like Broughton, Staffordshire, Lower Winchendon, Buckinghamshire, Worstead, Norfolk, and Compton Wynyates Chapel, 1665, Warwickshire.

The box-pew is a comely and functional piece of furniture, which deserved a better fate than to be ejected in favour of draughtier, less comfortable and less visually attractive Victorian pitchpine, as, alas, it so often was.[26] These honest pieces, now mellow with age, add a great deal to the character of the interior of any church still fortunate enough to possess them. Sometimes they rise in tiers towards the back like a lecture theatre, a practice more commonly associated with the Church of Scotland and English Non-conformity, but which occurs in Anglican churches at Chipping Warden and Stanion, Northamptonshire, Chicheley, Buckinghamshire, and Parracombe, Devon. It is an eminently practical form, though it would be visually harmful in the wrong church. At Torbryan, Devon, the box-pews envelop the original benches, emphasizing their draught-proofing role, and here the candle-holders are still in place, as they are at Staunton Harold, Leicestershire.

Older arrangements of furniture are still reflected at Well, Lincolnshire, where box-pews face the gang-way, and at Aldfield, West Riding, where they face the pulpit, and similar arrangements exist, as we have seen, at places like Teigh, Stapleford, and Little Gidding.

Most of the examples of box-pews mentioned here are taken from the late seventeenth and eighteenth centuries, their heyday, but they were introduced, perhaps from the Netherlands, as early as about 1580 at Brooke, Rutland. They became commonplace alongside benches in the Jacobean era, and were still occasionally being installed just as the ecclesiologists were beginning to tear them out. Victorian examples occur at Altham, Lancashire, where they have poppy-heads as a gesture to gothicism, St Mary-le-Belfry, York, and, dated 1858, at Bircham Newton, Norfolk.

Other pews occur occasionally, like the gothick ones at Shobdon (7) and Croome d'Abitot. At Shobdon they have arched tops to the ends, quatrefoil piercings, but rococo curves on the door tops and the sides of the ends, and rococo scrolls in the ornament. A purer rococo can be seen in the details of the pew doors at the back of Turner's Hospital Chapel, Kirkleatham, North Riding (66), and a purer gothick at Mildenhall, Wiltshire, c.1815.

Private pews for the wealthy, known as 'close seats', are referred to in late medieval documents, and if the custom of endowing family chantry chapels increased the tendency for the gentry to sit apart from the commonalty, the suppression of the chantries did nothing to check it. The Cowmire Pew at Cartmel Fell, Lancashire, looks late medieval, and the Fitz Warren Pew at Tawstock, Devon, with early renaissance details, was probably made about 1540–50. One of the first that can be fairly firmly dated is the Morgan Pew of c.1564 at Skenfrith, Gwent, and there are Elizabet-

han family pews too at Brooke, Rutland, Arlesey, Bedfordshire, and Whalley, Lancashire. A perfectly preserved Jacobean pew belonging to the Bluett family exists at Holcombe Rogus, Devon, screened, but not elevated, like the much better known Jacobean pews at Rycote, Oxfordshire (59). By the later part of the century, however, elevation was becoming a frequent practice. The Hastings Pew at Melton Constable, Norfolk, make about 1680, forms a sort of south transept to the church. It is raised up two steps, and the front is painted white with heraldic panels. Inside are chairs, elegant ones for the family and their guests, simpler ones at the back for the servants, and on the walls are numerous modest family memorial tablets. At Croft, North Riding, the Milbanke Pew of about the same date is not an adjunct to the building, but a piece of furniture within it – and what a piece of furniture! One ascends gently up a long staircase with twisted balusters, which turns through a right angle after a half-landing, eventually reaching the pew itself in the form of a double box with curtains, supported by Tuscan columns. It must have been difficult to pray humbly in such an exalted position (60). At Maidwell, Northamptonshire, the squire and his family sat in canopied seats at the back of the small church, placed either side of the tower arch in the manner of return stalls. Here the squire could see – or doze – without being seen.[27] Sometimes, as at West Ogwell, Devon, Stapleford, Leicestershire, Shobdon and formerly at Rycote, the squire's pew is even provided with a fireplace.

But the squire was not necessarily the only person to have a pew. At Rycote, the northern pew belonged to the Norreys family, but the southern one was probably made in 1625 for a visit by Charles I. At Longnor, Shropshire, there is a rector's pew, and Parson Woodforde often writes about his seat (i.e. pew) in the chancel at Weston Longville, Norfolk, which, being a bachelor, he often loaned to friends. Other dignitaries, too, sometimes had their special seats. Eighteenth-century mayors were well provided for in a number of town churches, like St Helen, Abingdon, Berkshire, 1706, where a sword rest also remains, Blandford Forum, Dorset, 1748, (65), and St Swithun, Worcester. At High Wycombe, Bucking-hamshire, a desk was provided for him too. Churchwardens also occasionally had their own pews, though the fashion seems to have been a short one, the dated examples at Upholland, Lancashire, Llananno, Radnorshire, and Whalley, Lancashire, being as close as 1679, 1681 and 1690 respectively. The general custom since has been for wardens' staffs to be placed by their usual seats. At Whalley, where the variety of

51 Dunsfold, Surrey: benches, probably late thirteenth century

53 Fressingfield, Suffolk: bench end, late medieval

54 Wiggenhall St Mary the Virgin, Norfolk: bench end, early sixteenth century

52 Tideswell, Derbyshire: pew front, late medieval

55 Bishop's Hull, Somerset: bench end depicting the resurrection, early sixteenth century

56 East Budleigh, Devon: bench end; dolphin, wool shears and heraldic unicorn, late medieval

57 Launcells, Cornwall: bench end, symbols of the Passion, late medieval

58 Crowcombe, Somerset: bench end with renaissance detail, c.1534

59 Rycote Chapel, Oxfordshire: fifteenth- and seventeenth-century woodwork

60 Above left Croft, Yorkshire: Milbanke Pew, c. 1670–80
61 Opposite West Grinstead, Sussex: benches with names of owners' farms inscribed, early nineteenth century
62 Above St Mary, Whitby, Yorkshire: a medieval church refurnished for Georgian sermons

63 Far left Buckland, Gloucestershire: aisle seating, 1615

64 Above left Bishop's Cleeve, Gloucestershire: west Gallery, Jacobean

65 Left Blandford Forum, Dorset: Mayor's chair, 1748

66 Right Turner's Hospital Chapel, Kirkleatham, Yorkshire: galleries, doorways, and pews, c. 1742

seating in the church is unusually interesting, a pew was provided for the constable in 1714. At Pickworth, Rutland, there is a special christening pew.

Family pews continued to be made even into the nineteenth century. At Selworthy, Somerset, one was economically and attractively contrived out of the parvise chamber over the south porch. Also elevated, and made in 1825, much the same time as the Selworthy pew, is the one at Rolvenden, Kent, which overlooks the altar rather than the pulpit, an unexpected siting for its date.[28]

As the population of some parishes increased, galleries were inserted to cater for the surplus, and many churches built in the eighteenth and early nineteenth centuries (and many nonconformist chapels into the twentieth) contained them as part of the original design. There were one or two small specialised precedents, like the Minstrels' Gallery at Exeter Cathedral of about 1350. The first in the modern sense date from the end of the sixteenth century, and some of these at least were designed primarily for musicians in the days when the choir and organ or band led the singing from the west end, acoustically a far more intelligent place for them to be than in the chancel, a Victorian innovation imitating cathedral and monastic choirs, where one sometimes suspects that they exist primarily to fill up the awkward chancel space and to provide visual decoration. At Bishop's Cleeve, Gloucestershire, there is a splendid Jacobean musicians' gallery (64), and there is another of about the same date at Abbey Dore, Herefordshire, while the one at Trentishoe, Devon, is as late as 1771. Of other galleries, the earliest may be at Melverley, Shropshire, which may date from 1588, while among the finest are those at Wren's St Martin, Ludgate, London, and Robert Adam's at Gunton, Norfolk, 1769. At St Martin, Ludgate, the gallery is above the narthex and contains three doorcases which must be among the best in any church in England. Adam's is more restrained, as one might expect, and holds the organ, as well as the choir. All the same, it is beautiful work, with a swag above the doorcase somewhat reminiscent of the Wren tradition. At Dorney, Buckinghamshire, there is a three-sided gallery of 1634, and such galleries on north, west, and south sides of churches were once a common sight. There is a very beautiful example of 1742 at Turner's Hospital Chapel, Kirkleatham, stepped at the west, with wrought iron railings and fine doorcases (66). Other excellent examples of three-galleried churches are St James, Whitehaven, c.1753, St Michael, Workington of 1770, restored in 1887, and All Saints, Wellington, Shropshire of 1790.

Sometimes galleries housed family pews. At Biddlesden, Buckinghamshire, there is a two-storeyed west gallery, in the upper part of which the squire and his family sat, while at Stapleford, Leicestershire, the family pew of the Earls of Harborough, with its Coade stone fireplace, is also in the west gallery. Cast-iron columns were often used as supports, especially from about 1790 to 1830. At London Colney, Hertfordshire, they are in the Norman style, and made in 1825, and there is a similar arrangement not far away at Markyate, while at St Peter, Belper, Derbyshire, built in 1824, all three galleries have cast-iron columns.

Inserted galleries often disfigured the architecture of medieval churches, and have since been rightly removed, though at Great St Mary, Cambridge, the galleries are elegant eighteenth-century affairs, possibly designed by James Gibbs, and still regularly used in this University church, and there are other churches where the galleries are the dominating feature of the interior and provide most of its character. In the octagonal church of St John, Chichester (5), built in 1813, they are on all four sides of the pulpit, as they also are at St Mary, Whitby, North Riding, (62). There is no interior in England like Whitby. The oldest gallery is the Cholmley Pew raised in the late seventeenth century on twisted barley sugar columns[29] across the chancel arch in the position once occupied by the rood loft. A west gallery was added very shortly afterwards, and galleries were added in the nave and transepts until the present state was reached in 1764. Obviously the pulpit must then have been inadequate, and the present tall three-decker, which puts the parson nearly on a level with his galleried parishioners, and which soars high above those accommodated in the box-pews, was put in in 1778. Very occasionally the addition of a gallery has been resorted to in modern times. At Millom, Cumberland, a west gallery was added in 1930, and at South Benfleet, Essex, the architect Sir Charles Nicholson, who was a parishioner, put one in in 1931.

Victorian and later seating is not on the whole interesting. At Hertingfordbury, Hertfordshire, there is the unexpected sight of rococo bench ends carved in 1890 by Joseph Mayer of Oberammergau, but even these are quite ordinary compared with those at St Stephen, Halgh, Bolton. This is a church built almost entirely of terracotta in the 1840s, and the bench ends and backs, even the organ case, are in the same material. As the church was paid for by the manufacturer, John Fletcher, to demonstrate the versatility of the material, it can, unkindly perhaps, be thought of primarily as a trade advertisement.[30]

Most Victorian seating was unadventurous, consisting either of inoffensive gothic pews or of chairs. It was the Victorians who introduced chairs for congregational seating, and the twentieth century has followed them with some enthusiasm, rarely altering the original design. Considered as an individual object, this standard design is pleasant and functional, as long as one squats rather than kneels, and as long as the church is draught-proof. Otherwise such chairs have grave disadvantages compared with fixed seating, and to be practical at all they need to be bolted to backboards, which reduces their one advantage of being more easily cleared from the floor should occasion arise. In modern churches like, say, Clifton Cathedral, where they are substantial and comfortable, and designed as part of the ensemble, chairs can be excellent, but few older than the Second World War are really suited to their purpose. Most could profitably be donated to the village hall.

Visually, too, seating can be disastrous: not in late medieval or subsequent churches where the design takes seats into account – the bases of late medieval piers are sometimes very high for that reason – but in early medieval churches, where arcades of great beauty can be partially obscured and their proportions spoilt. Indeed, this is a case where small congregations can have their compensations, for much of such seating is generally redundant, and simple stacking chairs which were put away when not in use would leave those naves looking as they should. Two churches which come to mind that would benefit from this treatment are St Mary, Barton-upon-Humber, and West Walton in the Norfolk marshland. The naves of medieval cathedrals need even more to be freed from the encumbrance of their rarely filled nave seating, none of which is historically important, and all of which detracts from the architecture. One only has to visit a cathedral when for some reason the nave has been cleared, or, failing that, to look at the prints in the volumes of Britton, published before the clutter was installed, to still any doubts. Perhaps, indeed, half our churches would be the better for less seating than they have now, better not only visually, but easier to keep clean, and, as our ancestors realized, more versatile in the ecclesiastical uses to which they could be put. Sometimes, as at Grosmont, Gwent, this has long ago been done, but here the chancel is so solidly screened off that it no longer seems to be one church, and that, though economical in heating, seems a pity in every other respect. Finally, small congregations for a communion service gathered into the chancel achieve an intimacy with the altar and the celebrant which has in most cases been lost since Stuart high churchmen insisted on the return of the communion table from the nave to the east end. A nave altar, which may be the right solution if the congregation is fairly large, has the unfortunate effect of blocking off the chancel, something one feels strongly in the present (1978) arrangements at West Wycombe. Coping with large churches in present-day conditions is not easy, but imaginative use – or disuse – of congregational seating is one of the keys to solving the problem.

Chapter 5
Other Nave Furniture

Pulpits

The word '*pulpitum*' means a raised place, and was used for two distinct pieces of furniture in a medieval church: the choir screen in a cathedral or conventual church, and a preaching or reading box. Pulpits in our sense of the word were used in monastic refectories for readings during meals long before they became customary in churches, and the pulpit at Beaulieu, Hampshire, where the parish church was formed from the abbey refectory, is the oldest still in use in the country. But pulpits were made at an earlier time than any which now exist, and Abbot Samson of Bury St Edmunds had one made as early as the end of the twelfth century so that he could preach to the people in English.

Whether the pulpitum in the sense of choir screen was ever a preaching platform is less certain. At Ripon Cathedral the now disused fifteenth-century stone pulpit is said to have stood on it until Victorian extensions to the organ. But even if this was its original site, it was unlikely to have been typical, for the rood screen generally stood one bay west of the pulpitum, and would have obscured the preacher. The use of the rood loft in parish churches for preaching is equally doubtful. The only evidence concerns one or two Devon churches where it was apparently the custom long after the Reformation. Admittedly at Walpole St Andrew, Norfolk, a bracket, obviously a pulpit base, is reached by an opening from the rood-stairs, but this is simply an example of economic planning. In fact, we know practically nothing about where medieval preachers stood before the introduction of pulpits.[31]

The earliest pulpits left to us seem to belong to the last years of the fourteenth century, and already both stone and wood were being used in different localities, materials which have remained standard ever since.[32] Metal pulpits, such as are sometimes found in Europe, were also made in medieval England – there was an iron one in Durham Cathedral – but there are none left. By and large, most medieval stone pulpits belong to the southern end of the oolitic limestone belt, while wood is usual in the stoneless areas of the south-east, and in other districts both materials are used fairly haphazardly.

A particularly fine group of dignified stone pulpits is found in the Bristol area, stretching into the Cotswolds, like the one at Northleach, Gloucestershire *(67)*, while further west in Devon, restraint is thrown off and they are encrusted with carving as rich as that found on screens. These were normally carved from Beer stone, hard chalk, widely used for carving capitals too, but further west still, at Egloshayle, Cornwall, Caen stone is used instead.

Like screens, most medieval pulpits were panelled with tracery recalling windows of the period, and, just as fifteenth-century glaziers commonly placed one figure in each light of a window, so painters often placed one figure in each panel of a pulpit, or of the dado of a screen. Most of these paintings have long since gone, but at Castle Acre, Norfolk, about 1400, and at Burnham Norton *(68)* nearby not long afterwards, the four Latin doctors – SS Ambrose, Augustine of Hippo, Gregory the Great and Jerome – can still be seen. In the west country, sculptured figures were sometimes used instead, as at Trull, Somerset *(70)* where there are a variety of saints depicted. Often medieval pulpits have been repainted in modern times, but never with figures. All the same, these pulpits, on their wine-glass stems, give a much better impression of the freshness and delicacy of the original conception. Notable examples are at Southwold, Suffolk, and at Fotheringhay and Warmington, Northamptonshire. At Fotheringhay there is a later tester, or sounding board, but the only contemporary one to survive, in the form of a typical late-medieval spired canopy, is at Edlesborough, Buckinghamshire *(69)*.

There is an early, Henry VIII, renaissance pulpit at Cockington, Torbay, in a remarkably convinced style. More often, renaissance motifs are combined with linenfold, as at Farcet, Huntingdonshire, and Catton, Norwich, dateable to 1537, and with balusters and arabesques as well, at Affpuddle, Dorset, 1547, and Chedzoy, Somerset, 1551. But the most beautiful pulpit of this time in its completely assured simplicity is the one in Wells Cathedral, made in stone about 1540 in memory of Bishop Knight *(71)*.

The north has its usual complement of flamboyant

tracery, probably about coeval with the earliest renaissance pulpits in the south. At Heighington, Co Durham, such a pulpit bears an inscription desiring prayers for the souls of the donors, Alexander and Agnes Fletcher, and others are at Hickleton, West Riding and Holme, Lancashire, in the latter of which the panels are pierced.

Initially it comes as a surprise to find that the Reformation led immediately to a decline in preaching, and, in consequence, to a similar decline in pulpit-making. So used are we to thinking of the reformed stress on the ministry of the word as against the catholic emphasis on the ministry of the sacrament, that it is easy to forget that revolutionary eras are not notable for freedom of speech. In 1548, preaching was forbidden except under licence from King Edward VI, Protector Somerset or Archbishop Cranmer,[33] and the minimum requirement in Elizabeth I's injunctions of 1559 is a mere four sermons a year, to be delivered by a licensed preacher. Fear of the rival sinister influences of Rome and Geneva meant that licences were not very freely granted, and Lord Keeper Bacon in 1578 felt moved to protest to the Bishop of Peterborough on the matter: 'Beholde in every Dioces the want of preachers, nay the greate discouragement that preachers find at yor hands...' But such protests had little effect, and in 1602, out of 433 clergy in the Diocese of Lichfield, only 82 were licensed to preach.[34] Since clergy who were not licensed had to read a set homily instead, few parishioners can have found enough inspiration from the pulpit to encourage them to spend lavishly on new ones. Nevertheless the Queen is praised, somewhat ambiguously perhaps, in 1580 on the base of the pulpit at Odstock, Wiltshire:

God bless and save our royal queen,
The lyke on earth was never seen.

Most Elizabethan pulpits were wooden, though the one at Fordington, Dorchester, of 1592, and the base of the one at Little Bytham, Lincolnshire, of 1590, are made of stone. One of the finest Elizabethan pulpits is at Orton Waterville, Huntingdonshire, originally in Great St Mary, Cambridge. It is ornate with caryatids, arabesques, and, less predictably, dogtooth. The panels contain blank arches, a common feature on any furniture when it was desired to elaborate plain wainscot panels. Although they are simply an updating of the gothic panels of the preceding period, they were never designed to contain paintings. Other specially good Elizabethan pulpits are at St Michael, Broadway, Worcestershire, and, with inlay, at Rudby-in-Cleveland, North Riding.

An order of Edward VI that a pulpit was to be placed in every church was clearly and predictably ineffective, but when, on the accession of James I in 1603, a similar canon was issued, the trickle of new pulpits became a flood. It was a period when preaching enjoyed a remarkable vogue, and outstanding men like John Donne, poet and romantic turned Dean of St Paul's, had a following reserved today to stars of the sporting or entertainment worlds. Indeed preaching was a form of entertainment. It was an age when religious passions ran high, and when the English language reached its apogee: the Authorized Version of the Bible appeared in 1611, and Shakespeare died in 1616. The best of Donne's sermons are certainly worthy of comparison even with these, and he did not stand alone. Lancelot Andrewes, Bishop of Winchester, and translator of much of the Old Testament for the Authorized Version, was a preacher of equal distinction, and there was no lack of others. Small wonder that new pulpits multiplied, and it seems as though almost every carpenter in England was making them. Only a relatively small proportion of seventeenth-century pulpits can be exactly dated, but there are just over 100 of them for the 22 years of the reign of James I, and nearly 150 more from the accession of his son Charles I in 1625 to the outbreak of the Civil War 17 years later. From 1642 to 1660, another revolutionary period with restricted freedom of speech, there are no more than 25, and though it must be added that by this time there can have been few churches left in need of one, the sudden decline is nonetheless significant.

The best of these pulpits are very fine, if ornate enough and naive enough to show that the spirit of the age of Elizabeth rather than of Inigo Jones dominated most joiners' shops and patrons' tastes. Indeed, Elizabethan style pulpits are found as late as 1636 at Ribchester and 1646 at Kirkland, Lancashire. Splendid Jacobean pulpits are found all over the country, and those illustrated, from St John, Briggate, Leeds, c.1634 *(72)*, Newport, Isle of Wight, 1636, *(73)* and Brancepeth, Co. Durham, c.1638, *(74)* are no better than dozens of others.[35] A simple pulpit of this time at Whitwell, Isle of Wight, 1624 could cost as little as £1, while even the one at North Elmham, Norfolk, which took 12 years to carve, presumably on and off, only cost £5.3s.4d. At the same time Nicholas Stone could charge up to £600 for a lavish monument.

Testers were often provided as sounding-boards, though many have been taken down since by less acoustically-conscious parishes to make such objects as vestry tables. Some inventiveness was applied to them, among the more interesting examples of which are the openwork ogee cupolas, like font covers, found notably at Brancepeth c.1638, *(74)*, Oxford Cathedral and at Husthwaite and neighbouring Carlton Husthwaite, North Riding, in the 1680s.

This was also the time of the introduction of the two-decker, where the parson read the service from the lower deck, ascending to the upper for the sermon. One of the earliest is at Leweston, Dorset, made about 1616, but there are others not much later at Alstonefield, Staffordshire, 1637, and Brancepeth *(74)*. The custom of a reader's desk in the nave was a fairly recent one, first mentioned in the Diocese of Norwich Visitation Articles in 1569,[36] and many were not physically attached to the pulpit. The most dramatic arrangement is at Leighton Bromswold, Huntingdonshire, where pulpit and reading desk were installed either side of the chancel arch about 1630 during George Herbert's incumbency. The two are almost identical, and both have testers. Clearly neither was to have precedence over the other. At Pembridge, Herefordshire, pulpit, reader's desk and lectern are also part of a Jacobean ensemble, all decorated with carved dragons, and at Ashington, Somerset, the reader's desk, probably made about 1631, is attached to the rector's pew.

In the eighteenth century, however, it was customary to attach desks to pulpits, and it is not until Victorian times that the two again became physically separate, frequently because of the Tractarian revival of the medieval practice of the parson officiating from the chancel. Most Victorian desks and their twentieth-century successors are unexceptionable objects bought from the ecclesiastical furnishers' catalogues of the day. The time will come when survivors will become collectors' pieces, but it has not arrived yet.

The most spectacular arrangement, however, was the three-decker. Here the lowest deck was occupied by the clerk, and the upper two by the parson as before. Shapes varied considerably, but the two Devon examples illustrated, from Branscombe and Molland, *(78, 79)*, are typical. The tester of the one at Boscombe, Wiltshire, is dated 1633, but that does not mean that it was all made at the same time, as three-deckers were commonly adaptations of existing pulpits. The medieval pulpit at Salle, Norfolk was made into a three-decker in 1611, which must make it one of the earliest in England. Kedington, Suffolk, of c.1620, and Foremark, Derbyshire, of the 1660s, look authentic enough, and there is one at Cartmel Fell, Lancashire, dated 1698, but the vast majority belong to the eighteenth and early nineteenth centuries like the one at Shobdon of c.1753 *(7)*. They were pulled down by ecclesiologists, needless to say, but conservative country areas untouched by Tractarianism cared little

67 Northleach, Gloucestershire: pulpit, fifteenth century

68 Below Burnham Norton, Norfolk: pulpit, fifteenth century
69 Right Edlesborough, Buckinghamshire: pulpit canopy, late medieval
70 Below right Trull, Somerset: pulpit, early sixteenth century

71 Left Wells Cathedral: pulpit, c.1540; Treasurer Sugar's Chantry, c.1490

72 Above left St John, Briggate, Leeds: pulpit and other woodwork, c.1634

73 Above right Newport, Isle of Wight: pulpit, 1636, by Thomas Caper

74 Left Brancepeth, Co. Durham: pulpit, c. 1638, by Robert Barker

75 Right Ingestre, Staffordshire: pulpit, c. 1676, probably designed by Sir Christopher Wren

76 Left St Mary Woolnoth, London: pulpit, c.1725, by Nicholas Hawksmoor
77 Right Royal Naval College, Greenwich: pulpit, c.1785, by William Newton

78 Above left Branscombe, Devon: three-decker pulpit, eighteenth century

79 Above right Molland, Devon: three-decker pulpit and box-pews, eighteenth century

80 Left St Martin, Scarborough, Yorkshire: Pre-Raphaelite pulpit, 1862

81 Right Chichester Cathedral: pulpit, 1966, by Geoffrey Clarke and Robert Potter

for such fashions, and three-deckers were installed at Boarhunt, Hampshire, probably in 1853, and at Murton, Westmorland in 1856. At Bawdeswell, Norfolk, the form was even revived in 1955.

The height of a three-decker, often considerable, was governed by the need of the parson to be able to overlook his flock hidden in the depths of their box-pews, or even to speak to those in galleries on fairly equal terms, as the plate of Whitby *(62)* demonstrates. They were thus practical pieces of furniture as most Georgian fittings were, and often quite simple. They were more commonly found in village churches than in the wealthy churches of the towns, for pulpits could, after all, be raised high enough to cope with galleries without subordinate decks, as numerous London churches show.

The Gibbons style, so strongly associated with Wren, and which gave London the finest pulpits in England *(3)*, can also be seen in places far removed from the capital, like Blisland, Cornwall, East Pennard, Somerset and Eynesbury, Huntingdonshire. Blandford Forum acquired one from a London church, but the one at Ingestre, Staffordshire *(75)* was made for it. The high raised pulpit with an access stair as beautiful as the pulpit itself could be a magnificent object, as the one of c.1725 at Hawksmoor's St Mary Woolnoth shows *(76)*, and an outstanding example from later in the century is at the Royal Hospital Chapel, Greenwich, installed as part of the restoration after a serious fire in 1779 *(77)*. Both these pulpits demonstrate the skill of the eighteenth-century cabinet maker in the use of curves – a highly sophisticated technique – and such pulpits, elaborate though they are, have nothing of the fiddly, all-over details of the Jacobean style, where the basic shapes were simple, and the visual effect relied largely on applied carving. The best eighteenth-century pieces, by contrast, impress first as pieces of design, which would still be beautiful even without the finely carved ornament.

The present position of pulpits, towards the east end of the nave, often close to one of the responds of the chancel arch, is Victorian, and Stuart and Georgian churches were by no means so standard. The pulpit was often the focal point of the church, as can be seen at Whitby *(62)* and St John, Chichester *(5)*. At Woodhey Hall Chapel, Cheshire c.1700, the pulpit is actually in the middle of the east wall, where it faced the family pew in the west gallery, with the communion table below and in front of it, and we have already seen that at Teigh, it was in the middle of the west wall. At Ravenstonedale, Westmorland, and Orton-on-the-Hill, Leicestershire, the pulpit still stands in the middle of the north side of the nave, and until recently at Orton the pews faced the pulpit. At Ashton-under-Lyne, Lancashire, it stands in the middle of the north arcade. All these pulpits are three-deckers, though the one at Ashton, as late as the 1840s, makes a concession to fashion by being in the gothic style. The box pews still face it, those in the chancel looking west. Gothic, or rather gothick, pulpits occur far earlier than the one at Ashton-under-Lyne of course, and the most notable is the one at Croome d'Abitot of c.1763.

Such an important piece of furniture had to be properly dressed in Stuart and Georgian times: so, for example, at St Edmund, Salisbury, the following entries in 1646–7 appear in the churchwardens' accounts:

Eleven yardes and a quarter of velvett at 15d the yard for the Pulpitt cloth and Pulpitt cusheon £3.8.9.
Eleven ounces of fringe ingraine and 3 quarters at 2s.6d per ounce £1.9.1.
Foure Tassells for the Cusheon 8.0.
Embroydering the figure on ye Cloth 12.0.
Buckrum and silke and making up the Pulpitt Cloth and Cusheon £1.4.0.
More to B.Beckham for woorke don, as by his bill £2.10.0.

Alas, by 1652 the laying of the pulpit cloth in this church was left to the discretion of the churchwardens as 'the Color is offensive to the sight of some of the parish.' But, expensive though this cloth and cushion were – more than the cost of the average pulpit – they were cheap compared with the ones of velvet provided for St Martin, Leicester in 1678–9, which cost £16.18.8.[37]

Virtually every seventeenth and eighteenth-century pulpit is made of wood, usually oak, though walnut and mahogany are sometimes used for more ambitious ones, but enterprising Victorian architects turned to a variety of materials. Iron, for example, was used by Street at Kingston, Dorset, and Kingsbury, Middlesex, and by other designers at Norton-sub-Hamdon, Somerset, Wem, Shropshire, and St Paul, Cheltenham. This last is movable, on runners, as are the pulpits at Langley, Shropshire, and Warehorne, Kent, an arrangement once commoner than it is today, for it allowed the altar to regain its focal position without the pulpit losing its place. Marble was sometimes imported for pulpits, as at Great Packington as early as c.1790, and Kirkby Stephen, Westmorland, 1872, but more commonly and less suitably alabaster was employed, its beauty and ease of carving outweighing the risk of damage to such a soft stone. So one finds it at Fonthill Gifford, Wiltshire, as early as c.1806, at Waddesdon, Buckinghamshire, in 1851, at Frant, Sussex, in 1892, and in many other places beside. More unlikely materials include plaster, at St Andrew Plymouth, 1851, and terracotta in the 'pot' church of St Ambrose, Widnes, Lancashire. Moving into the present century, Sandringham, Norfolk, has one basically of oak, but freely ornamented with silver. Mosaics, often used at this time for reredoses, were also used for pulpit panels, especially in ones made of alabaster, like the one at St Mary, Luton, designed by Street in 1882. Here the mosaics are by Jones and Willis, and the base of the pulpit consists of a pillar of Connemara marble, surrounded by smaller ones of 'Devonshire Red' on a base of 'Isle of Man Black'. Expense was certainly no object to secure the right blend of exotic materials.[38]

But freestone and wood never went out of fashion, and there are good Victorian examples of both, none better than the wooden pulpit at St Martin, Scarborough, c.1865, with ten panels painted by Campfield on a gold ground to designs by Morris, Rossetti, and Ford Madox Brown (80).

Twentieth-century examples begin with two lovely and restrained pieces, at Dullingham, Cambridgeshire, c.1905, where the beauty of the marble is what counts, and at St Bartholomew, Brighton, 1906. Henry Wilson, who designed the latter pulpit, was in different mood at Ripon Cathedral, 1913. Here the base consists of marble shafts round a marble core, but the pulpit itself is bronze with silver decoration. The access stair, by deliberate contrast, is beautifully simple.

Most modern pulpits are simple in shape, though St Paul's Cathedral has an attractive piece of Wren revival by Lord Mottistone, 1964, and St Leonard's Sussex has a wooden pulpit in the shape of a prow of a boat, a self-conscious conceit, perhaps, but an effective reminder of Christ's preaching on the shores of Galilee. The choir pulpit at Chichester Cathedral, 1966 by Geoffrey Clarke and Robert Potter, is made of stone-faced reinforced concrete and cast aluminium. Unusually, the front has a large abstract representation of the cross – a symbol one might have expected to find more frequently on a piece of furniture where Christ Crucified is to be preached (81).

Hour Glasses

Although there is a record of an hour glass being provided for the new pulpit at Lambeth in 1522, no pre-Reformation example exists, and only one bears a sixteenth-century date, that at Leigh, Kent, 15–7, the third figure being missing until recently, when a 9 was plausibly inserted. Most of the good examples left to us undoubtedly belong to the seventeenth century, and some to the eighteenth. At Binfield, Berkshire, the hour glass stands on an iron support with the arms of the Smiths' and Farriers' Companies. The one at Amberley, Sussex (82), in an iron stand, is supported by wooden winged cherubs' heads. At Compton Bassett, Wiltshire (83), the glass is again in a wooden frame, with turned and tapered balusters, in a wrought-iron stand, this time with elaborate finials top and bottom incorporating a three-dimensional fleur-de-lys, and which serve as a handle, enabling the preacher to reverse the stand and start the sand off for a second hour. Earl Stonham, Suffolk, has four glasses – one, on its own in an iron holder, for the hour; then a set of three, presumably later, for the hour, the half-hour and the quarter. An intriguing one at Pilton, Devon, is attached to the medieval pulpit by an iron arm and hand. At St Nicholas Hurst, Berkshire, the hour glass has quite elaborate, but naive, painting and gilding, with a lion and a unicorn supporting the date, 1636. Affixed to the same pillar is an iron scroll bearing the legend: 'As this glasse runneth, So man's Life passethe.'

Although this was an age of long sermons, they did not necessarily last an hour or more, as published examples prove, and in the nineteenth century they grew shorter. Queen Victoria, it is encouraging to learn, disliked long sermons, and the pulpit glass placed in the Chapel Royal of the Savoy in 1867 ran for only 18 minutes.[39]

Lecterns

The familiar feature of the nave lectern is a post-Reformation one. Lecterns were used in the middle ages, but they stood in chancels to hold gospel books. The oldest ones left in Britain were made of stone about 1200 or a little earlier, and are to be found at Norton and Crowle in Worcestershire. The one at Norton was found in the churchyard at Evesham Abbey, and consists of a sloping desk top with a high-relief figure of a bishop blessing on the fall-front. The rest of the carving consists of curling foliage in the stiff-leaf tradition. The one at Crowle (84) has been more heavily restored, but the central figure is in almost original condition, and is in higher relief than the Norton bishop. He grips the tendrils of the foliage with his hands, perhaps to support himself, as he kneels forward into thin air. The whole posture is extremely odd, but the thrust of the figure is upwards, as though he is supposed to be bearing the weight of the table top, though neither his hands nor his shoulders do so. A third similar lectern was found at Much Wenlock Priory, but this one has no central figure, and is a less ambitious piece in the same tradition.

Bookrests or gospel desks of stone are also found sometimes, usually built into chancel north walls. The one at Etwall, Derbyshire, may belong to the thirteenth century, but most of the rest seem to have been made in the fourteenth.[40] The fourteenth century also saw the making of the first surviving lecterns of the two types which have dominated the field ever since, the desk-top and the eagle. Both appear in wood or brass[41] quite frequently before the Reformation.

The desk-top comes in a variety of forms, depending on the number of sloping surfaces required to hold books. One of the earliest, made about 1325 judging by its carved foliage and arcading, is at Bury, Huntingdonshire. This has a single book-stand, like the early stone examples, and not unlike a Victorian schoolboy's desk. Not far away at Ramsey is a fifteenth-century wooden lectern with a much more elaborate base with openwork buttresses, and a double rotating bookrest. It probably came from Ramsey Abbey, and Boxley Abbey has been suggested as the place of origin of the superb timber lectern at Detling, Kent. This one *(85)*, the finest of its kind left to us, has four bookrests, all with pierced carving, and the top was originally surmounted by a statuette.

Among brass desk-tops, three are outstanding, those at Eton, King's College Cambridge, and St George's Windsor, all royal foundations. The Windsor one, made about 1500, may well have been imported from the Netherlands, whereas the others are probably English. The Eton lectern appears to be the older, though its basic design of a moulded base and stem, supported by four lions, and a double rotating bookrest is taken up by the even finer one at King's. The illustration *(86)* shows clearly the pierced tracery, the candle brackets, the chasing of the metal, the pierced rail along the top, and the finial statuette of Henry VI, founder of the college. Pevsner suggests that the same artists were responsible for this as for the screenwork in Henry VII's Chapel in Westminster Abbey. Certainly there can have been few people capable of this quality of design or execution.

Eagles were even more popular; inevitably in this case there was only a single bookrest, on the eagle's back, but the form was more imposing. The earliest eagles seem, like the desk-tops, to have been wooden, and there are fourteenth-century examples at Leigh-

ton Buzzard, Bedfordshire, and Ottery St Mary, Devon, the latter still gilded. A variation, probably as old, is the wooden cock lectern at Wednesbury, Staffordshire.

Most pre-Reformation brass eagles seem to hail from East Anglia, though the pelican at Norwich Cathedral seems to be Flemish work of about 1450, and since this is about contemporary with the earliest East Anglian products, like the one at Yeovil, Somerset, it could be that such imports stimulated local craftsmen. The place of origin of these eagles has never been determined, but there are several patterns, and the most likely sites for the workshops must be King's Lynn and Norwich.[42]

Some of these eagles have open beaks which form coinslots, and a stopper under the tail from which the coins could be extracted, gravity allowing natural functions to be emulated, enabling them to act also as offertory boxes. Another variation, the double-headed eagle, can be found at St Margaret's King's Lynn, and Redenhall, Norfolk. Many of these eagles stand on a moulded stem reminiscent of early Georgian wineglasses, and have a base supported by lions, *(87)*.

The iron lectern at Polebrook, Northamptonshire, is attributed to the middle ages by W.G. Hoskins,[43] but it is a difficult piece to date with any confidence. Iron, however, does not seem to have been used much for lecterns until the nineteenth century, though there is a strange sixteenth-century Spanish one at East Down, Devon, painted with the unexpected motif of dancing nudes on the shaft, which makes one doubtful about its ecclesiastical origin. There is also an attractive early eighteenth-century bracket lectern with scrolly ironwork, now under the tower at Alnwick, Northumberland, where it holds a Book of Homilies.

The Elizabethan period is, as so often, a lean one, though it is represented by a double desk-top at Cadbury, Devon. Equally predictably, the seventeenth century is rich in examples, and both eagles and desk-tops were revived. The earliest dated eagle of the revival, 1623, is at Wimborne Minster, Dorset. Oxford has a particularly fine accumulation of brass eagles – at Balliol, Exeter and Magdalen from the 1630s, at The Queen's and Wadham from Charles II's reign, and at Brasenose and University from the eighteenth century. There are wooden eagles too at Oriel, 1654, and St John's 1773. Two cathedrals acquired fine brass eagles at the Restoration, Canterbury in 1663, and Lincoln in 1667 both by William Burroughs. The brass double desk-top at Wells was made at about the same time. These were expensive items, and the one in St Paul's Cathedral cost £241 in 1720, not an excessive figure for fine materials and fine craftsmanship.

Although there was thus a revival of traditional forms in Stuart and Georgian days, there were also variations on the old themes, and one or two highly original pieces. At Blankney, Lincolnshire, the eagle puts a claw firmly on a serpent, a thoughtful piece of symbolism typical of the best of eighteenth-century piety, while at Tyberton, Herefordshire, in the 1720s, the wooden book-rest is supported by a chubby child angel in a pose which suggests that the designer was influenced by seventeenth-century Dutch work, like the example at Landbeach, Cambridgeshire, or even the ancient stone lectern at Crowle, *(88 cf 84)*. Nothing is known of the whereabouts of the Crowle one until 1845, when it was taken in from the churchyard, where it had been lying for some time, and restored, so the likeness could be completely coincidental.

But by far the most original eighteenth-century piece probably also served originally as a pulpit. Not surprisingly it is at West Wycombe, Buckinghamshire *(89)*. The desk is a small eagle on a fluted stem, while behind it is a comfortable Chippendale-style armchair in rosewood, finely carved and upholstered, originally with a dove hovering above, though this has recently disappeared. It all stands on a square platform with a semicircular projection for the eagle. It is movable, and has carrying handles, as does the access step. The whole design is splendidly conceived and executed, and there are two reading desks *en suite* with it.

Such originality extended into the nineteenth and twentieth centuries, though never to greater effect. As odd in its way is the lectern at East Hendred, Berkshire, with the strange motif at the base of a shod foot treading on three crocodiles. As an alternative to the still popular eagle, the pelican-in-her-piety was sometimes chosen,[44] as at Warborough, Oxfordshire, and Stanton Fitzwarren, Wiltshire, both Victorian, and at Bridgnorth, Shropshire, J. Phillips in 1929 discarded the wings of a bird in favour of the wings of a standing angel, perhaps an idea borrowed from Hardman's fine gilt angel of 1894 at Worcester Cathedral.

The great Victorian and Edwardian designers made their share of lecterns: one might pick out Butterfield's brass eagle at St Patrick, Brighton, which shows the saint and three Irish round towers at the foot, the Scott-Skidmore brass eagle of 1874 at Bibury, Gloucestershire, and Bainbridge Reynolds's iron and copper desk-top at St Cuthbert, Philbeach Gardens *(6)*. A much later Bainbridge-Reynolds piece is at St Osmund, Parkstone, Dorset, this time in bronze, a material Reynolds-Stephens had used both

for his lectern and his pulpit at Great Warley. At St Andrew, Roker, Sunderland, the lectern is by Ernest Gimson, *(90)*, made of ebony with the mother-of-pearl inlay of which he was such a master. Also inlaid with ivory and mother-of-pearl is the lectern of about 1930 at Chalford, Gloucestershire, by Peter van de Waals. Here the form is a double desk top, like the one at Roker, but the eagle also appears, in inlay, in the triangle formed between the bookrests. At Tarrant Hinton, Dorset, there is an Art Nouveau lectern by an unknown craftsman, given in 1909, and of very high quality, with something of the spirit of Charles Rennie Mackintosh *(91)*. It is made of iron, and iron was a popular material for lecterns from the early nineteenth century onwards. One of its most unusual manifestations must be the iron eagle at Attleborough, Norfolk, made in 1816.

Chests

In the middle ages there were several uses for chests in churches. One generally contained the parish records. It usually had three locks, so that it could only be opened in the presence of the incumbent and both churchwardens, though even greater security was provided for the chest at Stonham Aspal, Suffolk, which has 12 locks, and one at Boston, Lincolnshire, which has six. Plate might be locked in a chest if there was no secure wall-cupboard, or aumbry, for the purpose, and in larger churches there were vestment chests too. Medieval cope chests can still be seen in a number of cathedrals like the thirteenth-century examples at Salisbury and Wells.

The most primitive kind of chest consists of a single tree-trunk, hollowed out and sawn through longitudinally to separate the body from the lid. Unless they carry contemporary ironwork, such chests are impossible to date without dendrochronological techniques, but it is safe to assume that some are very ancient, dating from the twelfth century or even earlier while others are not as old as they may look. One at Bishop's Cleeve, Gloucestershire, has twelfth-century locks, whereas the ten-foot long one at Aldenham, Hertfordshire, is two centuries later.

The chest at Bishop's Cleeve is one of the earliest which can be dated with much confidence. Another, more interesting, is at Hindringham, Norfolk. This is of planked construction, with stout styles (end pieces extended downwards to form legs) characteristic of the thirteenth century, but the applied ornament consists of intersecting round-arched arcading, which makes a twelfth-century date possible, and anything later than about 1230–40 unlikely. At Hatfield, West

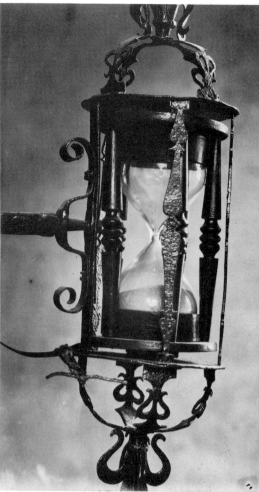

82 Left Amberley, Sussex: hour glass, seventeenth or eighteenth century

83 Above Compton Bassett, Wiltshire: hour glass, probably seventeenth century

84 Right Crowle, Worcestershire: lectern, c.1200
85 Below Detling, Kent: lectern, mid-fourteenth century
86 Below right King's College Chapel, Cambridge: lectern,
c.1515. Screen and stalls, c.1535 and c.1635

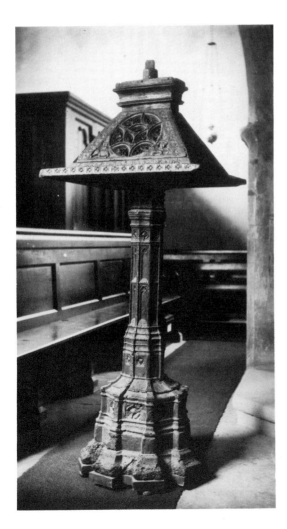

87 Above Wiggenhall St Mary the Virgin, Norfolk: lectern 1518
88 Above right Tyberton, Herefordshire: lectern c.1720
89 Opposite West Wycombe, Buckinghamshire: pulpit-lectern, c.1765

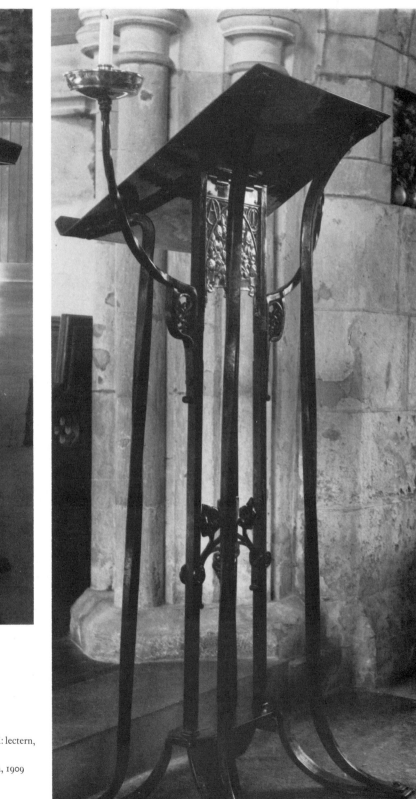

90 Above St Andrew, Roker, Sunderland: lectern,
c. 1907, by Ernest Gimson

91 Right Tarrant Hinton, Dorset: lectern, 1909

92 Top St John, Glastonbury, Somerset: chest, thirteenth century
93 Above York Minster: chest, early fifteenth century

94 Above left Newport, Essex: chest, late thirteenth century

95 Left Boston, Lincolnshire: iron-bound chest

96 Above right Adderbury, Oxfordshire: chest, 1725

97 Right Bedwellty, Gwent: vestment press, late fifteenth century (?)

98 Left Pinhoe, Devon: poor box, 1700
99 Right Butler's Marston, Warwickshire: poor box, 1902

Riding there is a similarly primitive chest with round-arched arcading, and incised patterns, drawn by compasses, one or two of which have been carved out.

Thirteenth-century ironwork is as characteristic on chests as anywhere. One at Church Brampton, Northamptonshire, has scrolly foliage; another, at Condover, Shropshire, has simple ironwork and simply carved styles. Rather later in the century in all probability are the chests at Icklingham All Saints, Suffolk, with ironwork very like the Eaton Bray door *(15)*, and at Malpas, Cheshire with delicate, free-flowing ironwork, which could even be after 1300. As at Condover, the styles are simply carved, in both cases seeming to form a handgrip to facilitate the none too easy task of moving these very heavy pieces of furniture.

Some chests are completely ironbound, like the one at Boston *(95)*, and these again are difficult to date unless there is an extraneous clue. There is a fine one, of the ark type, with a curved lid, at King's Langley, Hertfordshire. Less strong, but more in keeping with later medieval ideas of beautifying all woodwork with delicate carving, are the traceried chests. These follow window designs exactly, with lancets preceding tracery, as on the beautiful thirteenth-century chest at St John, Glastonbury *(92)*. The one at Saltwood, Kent, with its early bar tracery, could belong to the end of the thirteenth century, but most were made in the fourteenth, fifteenth and sixteenth. The finest carvings perhaps belong to the fourteenth century, as can be seen at All Saints, Hereford, and the three Lincolnshire churches of Fillingham, Glentham, and Huttoft. At Dersingham, Norfolk, the fourteenth-century chest has the symbols of the Evangelists carved on the front, and the walnut chest at Southwold, Suffolk, has a relief of St George and the dragon as well as rich tracery. About the middle of the fifteenth century, a further advance in construction was made, and framed-up chests appear for the first time, but planked chests with styles are still found, even when the carving is ambitious. Good fifteenth-century chests can be seen at Wilton, Norfolk, and Washingborough, Lincolnshire, the latter with roses instead of trefoils or quatrefoils in the heads of some of the arches.

More ambitious still is the splendid early fifteenth-century chest in York Minster *(93)*, with its highly spirited and crisp carving of the story of St George and the dragon, with a beautiful princess, a relief of a medieval town in the background, and the heads of the king and queen watching the saint's heroism from the discreet safety of the upper windows of a castle tower. About 1500, a fine chest was given to the church at Louth, Lincolnshire, with carved busts said to be of Henry VII and Elizabeth of York.

Church chests are not very different from secular ones, and a chest or coffer was the one piece of furniture nearly everyone possessed in days when most possessed very little. So some chests now in churches, whether medieval or later, may well be of secular origin. This is the case not only with locally made products, but also with the highly sought after Flanders kists, a term of which one has to be careful, since English-made versions were given the same name – they denoted an elaborately carved type in Flemish style. However, one or two Flemish-made chests do stand in our churches of which two can serve as examples. At Crediton, Devon, there is a superbly carved one with elaborate un-English gothic window tracery, while a later, sixteenth-century example at East Dereham, Norfolk, is in the renaissance style with arcaded female figures bearing religious emblems. Both have elaborate lock plates, and a little Nativity scene below.

There can be no doubt, however, about the most remarkable medieval chest in England, that at Newport, Essex *(94)*. This is a travelling chest, and the lid, when lifted, is painted to form a reredos, so that it could serve as a portable altar, the chest space no doubt occupied by eucharistic vessels and vestments, and the small superaltar, without which the wooden chest top could not be used for the celebration of mass, stored in the false bottom. Superaltars were small enough to be easily portable, but carved with the five consecration crosses to be found on full-size mensas. This chest can be dated by the paintings, said to be the earliest in oils on wood in England, to the late thirteenth century.

Another piece of medieval storage furniture was the hutch, which differs from a chest in that access is by means of a door in the front rather than by lifting the lid. They survive in a number of churches, including examples perhaps as early as the thirteenth century at Wennington, Essex, and South Mimms, Middlesex, and as late as the sixteenth century at Ruislip, and the seventeenth at Harefield, both Middlesex. One of the nicest, fitted out as a vestment press, which was probably a normal use for them, is at Bedwellty, Gwent. It has delicate flamboyant tracery with roses on the front *(97)*.

Post-Reformation chests are commonplace, but often excellent pieces of craftsmanship. One at Southwark Cathedral, probably made in 1588, has heraldic inlays, arabesques, and delicate Tuscan and Ionic pilasters. Among many Jacobean chests, one at Wishford, Wiltshire, may be singled out for excellence, another at Beaconsfield, Buckinghamshire, with painted landscapes, and a third at Rushbrooke, Suffolk, of yew wood with line drawings. At Woodbridge, Suffolk, the chest of 1672 has a gabled top and is covered in leather and bound with iron. By the eighteenth century, church chests had become for the most part simple utilitarian pieces made by the local joiner, and not to be compared with the best cabinet-making of the day. The chest at Adderbury, Oxfordshire *(96)* is typical, with the names of the churchwardens and the date, 1725, incised on the front, and ironwork so traditional it seems to be timeless. One of the most interesting later chests is the iron one, dated 1738, in St Asaph Cathedral, and made by the Wrexham smith Robert Davies to contain the cathedral plate. This chest is now used for freewill offerings, but at Purse Caudle, Dorset, there is a mid-sixteenth century chest made specifically for this purpose. Usually, however, alms were collected in smaller boxes.

Almsboxes

Almsboxes appeared in churches in early times, and a venerable age is claimed for the ones at Loddon, Norfolk, and Runwell, Essex, which are carved out of a single piece of wood in the manner of a dugout chest, and completely ironbound. Fifteenth-century examples are found at Kedington and Blythburgh, Suffolk, and Ludham, Norfolk. The one at Steeple Bumpstead, Essex, cannot be much later. At Bramford, Suffolk, the box looks medieval, but above it on the wall is painted the inscription: 'Remember ye pore. The Scripture doth record, what to them is geven, Is lent unto the Lorde 1591.' There is one at Dovercourt, Essex, dated 1589, but most surviving examples were made during the following century, and there are dated ones at Rewe, Devon, 1631, Monksilver, Somerset, 1634, Watton, Norfolk, 1639, Lostwithiel, Cornwall, 1645, and Grasmere, Westmorland, 1648. Several exhort the beholder to remember the poor, but one at Kingerby, Lincolnshire, dated 1639, is more ambitiously inscribed: 'This is God's treasury. Cast one mite into it.' One at Leyton, Essex, dated 1676, has the figure of a lame man on top, and another, at Pinhoe, Devon, 1700, a figure perhaps of a beadle; certainly he does not look like a pauper *(98)*. One of the nicest must be one of the latest, before the ubiquitous wall-safes took their places. This, at Butler's Marston, Warwickshire, and dated 1902, has an open hand carved on top *(99)*.

Collecting Shoes

Collecting shoes are also of some antiquity, though rarely used nowadays, being replaced either by the earlier custom of the almsdish (regarded as plate, and therefore not described in this volume), or by the more discreet, and therefore probably less productive, collecting bag. The shoe at Worlingworth, Suffolk, is dated 1622, and those at Troutbeck, Westmorland are dated 1692. The shoes at Blo Norton, Norfolk, are dated 1910, but it would seem that the carver got his 6 upside down, and that they are in fact Jacobean.

Chapter 6
Screens

From the earliest times the sanctuary of a church was railed off by a low screen. Later, when the choir was included in the eastern, clerical end of the church, it became customary to build a low wall to fence it off from the nave. These low walls were called 'cancelli', thus giving us the word 'chancel' for the area they enclosed. No early example survives here, though there are still a few in Italy, and there are a few fragments in England which could indicate similar arrangements in Saxon times. At South Kyme, Lincolnshire, there are some pieces of stone carved with foliage and trumpet spirals which could well be from cancelli, while it is just possible that some of the friezes at Breedon-on-the-Hill, Leicestershire, and some of the miscellaneous baluster shafts to be found in places like Hart, Jarrow and Monkwearmouth, Co. Durham, were too, for balusters could conceivably have supported an entablature like the ones at St Maria in Cosmedin, Rome, and formerly in Old St Peter's, and vine-trail friezes could have formed part of such an entablature.

Some early Saxon churches like Reculver, Kent, St Pancras, Canterbury, Bradwell-juxta-Mare, Essex, and Brixworth, Northamptonshire, had triple arches between nave and chancel. None remains intact, but the Reculver example, made about 670, stood until 1809 and is known from prints. The arches were equal in height, though the central one was wider, and turned in Roman brick. The responds were square, but the inner supports consisted of two quite elegant columns, now in the crypt of Canterbury Cathedral. The Reculver cross, fragments of which are also in the Canterbury crypt, stood in front of the middle arch, and appears to have been contemporary with the church. The siting may have been original, and it was certainly there in the early sixteenth century. The upper parts of the Brixworth chancel entrance lasted until the restoration of 1866. Here there was a stretch of solid masonry between the arches, and the central one was both taller and wider than those flanking it.

The triple-arched chancel opening seems to have been neglected after about the eighth century until the thirteenth. However, it is not surprising that Kent should be the scene of its revival, nor that the earliest, Westwell, should bear resemblances to its Saxon predecessors. The three arches are almost equal in height – the central one is very slightly higher than the others – and the two inner supports are tall, slender columns. At Capel-le-Ferne, near Folkestone, (100), the fourteenth-century screen is much lower than the one at Westwell, with three equal arches supported by octagonal piers and responds.

These two Kentish screens have solid wall above them, though this is in fact pierced at Capel-le-Ferne, but in East Anglia, the nearest parallels really are screens, as distinct from triple chancel arches, and set into a large conventional arch. The one at Bramford, Suffolk, made about 1300 is similar in its proportions to Capel-le-Ferne, and to another one of the same type at Welsh Newton, Herefordshire. The taller and more elegant screen at Bottisham, Cambridgeshire, is about a century younger, with the typical vertical emphasis of eastern work in the late middle ages. But the two most spectacular examples of this type are at Stebbing and Great Bardfield (105), Essex. Both belong to the fourteenth century and have elaborately cusped tracery, much restored. Whether the rood figures ever stood inside the apex of the central opening where they have now been restored is uncertain, but seems quite possible.[45]

From fairly early times the way churches were planned meant that the chancel screen came to stand below the Great Rood, though there was no necessary connection between the two. The Great Rood, so-called to distinguish it from the various other crucifixes in the church, was the dominant feature of the nave, standing or hanging where all eyes would be turned to it, either on the wall above the chancel arch, or within the arch itself. Some churches which have a central tower have an opening above the western arch which may have contained the rood, and a modern one in the great twelfth-century church at Melbourne, Derbyshire, gives an idea of the visual effect. Sometimes such an opening occurs in churches without a central tower, like the arrangement, remarkably solid even in its unfortunately Victorianised state, at Sandridge, Hertfordshire, though here it is too small to have contained the rood, which must have stood above it. At Capel-le-Ferne, (100), the opening looks older than the triple arch below it, suggesting a complex building history of uncertain interpretation.

The large chancel arches, or even the complete absence of chancel arches in the later middle ages were not designed to allow a flood of light from the east into the nave as they do now. In such cases, the rood was usually placed on a beam which stretched in tie-beam fashion across the church from north to south, and a boarded tympanum often filled the whole of the arch above the screen as a background to it. Such an arrangement survives in a few places, like Ludham, Norfolk, where a painted rood group is still visible. Though the style of the painting suggests the late fifteenth century – the date of the screen – it has been suggested that it belongs to the catholic revival under Mary Tudor, when roods destroyed during the iconoclasm of her brother Edward VI's reign had to be replaced in a hurry. Certainly carved roods were normal, even in remote little churches like Llanelieu, Brecon (112), where its white ghost can be seen against the otherwise painted tympanum.

The composition of the rood group varied, but normally the crucifix was flanked by figures of the Virgin Mary and St John, and churches which lacked these supporters were sometimes criticised during visitations. Less common were figures of Longinus the centurion, and the soldier with the sponge, though they occur in very early carved crucifixions in England at Daglingworth, Gloucestershire (236), c.1050, and the small rood of c.1000 at Romsey Abbey. The background of the rood group was often a painted Doom, or last judgement, either on the tympanum, as at Wenhaston, Suffolk, or on the chancel arch surround, as at St Thomas, Salisbury (174). At Attleborough, Norfolk, the painting surrounded a rood which must have stood in the tower opening in Melbourne-fashion.

No medieval rood group remains intact in Britain. Its sheer physical dominance and the veneration paid to it ensured that it became a prime target of the reformers, and an act of 1548 commanded that all images, including roods, whether 'abused' or not, should be 'extincted and destroyed'. Again in 1559–60, after the Marian interlude, they were ordered to be taken down. So thoroughly was this done that we are now left with only a few tantalising fragments. The most frequent survivor is the rood beam, itself unobjectionable, though often removed along with the rest, and even this is by no means common. At Cullompton, Devon, it is now surmounted by the Royal Arms, a telling substitution, and at Cullompton too, but *ex situ*, are remains of the carved Golgotha on which the rood stood (107). Very

few fragments of the rood groups themselves are known to survive, most of them now in museums. These include the head and right foot from the twelfth-century figure of Christ from South Cerney, Gloucestershire. However, there is some doubt about their original position, since the head of Christ has its eyes closed, whereas it was the normal custom at the time for the Christ of the Great Rood to be portrayed as Christus Victor in the Byzantine manner, with head erect and eyes open. Indeed the suffering Christ so dear to late medieval and later iconography was associated with the Albigensian heretics, and suspect for many years in consequence until the approval of St Francis overcame prejudice. The Christ figures from Cartmel Fell, Lancashire, Kemeys Inferior, Gwent, and Mochdre, Montgomeryshire, are also represented as suffering, but they are later, and since at Mochdre the figure of the Virgin also survived, it seems inescapable that here, at least, we have part of the Great Rood of the church. At Durham, part of one arm of a cross with holes showing where the arms of Christ were fixed to it was dredged up from the Castle well. And that, out of something like 9,000 medieval roods originally in our churches, is all that is known to survive.

As for the screens, the oldest now remaining is a matter for debate. The oldest piece of woodwork commonly classified as a screen is really the guard rail of the upper chancel chapel in the interesting two-storey arrangement at Compton, Surrey. Compton lay on the Pilgrims' Way, and it seems likely that it functioned as a pilgrimage church from shortly after the murder of Becket in 1170. The rail was probably made about 1200, and surmounts a low stone arch which leads into the lower chancel. The main chancel arch, of about the same date, is a little further west, and the Great Rood will have certainly hung over this.

The earliest true screens that survive with any degree of completeness belong to the thirteenth century. One, of stone, was the original choir screen of Salisbury Cathedral, removed by Wyatt at the end of the eighteenth century, and now reset in the Morning Chapel (102). Others, of wood, exist at Thurcaston, Leicestershire, Stanton Harcourt, Oxfordshire (103), Kirkstead, Lincolnshire, and Sparsholt, Berkshire. These are all rood screens, though the last is now in the south transept, but at Geddington, Northamptonshire, there is a thirteenth-century parclose, parclose being the name given to any screen used to fence off an aisle or chapel from the rest of the church. Such early wooden screens have quite a lot in common. They all imitate stone construction, they are all relatively simple, with the trefoiled arch as a usual feature, and none of them had a rood loft. Fourteenth-century screens are not very common either, and they can easily be distinguished from later work by their use of turned shafts instead of mullions in the lights.

The vast majority of medieval screens in England and Wales belong to the fifteenth and early sixteenth centuries, and though dated examples are not common, such dates as are known combined with stylistic evidence suggest that screen-making was a growth industry right up to the eve of the Reformation, many early and primitive screens doubtless being replaced by sturdier and more richly ornamented constructions complete with wide lofts and loft parapets. Lofts did exist as early as the thirteenth century, as the rood-stair doorways at Colsterworth and Thurlby, Lincolnshire, demonstrate,[46] but none earlier than the fifteenth century now exists.

These lofts fulfilled a variety of purposes: they housed the choir and sometimes carried a small organ as well; they provided convenient access to the rood, and they occasionally even carried an altar, as witnessed by the piscinas at Bettws Gwerfil Goch, Merionethshire, Great Hallingbury, Essex, and Blewbury, Berkshire, and the aumbry at Buckland, Gloucestershire. The association with the rood was enough in itself to secure the destruction of most lofts at the Reformation. Moreover, although the late sixteenth and early seventeenth centuries are rightly regarded as the golden age of English church music, the nature of most of the music is proof enough that this tradition belonged only to the great churches with choral foundations. In most ordinary parish churches music was discouraged in Elizabeth I's reign, and was not seriously revived until the seventeenth, the eighteenth or even the nineteenth century. So the lofts came down, though, sadly, some that survived the reformers and the puritans fell eventually to the Victorians, and only a handful remain today complete with their parapets, like the ones illustrated from Flamborough, East Riding (114) and Atherington, Devon (116).[47]

Far more, proportionately, survive in Wales, in spite of excessive Victorian rebuilding of church fabrics in the Principality.[48] Here the parapets vary from the plain wainscoting of Cascob, Radnorshire, to the elaborate examples illustrated (110, 115). Lofts in Wales are often wider than their equivalents in England, perhaps because the Welsh were ever a musical nation and had larger choirs. Accordingly screens were often of the verandah type, with open arcades to the east and west to give further support to the loft. Llanelieu (117), is a good example. The parapet has unfortunately disappeared, but the loft is

otherwise complete, and the tympanum is intact with ample traces of painting, not of a doom, but of a pattern of stars. The various squints cut into the tympanum must have been made to enable the choir to follow the celebrant's actions. But verandah screens were by no means confined to Wales, and good examples in England include the wooden one at Hexham Priory, Northumberland, and the stone one at Compton Bassett, Wiltshire, originally in Salisbury Cathedral.

Sometimes a loft exists without a screen below, or independently of the screen, as at St Margaret's and Pixley, Herefordshire, and Wingerworth, Derbyshire, but this arrangement, while it serves to underline the independent origin of the chancel screen and the rood and its appurtenances, can never have been common; indeed the normal late medieval name for the whole system of screen and loft was 'rood loft', and the word 'screen' is uncommon before the Reformation.

Medieval wooden screens have pronounced regional characteristics. Briefly, these are as follows: in south-west England they are long, low, and heavy. In this part of the country aisles frequently continued into the chancel and there was no structural division between nave and chancel. So screens often stretch right across a wide church from the north wall to the south, and sometimes, as at Dunchideock, Devon, even the intervening piers are encased in wainscoting. In a big church, like Dunster, Somerset, or Plymtree, Devon, such screens are tremendously impressive. The openings are usually in the form of four-light windows, with mullions running right through to the arches. The cresting is particularly richly carved, with several trails along the breastsummer, and the dados have paintings of saints, rarely, except notably at Ashton, Devon (108) of a quality to match the carpentry. At Ashton the painting is different in style from the usual rustic Devon work, and in some cases patently derived from woodcuts. Little carved figures form an alternative to two-dimensional painting on the dados of the screens at Bridford and Lustleigh, Devon, the first made about 1520, the second in the time of Mary Tudor. The execution is less happy than the idea, for the figures are rather small for their positions, but the Bridford screen (111) retains its colouring, glowing mysteriously in the rather dark little church in the manner of Byzantine iconostasis.

In the Gloucester area a number of parclose screens clearly depend on the early perpendicular work in the cathedral, whose main characteristic is the filling of stone arcades by complete windows of tracery. There is a good example at Mere, Wiltshire.

Welsh screens have much in common with those of

the west of England, and in strongly anglicised areas like the borders and the environs of the English bas- tides, English-style screens are found, probably made by English craftsmen.[49] Truly Welsh screens, and a few English ones, have rectangular tracery heads (whereas English ones are generally arched), and distinctive tracery, often in local groups, like those round Patricio (110), and a group in the Lleyn, of which Llanengan (115) is a good example. Dados tend to be lower than English ones, and the exuber- ance of the tracery together with the low dados suggest less emphasis on painting, and it has been seriously put forward that screens such as the one at Patricio were never intended to be coloured. All the same it is hard to accept that the plain loft parapet at Cascob was never painted with saints, like the one at Strensham, Worcestershire, or that the loft at Llananno, Radnor- shire, where there are now carved Victorian figures, was left bare.

The Patricio screen is sometimes attributed, ap- parently without evidence, to Italian workmanship. It seems very unlikely, and foreign craftsmen rarely seem to have been employed. Colebrooke (117), Coldridge and Brushford, Devon have exotic looking tracery, Franco-Breton according to Vallance, Franco- Flemish or Spanish according to Pevsner, Franco- Moorish according to Slader, and Holbeton, Devon, has Hispano-Flemish tracery according to Slader.[50] There is evidence of German influence occasionally in Kent, and of Scottish fashions in the extreme north of England. In the case of the German-style screen at St Stephen, Hackington, Canterbury, the contract still exists, dated 1519, under which Michael Bonversall undertook to copy the one then in Holy Cross church nearby, and most of these screens may well be by Englishmen who had travelled abroad, or their followers.

A peculiarity of some Midland screens is that the east face is left uncarved and looks unfinished, all the detail being reserved for the west face. East Anglian screens, on the other hand, are as scrupulously detailed as West Country ones. Like the churches they stand in, they tend to be tall and airy, with open tracery, and a lighter touch altogether in their design than in contemporary work further west. The one at Southwold, made sometime after 1460, is one of the best, and it is beautifully painted. East Anglian paint- ing seems to have been the best in England outside London at the time,[51] and the screens at Ranworth (109), Barton Turf, Worstead and Cawston in Nor- folk, and Somerleyton, Suffolk, have exceptionally fine work. Occasionally the tracery is in two tiers, a very impressive arrangement, to be seen for example

at Acle and Happisburgh, Norfolk, Castle Heding- ham, Essex, and unexpectedly at Queen Camel, Somerset.

In the east, screens are rarely carried across the whole width of an aisled church as they are in the west, though Attleborough, Norfolk, is an exception. Where there are chapel screens they are usually separate entities and often different in design from the rood screen. Where a screen arrangement survives fairly completely, even shorn of its lofts, as it does at such churches as Shillington, Bedfordshire, Hitchin, Hertfordshire, and, above all, Sefton, Lancashire, it is the most impressive non-architectural feature of the the church, while the absence of screens, especially in a large medieval church, makes it bare and barn-like. One only has to travel a few miles from Shillington or Hitchin to the grand but screenless church at Ashwell, Hertfordshire, to see the difference. Sadly, Ashwell's rood screen, which disappeared during a Victorian restoration, was of uncommon interest, with two tiers of tracery, and a tympanum above bearing a painting of the Royal Arms.

In aisleless churches screens often made provision for nave altars on either side of the central doorway. Memorable examples are to be found at Patricio (110), where the medieval altars survive, at Ran- worth, Norfolk, where there are charming little return screens, which guard the flanking altars to north and south, and at Nether Compton, Dorset, where the screen is of stone. When the nave was aisled, but not the chancel, the east bay of each aisle was usually screened off as a chapel, frequently a chantry. Den- nington, Suffolk (106), shows this arrangement at its best.

Not all screens retain their doors nowadays, and it is often forgotten that during the middle ages and beyond they were normally kept locked. The nave of the church was used for all sorts of secular, not to say profane, purposes, while the chancel was always regarded in its entirety as a sanctuary. Doors do in fact survive in many places, particularly in the west country. Winchcombe, Gloucestershire, has fine traceried doors, continuing the composition of the screen, an arrangement quite frequently found, as at Wysall, Nottinghamshire, where the doors are only dado-high, and Llangwm, Denbighshire, where they have a linenfold dado and square-topped Welsh tracery lights. At Ashby St Leger, Northamptonshire, the doors form a wider and flatter opening than the side-arches. The lock was normally on the east side, the priest, having locked up, departing through the door in the south wall of the chancel. An exception is the early screen of c.1260 at Stanton Harcourt,

Oxfordshire, where for some unknown reason the lock is on the west side. Some screens, especially in East Anglia, seem never to have had doors, and it has been suggested that in such cases there were fence screens further west to protect the nave altars as well.[52]

Before leaving the middle ages, we must return to look at some other screens of stone. Although there were still some made for parish churches in the later middle ages – the ones at Totnes, Devon, c.1460, and Arundel, Sussex, c.1470, are outstanding – most belong to cathedrals, abbeys, and the greater collegiate churches. Pulpitums stood to the east of the parochial parts of such churches, i.e. one bay to the east of the rood screen, making provision for a reredos for the nave altar and an effective choir screen. Those at Canterbury, c.1400, and York, c.1500, still retain their medieval statuary. Since they comprise sets of kings they were unobjectionable to the Tudor reformers, but they were lucky to survive the Commonwealth and Protectorate intact.

More beautiful are the early fourteenth-century screens, especially those carved by members of the East Midlands School, and chief among them are the

pulpitums at Lincoln and Southwell (104), the latter of the verandah type, and the screen behind the high altar at Beverley Minster. A similar school in Devon produced the Exeter pulpitum about 1340. In all these cases, the carving has to be examined in detail to be appreciated.

Virtually every great church has its share of chantries with stone screens, with particularly fine sets at Winchester, Wells, Canterbury and Tewkesbury. Some parish churches have them too, notably the Wenlock screen at Luton, a large open construction made about 1392 between the chancel and the north transept chapel, the Kirkham chantry at Paignton, Devon, and the Harrington tomb of c.1350 at Cartmel Priory.

Earlier than all these are the fragments at Chichester Cathedral (101), which are among the finest pieces of twelfth-century sculpture in Europe, and which are presumed to have formed part of the choir screen made about the second quarter of the twelfth century. What is so memorable is the expressiveness of the faces, so rare in the sculpture of the time. The two panels depict the story of the raising of Lazarus, and

100 Capel-le-Ferne, Kent: chancel screen, fourteenth century

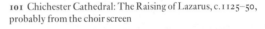
101 Chichester Cathedral: The Raising of Lazarus, c.1125–50, probably from the choir screen

102 Top Salisbury Cathedral: detail of the rood screen, c.1235–50, now in the north-east transept

103 Above Stanton Harcourt, Oxfordshire: rood screen, mid-thirteenth century

104 Right Southwell Minster, Nottinghamshire: detail of pulpitum, c.1330

105 Right Great Bardfield,
Essex: rood screen, late
fourteenth century; restored by
G.F. Bodley, 1892

106 Centre right Dennington,
Suffolk: parclose screen,
fifteenth century

107 Bottom right Cullompton,
Devon: Golgotha from the rood
group, late medieval

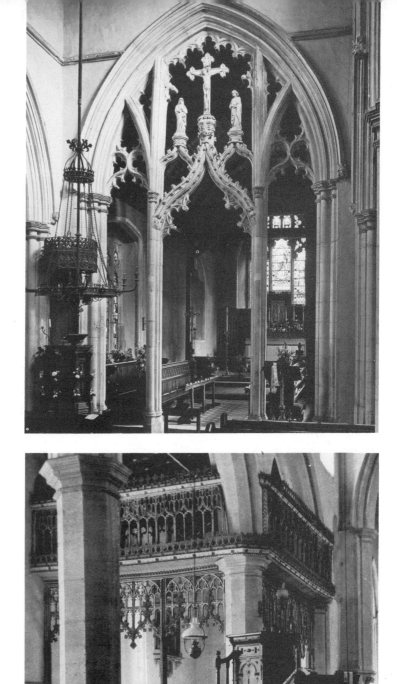

Opposite

108 Far left Ashton, Devon: parclose screen, late fifteenth century

109 Left Ranworth, Norfolk: screen panel of St Michael and the Devil, mid-fifteenth century

110 Below left Patricio, Brecon: rood screen, early sixteenth century

111 Above right Bridford, Devon: rood screen, c. 1520, detail of dado

112 Above centre Llanelieu, Brecon: rood screen, verandah type, with tympanum, fourteenth and early sixteenth century (?)

113 Right Compton Bassett, Wiltshire: rood screen, verandah type, early sixteenth century (?)

114 Left Flamborough, Yorkshire: rood screen, fifteenth century
115 Right Llanengan, Caernarvonshire: rood screen and stalls, early sixteenth century

116 Atherington, Devon: screen, c.1530–40 by John Parrys

118 Carlisle Cathedral: Dean Salkeld's screen, after 1541

117 Colebrooke, Devon: parclose screen showing foreign influence, early sixteenth century

119 Foremark, Derbyshire: detail of chancel screen, 1662

120 Above Abbey Dore,
Herefordshire: screen, c. 1633

121 Left St Paul's Walden,
Hertfordshire: screen, 1727

122 Right St Mary-at-Hill, London: arms of Charles II

123 Below Winchester Cathedral: wrought iron grille, probably twelfth century

124 St George's Chapel, Windsor: grille of Edward IV's tomb, c.1480 by John Tresilian

126 Ely Cathedral: iron gate to Bishop West's Chantry, c.1525

125 Westminster Abbey: bronze gate to Henry VII's Chapel, c.1515

127 Derby Cathedral: chancel screen, c.1730 by Robert Bakewell

128 Coventry Cathedral: crown of thorns screen to the Chapel of Gethsemane, c. 1962, by Sir Basil Spence. Panel of sleeping disciples by Stephen Sykes

129 Lichfield Cathedral: choir screen, 1859–63, designed by Sir Gilbert Scott, and made by Francis Skidmore

the sculptors display an exceptionally sensitive insight into the feelings of the characters. There is nothing so powerful emotionally in English sculpture until the best of the baroque funerary monuments.

Gothic-renaissance screens are found in a number of places like Foy and Llandinabo in Herefordshire, and the Spring Chantry at Lavenham, Suffolk. A pair of rustic early renaissance parclose screens exists at Orford, Suffolk, but the first accomplished piece of

English renaissance screenwork left to us is Dean Salkeld's screen at Carlisle Cathedral, given in the 1540s. Mullions have turned into balusters, rows of saints into medallion busts, tracery into affronted pairs of dolphins, and so on, but the underlying forms are virtually unchanged, and the screen represents an evolution rather than a revolution from late gothic forms. The more radical Continental approach to renaissance forms is seen in the screen at King's

College Chapel, Cambridge *(86)*, made about 1535, and designed and produced either by Frenchmen or Italians.[53] Here there is total assurance in design, and the quality of the carving is wonderful. English carpenters have produced equally good work over the centuries, but not in that style at that time, and the King's screen is one of the few foreign incursions into the field of English woodwork. It set no fashion, and stands in superb isolation.

When the order for the destruction of roods went out in 1548, so closely had the screens become associated with them that not only the lofts, but also the whole screens were sometimes destroyed: Bishop Hooper of Gloucester was particularly keen on their removal. But medieval and later screens were vulnerable to destruction right up to the present century, generally under the guise of restoration.[54] Since rood screens were the focal point of the church their removal has been disastrous visually, and although their original purpose has long since ceased, sensitive spirits from Elizabethan times onwards have sought to plug the ugly gap.

After the Lustleigh screen of the 1550s there is admittedly a pause of about 20 years until the next datable example, that at Morwenstow, Cornwall, made about 1575, and repaired and restored by an unusually enlightened Victorian parish. Then, about 1580, comes the simple screenwork at Brooke, Rutland; St Margaret's King's Lynn has one of 1584, Emmanuel College Cambridge one of 1588, and Hardwick Hall Chapel, Derbyshire, one of about 1597. Screens of 1602 exist at New Romney, Kent, and North Baddisley, Hampshire.[55]

Jacobean screens are numerous and often excellent. At Rodney Stoke, Somerset, the screen of 1625 even has a false loft parapet – there is no loft – and other churches too, like Croscombe *(2)*, show that people were still aware of the imposing nature of the medieval lofts. The Croscombe screen was made about 1616, and has two-tier tracery, then a solid, heavily ornamented cornice, reminiscent of a loft parapet, and finally an elaborate framing for the Royal Arms at the centre of the cresting. Lord Scudamore's screen at Abbey Dore *(120)* also has ornamental cresting surrounding the Royal Arms, but it is a rather heavier, lower screen, with a stronger horizontal emphasis.[56]

A few screens were even made during the temporary proscription of the Anglican church after the Civil War, four of which can be certainly dated, at Campton, Bedfordshire, 1649, St Bartholomew's Hospital Chapel, Oxford, 1651, Iwerne Courtenay, Dorset, 1654, and Cholmondeley Castle Chapel, Cheshire, 1655.

After the Restoration there was a continuation of screenwork in the Jacobean style, as the one at Foremark, Derbyshire *(119)*, made in 1662, shows, but by the late 1670s, when the screen was put in the church attributed to Wren at Ingestre, Staffordshire, the change of style is apparent. This screen revives the triple arches of very early work, but it only fills the lower part of the chancel arch. The detail is now much more classical, with delicate pilasters, and there is no fussy cresting to detract from the Royal Arms, which here achieves a dominance comparable to that of the medieval rood. A very strange screen at How Caple, Herefordshire, put up in the 1690s for the evident purpose of supporting the Royal Arms, takes the contemporary passion for twisted balusters to an extreme. The columns, and even the arches have twisted members. Odd though this screen is, it is in some ways a country cousin to the Wren screen at St Margaret Lothbury, London, of about 1690 and originally at All Hallows the Great. This is very open, with intertwining pairs of spiral-twisted columns supporting the side pieces, and a heavy central section with a large Royal Arms., and a development of Wren's earlier screen at St Peter-at-Cornhill.[57]

The revival of church carpentry in Co. Durham inspired by Bishop Cosin produced some splendid screens still reminiscent of gothic precedents, best of all perhaps at Brancepeth and Sedgefield. In both cases, and at Bishop Auckland Palace Chapel, there is even a zig-zag ornament clearly copied from the piers in Durham Cathedral, though the rest of the medieval details belong to the fourteenth and fifteenth centuries. The cresting of tabernacle work derives clearly from the high altar reredos in the cathedral *(159)*.

Another early gothic revival screen is Hawksmoor's in the north chancel aisle of Beverley Minster,[58] but few eighteenth-century screens survived the nineteenth. The one at St Paul's Walden, Hertfordshire, which in 1727 turned the chancel into a glorified family pew, is a lovely exception, with triple arches supported by Corinthian columns standing on a plain wainscoted dado *(121)*. It is all restrained except for the cresting, which is exuberant with scrolly candelabra and in the centre a rayed disk containing the sacred monogram. It is reminiscent of the slightly earlier and also excellent screen at The Queen's College, Oxford. At Cruwys Morchard and Georgeham, Devon, are two later eighteenth-century Corinthian screens, not in the least ornate, but models of quiet dignity.

Right at the end of the seventeenth century the idea of a screen carrying the organ, last seen at King's College Chapel, Cambridge, was revived at Oxford and Cambridge, and typical examples survive at Trinity College, Oxford c.1694, and St Catharine's College, Cambridge, c.1700. William Kent designed an organ screen for Gloucester Cathedral in 1741, but, Britton tells us, it 'was taken down in 1820 to give place to the present more appropriate design.' Later still, a Coade stone screen was built in 1792 to carry the organ at St George's Windsor, and the Victorians continued the tradition, Scott's fine work at Chester Cathedral being one of the best *(251)*.

The eighteenth century also saw the revival of wrought-iron screenwork. Iron was used extensively and beautifully in the middle ages, and iron grilles and gates at places like Winchester *(123)* and Lincoln Cathedrals have a limpid beauty which puts them into the front rank of design and craftsmanship alike. They were made in the twelfth or thirteenth century, and are related to contemporary scrollwork on doors. A different style, more purely geometrical, is found in the thirteenth-century grille re-used in the chantry of Duke Humphrey of Gloucester at St Albans, and there is similar work of c.1310 in the gate of the choir screen at Canterbury Cathedral. In the later middle ages, iron imitated woodwork, just as early wooden screens had imitated stone. The iron grille of Edward IV's tomb at St George's Windsor *(124)* is very like contemporary stallwork, not only in its design, but also in its construction, being jointed and pegged together with cotter pins.[59] More independence was used in bronze, probably due to renaissance influence, and the magnificent gates to Henry VII's Chapel in Westminster Abbey of c.1515, *(125)*, and to Bishop West's Chapel in Ely Cathedral c.1525, *(126)*, have no real parallel in ironwork.

Iron stanchions were sometimes inset in the open late medieval tracery of screens to secure chancels against intruders, as in the stone screen at Totnes, and the wooden parcloses at Hitchin and St Margaret's, King's Lynn. Stone screens, too, often had iron gates as the pulpitums at Canterbury and York still show.

After the Reformation the custom of locking the chancel slowly fell into disuse, though at Knotting, Bedfordshire, iron gates were set up in the chancel arch in 1637 after the rector and churchwardens had been found present at a cock-fight in the chancel,[60] but the real revival was probably sparked off by Wren's employment of Jean Tijou to make the chancel gates for St Paul's. Scandalously, these were dismantled in 1890 and now stand in the eastern bays of the chancel arcades with the sanctuary screens, while Grinling Gibbons' woodwork has been partly re-used as a doorcase in the south transept. Still in place, however, are Tijou's gates to the chancel aisles.

Tijou's craftsmanship was matched by his pupils William Edney and Robert Bakewell, so much so that it is uncertain whether the screens at Staunton Harold, Leicestershire, and Birmingham Cathedral are by Tijou or Bakewell. The screen at Derby Cathedral *(127)* was undoubedly made by Bakewell and his pupil Benjamin Yates, about 1730. Edney's work suffered badly in the bombing of Bristol, but his beautiful chancel screen of 1710 in St Mary Redcliffe, now unfortunately under the tower, shows his work at its best.[61] The contemporary gates to the north choir aisle at Beverley Minster are perhaps London work, but excellent provincial work can be found in the late seventeenth-century screen at Wrexham, said to have been given by Elihu Yale, and the gates at Boston, made for the chancel in 1743, but now, like Edney's Bristol gates, relegated to the tower.

The great Victorian architects used wrought iron to considerable effect in screens. Among them are Street's at East Heslerton, East Riding, 1877, and Kingston Dorset; St Peter, Parkstone, Dorset 1877 by Pearson, and St Bees, Cumberland, 1886, by Butterfield. Street used brass for the fine screen at Fimber, East Riding, in 1871. But the finest of all these Victorian pieces, though rather belatedly recognized as such, are those designed by Scott and executed by Francis Skidmore. They have suffered because they were not always sensitive to the *genius loci*, but the one at Lichfield Cathedral *(129)*, made between 1859 and 1863, and recently beautifully restored, is easy to appreciate, being the gateway to one of the finest of Victorian choirs.

Near the beginning of the present century one of the most remarkable of all English metalwork screens was installed in the new church at Great Warley, Essex, by William Reynolds-Stephens, and is described in the first chapter (page 29). Another Art Nouveau composition, installed five years earlier in 1899, is the iron screen at Busbridge, Surrey, designed by Lutyens, and executed by Starkie Gardner. The base, of stone and marble, is reminiscent of cancelli, and the ironwork is in the upper part of the chancel arch only, forming a base for the rood group. For this is a rood screen, and rood figures, though hardly common, were by this time perfectly possible in Anglican churches. Important though they may be devotionally, not many need singling out as works of art. At Blisland, Cornwall, the rood forms a worthy climax to a traditional screen mostly by F.C. Eden, 1896; at Eye, Suffolk, the rood group is by Sir Ninian Comper, but the screen, including its loft, is basically medieval. Sometimes a cross is used instead of a rood, and the fine one at Dunham-on-the-Hill, Cheshire, is a Scott-Skidmore piece, made for Chester Cathedral, whence it was removed in 1913 in favour of a rood by Scott's grandson, Sir Giles Gilbert Scott, the architect of the Anglican cathedral at Liverpool.

Even the most medievalizing of Victorian architects were unenthusiastic about heavy chancel screens except to enclose a cathedral choir, or to divide a chapel from its ante-chapel, as Pugin's screen does at Jesus College, Cambridge. Some Victorians went to the other extreme, and installed cancelli to provide a punctuation mark between nave and chancel, while leaving open to view all that went on inside it. Exceptionally one was made for the church at Wighill, West Riding, as early as the later seventeenth century, but serious revival only began about 1850, the year Butterfield made one of Sussex marble for West Lavington, Sussex, a screen described by Ian Nairn as 'incredibly moving, and so natural that it looks as though the stone itself had been metamorphosed into simple Gothic detail.'[62] Others, made of coloured marbles, are at Westminster Cathedral, and the Roman Catholic church at Lynton, Devon, 1910.

Twentieth-century screens tend to be simple, especially in recent churches where an atmosphere of peace, so necessary to the present-day soul, seems to have been of prime concern to architects and craftsmen. Typical pieces, in fine metal-work, are the gates to the baptistry of Liverpool Metropolitan Cathedral, by David Atkins, and the screen added in 1965 to give the Lady Chapel at Coventry a sense of identity it lacked in the original open arrangement. At Coventry also is a rare symbolic piece of screenwork, the Crown of Thorns, designed by Sir Basil Spence to stand at the entrance to the Chapel of Christ in Gethsemane *(128)*. These modern screens are all open in character, neither visual nor physical barriers, and making no attempt, as medieval screens did, to impart a sense of mystery to what lay beyond. Rather they are visual foils, creators of depth and perspective, serving to identify areas which might otherwise seem amorphous, and for this purpose metalwork is obviously more appropriate than wood or stone. While participation rather than mystery remains the keynote of the interpretation of the Eucharist, screenwork of any sort is likely to be rare in new churches with only a single altar, and traditional screens will perhaps only be commissioned to make proper divisions in large medieval churches which have been wrongly opened

up. One such, and a suitable piece of work to form a tailpiece to the chapter, is the screen made for Bangor Cathedral between 1954 and 1960 by the Yorkshire carver Robert Thompson the Mouseman, so-called because of the mouse that formed his invariable signature, and which is continued by his successors in his firm today.

Royal Arms

Although not all Royal Arms were made for the head of the chancel screen, and many that were have subsequently found more modest homes, the practice of using them to take the place of the vanished rood was so prevalent for so long that it is useful to mention them here. Many are painted on canvas, or on panels; some were painted directly on to tympana; others are carved in wood or plaster, and a few have even been made in cast iron. By Victoria's reign the Royal Supremacy was so taken for granted that the custom fell into disuse, though there are examples of her reign, including one at Catfield, Norfolk, prudently inscribed 'V 1st R.' There is at least one example of Edward VII's reign, at St Luke, Birmingham, and of George V's at Trentishoe, Devon, as well as a few of Elizabeth II's.

Some Royal Arms are crude village work, but the best are masterpieces, and deserve more attention than they are usually accorded. The one at St Mary-at-Hill, London *(122)* depicting the arms of Charles II, is typical of metropolitan work, but some villages, like Shelton and Ingworth in Norfolk, have examples that are every bit as good. Very early ones are rare: Henry VIII's are now only found at Rushbrooke, Suffolk, and Cirencester, Gloucestershire; Edward VI's only at Westerham, Kent; Mary Tudor's only at Waltham Abbey; and there are few of Elizabeth I's reign.[63] The only Commonwealth example to survive is at North Walsham, Norfolk, and that only because the Arms of Charles II were painted on the back. James II's Arms are also rare, more perhaps due to the brevity of his reign than to his unpopular Roman Catholicism, though there is a fine carved example at West Malling, Kent. The other Stuart monarchs and all the Hanoverians are well represented. An unusually interesting example of Charles I's reign at Burstwick, East Riding, has a painting of his execution on the back.

Chapter 7
Chancel Seating

Long before the laity had anywhere to sit, seats were provided for bishops, clergy and choir monks, all of whom, after all, spent very much longer in church. Bishops' thrones were originally placed in the apse, behind the high altar, and raised up, facing the congregation. The much-restored Saxon throne in Norwich Cathedral has been returned to this position, although the ambulatory behind the apse compromises the dramatic effect it would have had in the small cathedral at North Elmham where it must once have stood.

Only fragments of the Norwich throne are original, but two similar ones remain entire. One is at Hexham Priory, and there is no reason to doubt the tradition that is was Wilfrid's, made in the seventh century when he built Hexham as his cathedral (130). The other is at Beverley Minster, and although the Minster has never been a bishop's seat, it functioned as a sort of suffragan cathedral to York during the middle ages. This practice might go back to Saxon times, when it was already an important collegiate church. Certainly the throne, known as the Frith Stool from its connection with the right of sanctuary, has every claim to be pre-Norman, and it resembles the Hexham throne in its shape, and in the fact that the back and arms are of equal height. Two other seats once thought to be Saxon appear to be much later. The Purbeck marble throne known as St Augustine's Chair, and used for the enthronements of Archbishops of Canterbury, is now thought to belong to the thirteenth century, while the wooden chair at Jarrow known as Bede's, is so plain that it is difficult to date with confidence. Pevsner suggests the fourteenth century.

There are a variety of medieval stone seats in churches whose original purpose is sometimes rather obscure, like the one at Barnack, near Peterborough, where there is a recess in the west wall of the eleventh-century tower in the form of a seat with a triangular-headed canopy. At Linslade, Bedfordshire, there is a thirteenth-century stone seat just inside the chancel on the south side, and a similar seat at Farcet, Huntingdonshire, now forms a sedile, though that was probably not its original purpose. A stone seat at Welsh Newton, Herefordshire, is on the north side of the chancel. At Sprotbrough, West Riding, the stone seat recalls the twelfth-century sedile at Halsham, East Riding, but the details are fourteenth century, and Pevsner suggests that it was reworked then.

A few medieval bishops' thrones remain. The finest is at Exeter (132), designed in all probability by Thomas Winton in 1313, and completed about four years later. Winton was a forward-looking man, among the most distinguished of his generation, and his use of the nodding ogee arch in the canopy is one of the earliest known. Another good wooden throne was installed at St David's in the time of Bishop Gower, 1328–47. It is simpler than the one at Exeter, but may well derive from it, as there was a good deal of cultural contact between St David's and the cathedrals of south-west England during the middle ages. The later fourteenth-century throne at Hereford has a subordinate seat either side forming part of the composition, and used by the bishops' chaplains. This too has nodding ogee arches and a spired canopy, though it does not really resemble the Exeter one.

The throne at Durham is unique as it is built on a platform created by the roof of Bishop Hatfield's chantry. It was erected during the lifetime of the bishop, who died in 1381, and was presumably his idea. The throne proper is in the centre of a screen. The balustrade of the staircase and the front parapet are good seventeenth-century woodwork, and the whole composition has recently been recoloured (133).

In the nave of Canterbury stands the grand canopy which originally stood over the throne given by Archbishop Tenison in 1704. Its design has been attributed to Hawksmoor, and the carving is by Grinling Gibbons. The composition is based on clusters of Corinthian columns, the canopy itself projecting from a segmental-headed pediment. Although there are a few other pre-Victorian pieces, like the Georgian one in the nave at Gloucester, and the one at Winchester of about 1820 made by Garbett, most of the rest are Victorian or later. Among them are ones designed by Pearson at Truro and Norwich, by Street at Carlisle, by Scott at Worcester, Lichfield and elsewhere, and by Slater and Carpenter at Chichester.

These all continue the medieval tradition of grandeur, but twentieth-century work, in harmony with more democratic ideas of the episcopate, is more modest. At Coventry Spence designed a throne which forms part of the same composition as the choir stalls, but more typical of the present mood are R.D. Russell's at Liverpool Metropolitan Cathedral, very plainly canopied, and the simple chair at Clifton.

Wooden chairs for various purposes seem to appear in the thirteenth century, with the strange object in Hereford Cathedral, a triumph of the turner's art, more curious than beautiful, and similar to another chair in the Victoria and Albert Museum. The earliest gothic chair in our churches is the famous Coronation Chair in Westminster Abbey, made specifically about 1300 to accommodate the Coronation Stone stolen from the Scots.[64] Post-medieval chairs have mostly been inserted for the occasional visits of bishops. There is rarely any certainty that they were made for the church, and some were doubtless given long after they were made, as suitably august and venerable pieces for their purpose. An exception is Cosin's chair at Bishop Auckland, dated 1638 *(131)*.

Stalls are much more important than chairs. Every cathedral, monastery or collegiate church in the middle ages possessed a set, and many of these still exist, either in the churches for which they were made, or in the churches that acquired them at the Reformation.[65] Early stalls seem to have been simple, extreme examples of which may be the stone benches along the north and south walls of the chancel at Chipstead, Surrey, and the stone benches east of the screen facing the altar, like return stalls, at Gumfreston, Pembrokeshire. Both these are probably thirteenth century. However, wooden stalls with misericords, that is, tip-up seats with projections against which participants could rest during the standing parts of the long choir offices, were in use at least as early as about 1200, as the single example at Hemingborough, East Riding, proves.

More substantial remains of early stalls are to be found at Rochester Cathedral, where they are mixed up with early renaissance pieces and much work by Scott. The original fragments date from about 1227 and comprise trefoiled arches in the back stalls and part of the return stalls. At Peterborough there are scanty remains of the stalls of about 1240, shafted, and with stiff-leaf capitals, and Exeter Cathedral has a wonderful set of misericords, carved between about 1230 and 1270, and incorporated first into the stalls of c.1310, and then into Scott's stalls of about 1870.

The earliest complete set of stalls remaining was made about 1308 by William Lingwood for Winchester Cathedral, with beautiful tracery in the back panels and elegant canopies *(134)*. Later in the fourteenth century several justly famous sets were made, like those at Hereford, Gloucester, Chester, Nantwich and Lincoln. The Chester set, *(136)*, made about 1390, is one of the best in England. By now the canopies have become spiky with little pinnacles, a froth of lacy but constructionally sturdy woodwork. Stallends, armrests, and misericords are all carefully carved, and Victorian restoration work is so good that it is often difficult to tell from the original.

This style of canopy work remained popular in the north of England until the Reformation, as stalls at Whalley, c.1420–30, Ripon, 1489–94, Manchester, c.1505–10, and Beverley Minster, c.1520, *(137)* show. It is interesting to compare the ones at Beverley Minster with the simpler set a century older along the road at St Mary's. At Manchester Cathedral there are actually two tiers of canopies, giving an unrivalled sense of opulence. However, this was not the only tradition in the north. At St Mary, Lancaster, are stalls which probably came from Cockersand Abbey. They are earlier than the stalls at Chester or Nantwich, but even richer in detail, in that particular version of the Decorated style which, when exported, was a progenitor of the Flamboyant of France. It was reintroduced in its Flemish form into the south of England about 1520 for the stalls of Henry VII's Chapel in Westminster Abbey, and for Bristol Cathedral.

Among other medieval stalls, those at St David's are an attractive set, and much simpler, but pleasing in their modesty, are the set at St Asaph made about 1480. Stalls in smaller establishments generally lacked canopies, but Nantwich and Ludlow are notable exceptions, and even the simplest sets could have ornately carved fronts and good misericords. Jarrow has North Country flamboyant tracery of some beauty, though the scale is small, and at Noseley, Leicestershire, the fronts have poppy-heads and well-carved cockerels.

Almost all medieval stalls have lost any colouring they once had, though at Astley, Warwickshire, the backs have paintings of figures carrying scrolls, much restored but still effective, and originally dating from about 1400, while at Carlisle Cathedral the earlier stalls carry not very exciting paintings of about 1500 depicting the apostles and lives of the saints.

Medieval misericords form a study of their own *(138, 139)*.[66] The most striking thing about them other than skill of execution is the variety of subject matter. Only roof bosses, and then by no means always, seem to have given the individual carver so much freedom of scope. M.D. Anderson has investigated the origins of some of the carvings, and has suggested that the main source of inspiration was manuscript illuminations, while others may have been derived from wall-paintings which themselves often had manuscript sources. She suggests that in some cases forms of the stories were circulated with rough drawings which each individual carpenter interpreted according to his lights. For example, she quotes the theme of the mermaid suckling a lion, found at Hereford and Norwich Cathedrals, and Edlesborough, Buckinghamshire, and, more remarkably, the scene from Tristan and Iseult where Sir Yvain, pursuing an enemy into his castle, is trapped by the portcullis falling on the hindquarters of his horse. This design is found at Chester and Lincoln Cathedrals, at New College, Oxford, at Boston, and at Enville, Staffordshire, and in each case the supporters, which, in English misericords almost always flank the main subject, are the soldiers who tried to seize him.

Some subjects are purely domestic, like the scene illustrating January from the labours of the months at Ludlow *(139)*, and the innkeeper in the same church, drawing ale from a cask. At Boston, and several other places, a schoolmaster is shown caning a pupil. Obviously there were religious themes too, from the Bible, from moralising tales, like the Fall of Pride at Lincoln Cathedral *(138)*, and from bestiaries. Thus we find the familiar mermaid as a symbol of temptation, but doubtless also a pleasure to carve, and a more popular subject than most. The elephant and castle also intrigued a number of carvers, though it is clear that not all of them had seen an elephant, and fewer still a howdah.

The finest Early Renaissance stalls in England by far are those at King's College Chapel, Cambridge, *en suite* with the screen, and put in about 1530–35 *(86)* and owing little to medieval precedent. Apart from the misericords, which seem to be English carving, they are probably by French or Italian craftsmen. Surprisingly the balusters, cornice, and coats of arms were not part of the original design, but a remarkably sympathetic addition of 1633 by William Fells. Between these two phases at King's, there was not very much activity. Gothic survived till the middle of the sixteenth century at Farewell, Staffordshire, and there was a little more Renaissance work at Cambridge. The stalls at Trinity College Chapel were made about 1560 in a modest English version of the style, and the stall-backs at Corpus Christi were made about 1580.

The early seventeenth century saw much more activity, and among many sets one might single out the ones at Passenham (see p. 15), at Abbey Dore, and

the florid additions to the modest fifteenth-century stalls at Cartmel Priory *(135)*. The backs, together with the screen, were given about 1620 by George Preston, who did a great deal to restore the church at that time. The style is north of England flamboyant, with some concessions to classical taste in the pilasters, columns and cornices, but giving an overall impression of the gothic-renaissance overlap of the previous century.

The one complete set of puritan chancel seating remaining in England is at Deerhurst, Gloucestershire *(148)*, where the communicants sat on the north, south, and east sides of the communion table, which is free-standing. The Directory of Public Worship in 1644 states that 'the table being before decently covered, and so conveniently placed that the communicants may orderly sit about it or at it, the minister is to begin the action with sanctifying and blessing the elements of bread and wine set before him.'[67] Clearly the Deerhurst seating was made in accordance with this injunction.

Cosin-inspired stalls appear in several churches in County Durham including the cathedral, all of the high quality and excellent design one expects from this school of craftsmanship. The tradition even lasted into the eighteenth century with the work of c.1707 in St Mary-le-Bow, Durham, but the great work of this time is in the classical, not the gothic tradition. The elegant composition and lively detail put Grinling Gibbons' stalls in St Paul's Cathedral into a class of their own *(142)*, and an interesting and characteristic feature is that the backs, as seen from the aisles, are as carefully designed as the fronts.

After the great fire in York Minster in 1829, Smirke replaced the destroyed work successfully and in the same spirit, as can be seen from surviving original fragments, and later nineteenth-century stalls are also gothic. At Wells, the stone canopies with their polished columns and their nodding ogee canopies, presumably by Salvin, who was working on the pulpitum at the time, replaced medieval ones in 1848. They incorporate the original splendid misericords of c.1340, and a very effective feature is the needlework used for hangings in the canopies, backrests and cushions, designed by Lady Hylton, and made by local ladies between 1937 and 1948. But the best Victorian stalls are by Scott, who had a good deal of experience of restoring, not always discreetly, medieval ones. At Worcester they incorporate medieval misericords, and at Lichfield they are more frankly High Victorian, with Skidmore ironwork which helps tie the composition to the screen.

Most twentieth-century stalls are plain, like Eric

Gill's at Mount St Bernard Abbey, Leicestershire, made in 1938, and Waring and Gillow's in the Anglican cathedral at Liverpool. The two outstanding sets are at Coventry and Westminster Cathedral. Ernest Gimson's work at Westminster is in the Chapel of St Andrew *(141)* tall and elegant in the best Art Nouveau tradition, and made of ebony with ivory inlay. Spence's stalls at Coventry, like so much else of his work there, manage to look forward and backward at the same time *(10)*. The canopies give the impression of fluttering angels as vividly as Ripon's, but the means of expression is abstract-symbolic. The bishop's throne forms part of the same composition, with a towering flutter of the triple symbols, culminating in a gilded copper mitre, designed by Elizabeth Frink, and decorated with nuts and bolts as becomes the seat of the bishop of so industrial a diocese.

130 Below Hexham Priory: Wilfrid's Throne, probably late seventh century

131 Right Bishop Auckland Palace Chapel, Co. Durham: Cosin's chair, 1638

132 Exeter Cathedral:
Bishop's Throne, 1313–17 by
Thomas Winton

133 Right Durham Cathedral:
Bishop's Throne and Hatfield
Chantry, c.1380

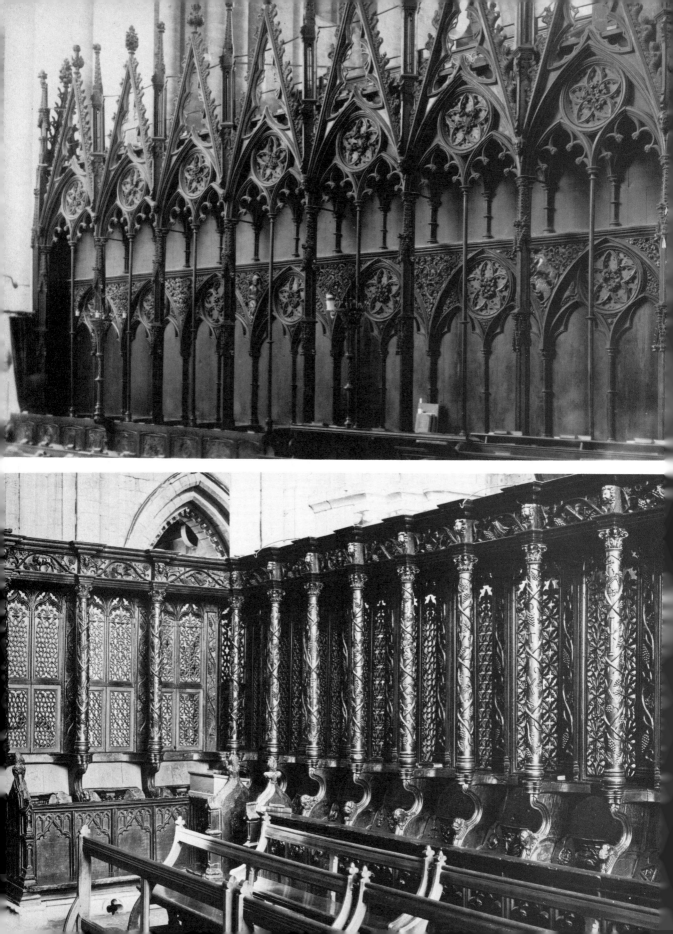

134 Left Winchester Cathedral: stalls, c.1310 by William Lingwood

135 Below left Cartmel Priory, Lancashire: stalls, fifteenth century; backs and screen c.1620

136 Right Chester Cathedral: stalls, c.1390

137 Below right Beverley Minster, Yorkshire: detail of stall canopy, 1520

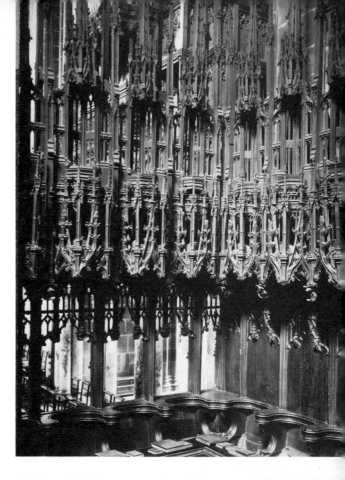

138 Below Lincoln Cathedral: misericord, the Fall of Pride, c.1365–70
139 Bottom Ludlow, Shropshire: misericord, January, 1447
140 Right Cholmondeley Castle Chapel, Cheshire: pews and screen, 1655
141 Far right Westminster Cathedral: stalls in St Andrew's Chapel, c.1912 by Ernest Gimson
142 Bottom right St Paul's Cathedral: detail of stalls, 1695–7 by Grinling Gibbons

Chapter 8
Eucharistic Furniture

Altars and Communion Tables

At its simplest a church was a shelter for an altar, and occasionally among the earliest churches in Ireland, they were just that and no more. Similar tiny chapels once existed in Cornwall and Wales, perhaps originally the private oratories of Celtic saints, though they will certainly sometimes have attracted congregations, who must have stood outside, and watched the celebration through the west door.[68]

Medieval altars survive throughout Britain, and some, ejected by the reformers, have since been restored to use. They usually had a stone base with a hollow for the insertion of relics, and they always had a stone slab, known as a mensa from the Latin word for table, on top. Five crosses, representing the wounds of Christ, were incised on the top for anointing during the consecration ceremony, but they were otherwise usually plain, and covered in use by an embroidered frontal and a linen cloth on the top. Sometimes however, especially in early days, the frontal was of carved stone. One at Hovingham, North Riding, now sadly worn, has eight figures in an arcade and a vine-scroll frieze, and must once have been like the much better preserved miscellaneous carvings at Breedon-on-the-Hill, Leicester. It probably belongs to the eighth or ninth century.

Complete medieval altars can be seen at Porthcawl, Glamorgan, and in the crypt at Grantham, Lincolnshire, but the most remarkable survival of medieval altars is at Patricio, Brecon, where there are three, one either side of the chancel arch, and another, with six consecration crosses, in the western chapel.[69]

After the Reformation, altars were replaced by wooden communion tables, as ordered by an injunction of 1550. It was not universally obeyed, and Elizabeth I's injunction of 1559 makes the substitution optional. One of the earliest communion tables ever made is at North Walsham, Norfolk, where the quotation from the first Prayer Book of Edward VI carved on the front puts it between 1549 and 1552. The insertion of 'and blood' after 'body', clearly as an afterthought, suggests that the carver still thought in terms of communion in one kind. The administration of the cup to the laity was only authorized at the end of 1547, and probably not practised till 1548.[70]

Elizabethan communion tables are probably fairly common, though not noticeable if they are covered by frontals. They frequently have the bulbous turned and carved legs of the period, though the characteristically Elizabethan table at St Marcella, Denbigh, was made in 1623, a date which more obviously fits the contemporary communion rails. However, an ensemble of table and rails as early as this is still a precious survival, *(144)*. St Saviour, Dartmouth, has an ambitious table, dated 1588, with carved figure supports, while one at Southwold, Suffolk, is round.

Many churches still possess seventeenth-century tables: Cautley noted 208 in Suffolk alone, though only one, at Carlton, 1630, is dated. Little carved crosses on the apron sometimes distinguish ecclesiastical from similar secular pieces, but most are plain, and two simple puritan examples can be seen at Irstead, Norfolk, 1650, and Avening, Gloucestershire, 1657. Richer tables can be seen at Tickhill, West Riding, with inlay of birds and flowers, and at Astbury, Cheshire. Much more elaborate are the one at Brancepeth, part of Cosin's refurbishing and such Wren tables as the one at St Bene'ts, Paul's Wharf, but the greatest contrast between the simple Jacobean tables and the height of Metropolitan fashion of the latter part of the century can be seen at Burnham-on-Sea, Somerset, where what is left of the Whitehall altar now stands. This was designed by Wren, and executed, for £1875, by Grinling Gibbons and Arnold Quellin for the Chapel Royal, Whitehall, in 1686, when the ardently Catholic James II was king, which explains the angels venerating the sacrament, and a cherub with a censer. The altar was moved first to Hampton Court, then to Westminster Abbey, and only came to Burnham in 1820. A great deal was lost during its travels, but it is still impressive.

By Georgian times the Protestant prejudice against stone-topped tables as symbols of popery was wearing thin. Marble was fashionable for tables in great houses, and some complete altars were made of marble, among them Steane, Northamptonshire, 1720, Hugill, Westmorland, c.1743, and Theddlethorpe All Saints, Lincolnshire, and one in the Catholic chapel at Wardour Castle, Wiltshire, c.1773.

At Redland, Oxfordshire, the altar consists of an eagle supporting a marble top in the manner of William Kent, and Loughborough, Leicestershire, St Swithun, Worcester, and Birtsmorton, Worcestershire, have altars of wrought iron carrying marble tops. At Milton Abbey, Dorset, Wyatt installed an altar of alabaster about 1789.

Nevertheless, wood was still usual, and styles followed the secular fashions of the day. The tables at Rye, Sussex, *(147)* and Wheatfield, Oxfordshire, are elaborately carved, with cabriole legs and the use of such expected motifs as ball-and-claw or scroll feet, lion masks, and acanthus foliage. Cherubs' heads declare the religious purpose of the tables, and the one at Wheatfield also has Greek key ornament, and a delightful apron where cherubs' heads in the centre and at the corners are linked by their wings and by symbolic trails of wheatears and bunches of grapes.[71]

Victorian altars are generally unimportant: they were made to be covered, though at Wreay, Cumberland, the altar, described in the introduction (page 27) is worthy of the church. Most twentieth-century altars fall into the same category. Notable are the Arts and Crafts altar by C.R. Ashbee, c.1905, at Calne, Wiltshire, the altar in the Chapel of the Incarnation at St Osmund, Parkstone, Dorset, with inscriptions by Eric Gill, and the silver altar at Sandringham by Barkentin and Krall, 1911, with a silver reredos by W.E. Tower, added in 1920. Really new ground, however, was only broken in the 1960s, with such finely designed plain pieces as those at St Agatha, Sparkbrook, Birmingham, the south-east chapel of Chichester Cathedral, and the high altar at Liverpool Metropolitan Cathedral, which is made of a 19-ton, 10-foot block of pure white Skopje marble *(158)*.

Ancient frontals are rare. Baunton, Gloucestershire, possesses a fine fifteenth-century one embroidered in appliqué work on a damask cloth, with a rebus of the place name incorporated in the design *(152)* and there is another similar one, with figures of the Virgin and angels, not far away at Chipping Campden *(151)*. A third, at Alverley, Shropshire, shows Abraham with souls in his bosom, and a variety of cherubs and foliage, and there is a fourth at Romsey Abbey with gold embroidery on green velvet. Other apparently medieval frontals turn out on inspection to be re-used copes, and at Winchcombe, Gloucestershire, fourteenth-century copes were made into a frontal as early as the time of Catherine of Aragon, that is, before the Reformation, as is proved by her pomegranate badge, clearly added as part of the conversion.

Linen cloths for the top of the table are regrettably perishable, but early examples made in 1632 and 1633 respectively exist at Shadingfield, Suffolk, and North Curry, Somerset. At Shadingfield, the original box with an inscription inside the lid recording the donation survives with it. Even frontals of this period are surprisingly rare; one of the late seventeenth century at St Michael, Spurriergate, York, is made of stamped leather, and at Axbridge, Somerset, a needlework piece made by Mrs Abigail Prowse, daughter of the Bishop of Wells, between 1713 and 1720, shows how the communion vessels were arranged at the time *(153)*. Among later frontals one can single out those at Busbridge, Surrey, by William Morris, c.1870, at St Bartholomew, Brighton, by Henry Wilson, at Bosham, Sussex, reproducing a scene fron the Bayeux tapestry, and at King's College Chapel, Cambridge, by Joyce Conwy Evans. This last is an attractive feature of the otherwise unfortunate recasting of the east end to accommodate Rubens' 'Adoration of the Magi' as an altarpiece, a woven tapestry of octagons in browns and yellows, with gold appliqué work forming a cross as the central motif. Finally, at Bangor Cathedral, Caernarvonshire, there is a frontal made by Celtic Studios, Swansea, of Welsh flannel in 1975.

Altar crosses and candlesticks are almost invariably recent, or, if old, brought in recently. Medieval examples were prime targets of the reformers: like shrines, they excited both Protestant ardour and materialistic greed. One of the most remarkable English medieval altar crosses to survive was made of ivory about 1150 at Bury St Edmunds, possibly by Master Hugo, a gifted craftsman who made bronze doors for the abbey, and who was a first class illuminator. The cross is a beautiful object, as can be appreciated from the photograph *(143)*, and is now in the Metropolitan Museum of Art in New York. A fifteenth-century cross, found at Lamport Hall, Northamptonshire, and given to the church there, is made so that it can stand on an altar or be fixed to a staff for processions, and there is a similar one used as an altar cross in St David's Cathedral.

Many crosses presently in use are Victorian, like the one by Butterfield at Barnsley, Gloucestershire. There is an Arts and Crafts cross of 1892 at Carshalton, Surrey, by A. Blomfield, and two in the same style by Bainbridge-Reynolds, of 1898 at Bridgnorth, Shropshire, and of 1916 at St Osmund, Parkstone, where he also made candlesticks and a tabernacle. He also made a further altar cross and candlesticks there in 1925. Both the altar and the processional crosses at Roker, Sunderland, are fine Edwardian pieces by Ernest Gimson.[72]

At Shere, Surrey, the cross and candlesticks made

in the 1950s by Louis Osman, are of wrought iron with bronze reliefs, and another good set of this period are at All Saints, Leamington, by Gerald Benney. At Birmingham Cathedral, John Donald's altar cross consists of a lump of crystal quartz from which a cluster of silver-gilt spokes radiates, while Coventry Cathedral has a high altar cross by Geoffrey Clarke, abstract, but vividly conveying the agony and contortion of crucifixion. The crucifix and candlesticks at Liverpool Metropolitan Cathedral, *(158)* are by Elizabeth Frink and R.Y. Goodden, more conventional perhaps, and pleasingly simple. The movement now, indeed, is towards simplicity, and sometimes altars, like the ones in Clifton Cathedral, carry no cross or candlesticks at all, especially where the celebrant faces the congregation.

Altar candlesticks are a study on their own, and no attempt will be made to embark on them here. Owing to the depredations of the Reformation and the Civil War, only one medieval set seems to be in use which has not been imported since. It is at Southwell Minster, where, like the lectern, they were dredged up from Newstead Abbey fishpond. These are of brass, or rather latten, but other materials are sometimes found: late seventeenth-century pewter at Cowley, Gloucestershire; wood, made about 1640, at Lydbury North, Shropshire; alabaster at Wreay; marble, designed by Clutton in 1853 at Dunstall, Staffordshire, and sometimes silver, though the increase in thefts from churches recently has meant that few candlesticks of any merit are left on display, and many small portable pieces are now locked away with the church plate.

Reredoses and Retables

A reredos is a decorated wall or screen rising from ground level behind an altar, and a retable (which means 'rear wall') stands either on the back of the mensa or on a pedestal behind it. A medieval altar always had one or the other, and sometimes both.

Few medieval reredoses retain more than a fraction of their figures. The huge screen-reredoses at New College Oxford, 1447, St Albans Cathedral, 1476–92, and Winchester Cathedral, c.1500, all underwent extensive Victorian restoration. Since colour has not been reintroduced, and since Victorian statuary is invariably quite different in inspiration from its medieval prototypes, the effect has been to give these elephantine structures a pervading and unfortunate Victorian flavour. Unrestored reredoses, like the one at Christchurch Priory, in their sadly damaged state, are far more moving. In a class of its own is the reredos at Durham Cathedral, the so-called Neville Screen,

probably designed by Henry Yeveley and completed in 1380 *(159)*. Originally it contained 108 alabaster statues, but even in its present denuded state, its freedom of composition and spiky tabernacle work give it a life and vigour that the great square-topped reredoses of the later middle ages conspicuously lack. In its original state, with statuary, colour, and gilding, it must have been magnificent.

Earlier reredoses survive occasionally, and one of the most interesting is at Adisham, Kent, made of wood about 1250, and originally belonging to Canterbury Cathedral. At Llantwit Major (Llanilltyd Fawr), Glamorgan there is a thirteenth-century Jesse niche, the sleeping Jesse as usual at the bottom, and heads peering out of the foliage in the sides of the frame, with the head of Christ in a nimbus at the apex of the trefoiled arch *(156)*. The central area would have contained the rest of the composition, probably painted on to the flat surface. It has been very plausibly suggested that this was originally the high altar reredos.[73]

Not much needs to be said about other medieval reredoses, though plenty survive in whole or part. One of the nicest, at St Issey, Cornwall, made by the Master of St Endellion, was originally the front of a tombchest. Many were made of alabaster, of which perhaps the best now left in a church is at Yarnton, Oxfordshire, with four panels of scenes from the Life of Christ.

A few painted retables survive. The most famous is the Wilton Diptych in the National Gallery, and there are a few small post-medieval ones, like the one at Melton Constable, Norfolk. A diptych is a retable which consists of two hinged panels. A triptych has a centre and two wings, but no medieval one of importance survives in a church.[74] However, there are several fine medieval retables without wings, among them the one at Westminster Abbey, painted about 1280 *(160)* and another about 20 years later, now at Thornham Parva, Suffolk, but also London work, related to the sedilia paintings at Westminster Abbey. In 1381 Norwich Cathedral was given the retable now in St Luke's Chapel. This piece, together with the panels from St Michael-at-Plea nearby, now made up into another retable in St Saviour's Chapel, enables the fine quality of East Anglian painting found in early fifteenth-century screens to be traced back for another generation, a quality which some critics have even compared honourably with the best contemporary Flemish work.

Early post-Reformation reredoses are rare. Braunton, Devon, has an altar-back of 1563, surprisingly simple for an Elizabethan creation, but there are few, if any, others before the early Stuart revival. At Little Gidding, Nicholas Ferrar's reredos is an early example of the type containing the creed, Lord's Prayer and Ten Commandments, but, exceptionally, it is made of brass, set in a wooden frame. In 1635 the Brudenells of Deene, Northamptonshire, were Roman Catholics, and commissioned a reredos depicting the Sacred Heart, originally, no doubt, for their private chapel, but now a rather unlikely object to grace an Anglican parish church, though certainly a fortunate one to survive the Commonwealth.

The Restoration produced some sumptuous reredoses, evocative of the confident splendour of triumphant Anglicanism, and witness to the exceptional skill of the craftsmen of the day. The Temple Church, London, has the reredos made for it in 1684 by Emmett, and possibly designed by Wren. Corinthian columns carry a central pediment and pilasters support the side pieces. It was removed from the church in 1840, and thus survived the blitz, being returned in 1953. At about the same time Wren designed the more ornate piece carved by Grinling Gibbons for St James Piccadilly, but even finer is the Grinling Gibbons reredos at St Mary Abchurch, 1686. So well has it been restored that is is difficult to believe that it was blown into two thousand fragments during the blitz. Corinthian columns supporting a broken pediment, exquisite swags and garlands, and fine panelling combine into a glorious composition. A little earlier than these, the reredos of about 1676 at St Magnus the Martyr, Lower Thames Street, London Bridge *(3)* still has its painting of Moses and Aaron, an early example of a popular subject, especially when the reredos contained the ten commandments.

Outside London, two Oxfordshire reredoses are carved in the same manner, with delicate limewood details that recall the work of Gibbons. That at St Michael's Chapel, Rycote, is dated 1682 *(59)*. Five panels of texts have acanthus frames and their own pediments, while between them rise four fluted Corinthian demi-columns to support a segmental pediment with fruit and flower swags. At Trinity College, Oxford *(1)* the reredos is slightly later, c.1694, an elegant composition with plain surfaces veneered in juniper tellingly contrasted with fruit and foliage, and two well-proportioned Corinthian columns to support the central pediment.

The reredos in the Chapel at Chatsworth, Derbyshire, was also made in 1694. Although the side walls of the chapel are panelled in cedarwood with limewood carvings by Samuel Watson, the reredos, probably also Watson's work, is made of alabaster, a piece of truly ducal splendour, with Ionic columns

and pilasters, subtly curving side-panels, and an apsidal central niche, with, above it, Corinthian pilasters supporting a segmental pediment which together frame Verrio's painting of Doubting Thomas. At the base of these flanking pilasters stand two statues by Cibber.

This was a prophetic piece, for as the eighteenth century progressed, stone again came into use, for example at Chicheley, Buckinghamshire, not later than c.1710, Painswick, Gloucestershire, 1743, Holkham Hall Chapel, Norfolk, c.1750, and Otterden, Kent, 1759. Alabaster was used for the Holkham reredos, which contains a painting of the Ascension in three panels, while at Otterden, the reredos is a marble version of the customary wooden type, with Lord's Prayer, Creed and Commandments in gilt letters.

The romantic and classical streams of taste in the eighteenth century can be neatly contrasted in two reredoses made in 1769. Essex copied details from the tomb of Bishop de Luda of Ely for the surprisingly convincing medievalizing piece in the Angel Choir at Lincoln, while at Gunton, Norfolk, Robert Adam used wooden Corinthian pilasters and columns to support a pretty floral frieze in plaster. In the centre is a painting of the Adoration of the Shepherds.

Coming into the early nineteenth century, there are altar paintings by John Constable of 1804 at Brantham, and 1809 at Nayland, both Suffolk. The Christ and the Children at Brantham is still in the eighteenth-century studio convention, but his Christ Blessing the Bread and Wine at Nayland is a much more original work.

Pride of place among Victorian reredoses must go to the elaborate Scott creations at Gloucester, Lichfield and Worcester Cathedrals, and they are undeniably impressive. Livelier if not lovelier are the gaudy tiled reredos at Bishop's Tawton, Devon, and Woodyer's pale blue cross on a yellow stone background, made in 1865 for St Mary, Gosport. Burmantofts, Leeds has a reredos of 1891 made of local faience, and Shields and Heaton vividly depicted the Risen Christ in cloisonné work at St Mary-without-the-Walls, Chester, in 1888.

The Burne-Jones retable of 1861 at St Paul, Brighton, a very early Morris & Co. piece, is characteristic in its portrayal of various members of the brotherhood. William Morris is one of the Magi, while Swinburne and Burne-Jones himself appear more humbly as shepherds. Comparable in this respect is the reredos in Llandaff Cathedral, where Rossetti used Morris and his wife, Swinburne, and Burne-Jones as models to illustrate his theme, the Seed of David. Few furnishings can have caused **more**

143 Left Metropolitan Museum of Art, New York: ivory altar cross from Bury St Edmunds, c.1150 possibly by Master Hugo
144 Below St Marcella, Denbigh: communion table and three-sided rails, 1623
145 Bottom Branscombe, Devon: communion table and four-sided rails, c.1690

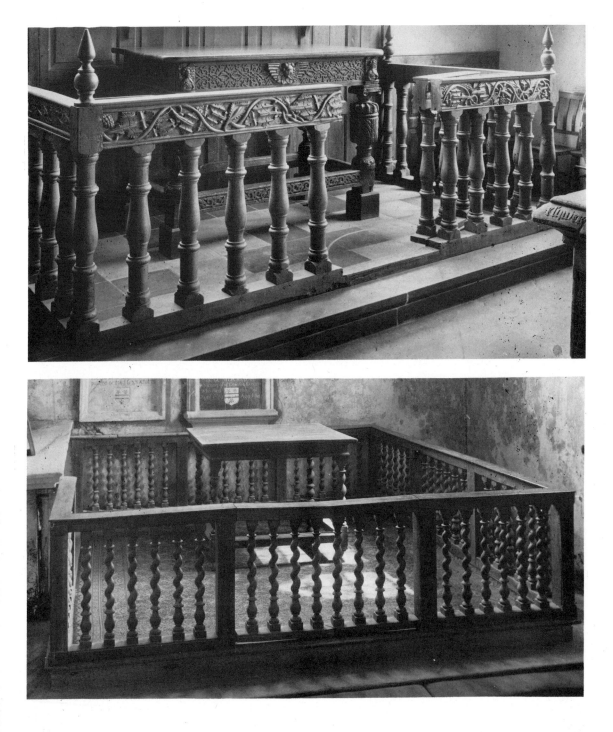

146 Left North Molton, Devon: chancel panelling and communion rail, c. 1640 (?)

147 Below left Rye, Sussex: communion table, c. 1740

148 Right Deerhurst, Gloucestershire: Puritan chancel seating, mid-seventeenth century

149 Below right St Martin-cum-Gregory, York: reredos, 1749; communion rail, 1753

trouble than this. It took several years for Chapter and architects to persuade Rossetti to finish it, after a good deal of haggling about the price, and when, in 1864, it finally appeared, it could hardly be seen in the darkness which shrouded the high altar. The illustration *(157)* shows it in its original sumptuous stone setting, but in the post-war reconstruction of the cathedral, a virtue was made of necessity, and Rossetti's paintings were moved to St Illtyd's Chapel, and set in a gentle blue and gold triptych frame, in good light where it is at least possible to enjoy the painting.[75] The pre-Raphaelites also produced tapestry reredoses, like the one at Roker, Sunderland, woven by Morris & Co., from a Burne-Jones design in 1906 *(262)*.

Between then and 1960, there are some impressive Comper pieces, rather in the same spirit as Scott's earlier work, and two with paintings set in beaten metal frames made by the Bunce sisters, Kate and Myra, at Longworth, Berkshire, and St Alban, Bordesley, Birmingham, 1919.

The tendency for free-standing altars has not prevented some striking work in the 1960s. Hans Feibusch transformed the undistinguished church of St Mark, Coventry, by his painting of the Resurrection covering the whole east wall, finished in 1963, but even this is small compared to the huge tapestry of Christ in Majesty at Coventry Cathedral, designed by Graham Sutherland. Perhaps no other single fitting dominates a large church to the same extent, and the figure of Christ has something of the same visual impact as the most dramatic Romanesque apse-mosaics, like those at Cefalù Cathedral, Sicily. Certainly the contrast between the gigantic figure of Christ and the diminutive, but, incredibly, life-sized figure of man similarly emphasizes the difference in stature between Christ and ourselves.

Smaller in scale, but equally striking, is John Piper's tapestry reredos in Chichester Cathedral, installed in 1966. Seen from the west through the Bell-Arundel screen, it glows with colour, bringing much-needed warmth to an otherwise grey vista. Close to, it reveals symbols of the Trinity at the centre, and of the four elements and the four evangelists flanking them. The background colours, in strong red, green and blue swathes at the centre, shading to softer green and mauve at the sides, emphasize the symbols, which contain a good deal of white, with great clarity. Both the Coventry and the Chichester tapestries were woven by Pinton Frères near Aubusson.[76]

The Piper tapestry is not the only distinguished modern altarpiece at Chichester. The Chapel of St Mary Magdalene has a painting by Graham Sutherland, '*Noli me Tangere*', which, while painted in a properly modern idiom, nevertheless seems to allude to the early fourteenth century in the postures of the figures *(161)*. Although quite small, it can be seen for the length of the cathedral, and from the west, like the tapestry, it forms a distant and exciting pool of colour.

Canopies and Baldacchinos

A few altars are surmounted by baldacchinos supported by columns, or by coronas suspended from the ceiling. The baldacchino at Peterborough Cathedral, made in 1894, is attributed to J.L. Pearson, who was working at the cathedral at about this time, and the marble baldacchino at Westminster Cathedral was designed by Bentley in 1901, though not made until after his death. Wren had contemplated one for St Paul's, but the realisation of the idea had to wait until the 1960s, when it was designed by Stephen Dykes Bower and Godfrey Allen. In a more modern style, the Church of the Ascension, Crownhill, Plymouth, has a concrete baldacchino of 1956, delicately curved, its simplicity nicely contrasted with Geoffrey Clarke's granite and glass wall behind it.

Suspended canopies in the form of coronas, both made in the 1960s, can be seen in the Roman Catholic Cathedral at Liverpool and the Anglican one at Blackburn. The Liverpool one, consisting of vertical tubes, was designed by the cathedral's architect, Sir Frederick Gibberd. Blackburn's, by Lawrence King, likewise crowns a central altar – the point of such a canopy would be lost over an altar at the east end – and it too has vertical tubes, but there is also a symbolic allusion to the crown of thorns, while lumps of crystal glass, faceted like diamonds, simultaneously suggest a diadem. Sanctuary lamps are suspended from it.

Communion Rails

During the middle ages the altar was effectively fenced by the rood screen, but after the Reformation, as the chancel became accessible to the congregation and many rood screens either had their doors removed, or were taken down altogether, the problem of the profanation of the communion table by dogs had to be tackled. It was also desirable to define the sanctuary area. Low rails were introduced with vertical balusters set close together to exclude dogs from the sanctuary, and, when it became customary for communicants to receive the elements kneeling at the rails, their height was convenient, though the primary reason for their lowness was undoubtedly to ensure that the congregation's view of the celebrant was not obscured. Bishop Wren of Norwich ordered in 1636 that 'the Rayle be made before the Communion Table reaching crosse from the North wall to the South wall, neere one yarde in height, so thick with pillars that doggs may not gett in.'[77]

Not many Elizabethan rails survive. At Sutton, Shropshire, they were installed in 1582, and on stylistic grounds – always an uncertain criterion – a number of other sets can be attributed to the same period.[78] One of these, at Woodbury, Devon, has fluted columns, and, very unusually, another set of similar rails encloses the font. Font rails also occur a century later at Wren's church of St Edmund the King, London.

There is no doubt that the impetus to provide communion rails came about through the Laudian revival, and the rails Laud himself installed at Gloucester Cathedral during his days as Dean can be seen in the Lady Chapel. Vertically symmetrical balusters were the normal supports, and although these later gave way to other fashions, they are still found as late as 1684 at Altarnun, Cornwall, where, exceptionally, they stretch right across the width of the church, 1686 at Burton Bradstock, Dorset, and even 1720 at Hardham, Sussex. An occasional Jacobean eccentricity was to alternate balusters with stalagmite-stalactite pairs of demi-balusters which do not quite meet in the middle. At Chediston, Suffolk, the stalagmites are slender cones, while the stalactites are like elongated acorns. The more elaborate set at Isleham, Cambridgeshire, has spiky demi-balusters and much attached ornament in the form of jewels and panelling in the framework, while at Wormleighton, Warwickshire, the balusters are closely set, so that the alternating stalactites, without stalagmites, are purely ornamental and do nothing to exclude dogs.

Vertically symmetrical balusters were succeeded in fashion by dumb-bell balusters later in the seventeenth century; then, at the end of the century and the beginning of the next, balusters with a barley-sugar twist were used – the conventions thus keeping parallel to fashions in domestic furniture during the same years. The two styles overlapped for a quarter of a century and more, and occasionally dumb-bell and twisted balusters were used alternately as at East Ilsley and Leckhampstead, Berkshire, and at King's Somborne, Hampshire. Cumnor, Berkshire, has alternate twisted and fluted balusters.[79]

More expensive sets at this time sometimes had foliage motifs, especially acanthus. At Burnham, Buckinghamshire, they were made about 1680; at Eckington, Derbyshire, and Chalfont St Giles, Buckinghamshire, about 1700. Milton, Cambridgeshire, has a rail from King's College Chapel, which is panel-framed and has small obelisks on the rails.

The revival of wrought-ironwork at the beginning of the eighteenth century has given us some of the most beautiful altar rails we possess. The finest of all are perhaps the earliest, at Lydiard Tregoze, Wiltshire *(150)*; rightly or wrongly they have been attributed to foreign workmanship, but they were clearly made for the church. They are probably about contemporary with Tijou's rails of 1704 at St Andrew Undershaft, London. Robert Bakewell may have made the rails at Wimpole Hall Chapel, Cambridgeshire and Foremark, Derbyshire, but it is not known who made the equally fine ones at Turner's Hospital Chapel, Kirkleatham, North Riding and Castle Bromwich, Warwickshire in the 1740s. Occasionally in the early nineteenth century, cast-iron was used instead, as at Pavenham, Bedfordshire.

Other materials were rarely used in the eighteenth century, though Great Packington, Warwickshire has a marble set made in 1790, but the nineteenth century was as usual more eclectic. Victorian communion rails have not yet been paid adequate attention, but various metals were used as well as wood, and sometimes they were inset with cabouchons of marble and other exotic stones, as at Norwich Cathedral. The superb metal rails at Elford, Staffordshire, *(155)*, may perhaps have been designed by Street, who worked there in 1869–70,[80] and it will be seen that by then it was no longer customary to take one's dog to church, so that the rails now only had to provide a place for communicants to kneel and delineate the area of the sanctuary. Thus designs could be much freer. Many twentieth-century sets, indeed, have only the minimum number of supports necessary for stability.

So far nothing has been said about the shape of the rails. Until the time of Laud, and sometimes much later, it was customary for the communion table to stand in the body of the church or the middle of the chancel. The communicants gathered round, and the celebrant usually faced west. Thus the rails were either four-sided, going right round the communion table, or three-sided, the north and south arms abutting the east wall if the table stood in the chancel. In spite of the insistence of Laud and his bishops that the rails should go straight across the chancel from north to south, the three-side custom even survived into the early nineteenth century in low-church circles, and many presently straight sets of rails may prove on inspection to have been originally three- or four-sided.[81]

Not many four-sided sets survive. There is one at Lyddington, Rutland, dated 1635, one at Branscombe, Devon, *(145)*, dating from the end of the

150 Above Lydiard Tregoze, Wiltshire: communion rail c. 1700

151 Left Chipping Campden, Gloucestershire: detail of altar frontal, fifteenth century

152 Baunton, Gloucestershire: altar frontal, fifteenth century

153 Bottom Axbridge, Somerset: altar frontal, 1713–20, by Mrs Abigail Prowse

century, and one at Gibside Chapel, Co. Durham. Gibside, built in the shape of a Greek cross, was built in 1760 as a mausoleum, but converted into a church between 1809 and 1812, with the communion table placed under the dome at the crossing. Such a central communion table was revolutionary indeed at that time, and the four-sided rails are of course the only way of protecting the sanctuary. At Deerhurst, Gloucestershire, the communion rail is a very early one of about 1600, and runs across the sanctuary in the manner later approved by Laud. It was unobjectionable to the Puritans who installed the communicants' seats, for they were placed inside the rail, within the sanctuary.

Three-sided rails are still relatively common. Among those of interest may be selected the pre-Laudian ones at St Marcella, Denbigh, *(144)*, sets with twisted balusters at Llangelynin, Caernarvonshire, Boxted Suffolk, and Brent Eleigh, Suffolk, and a set with dumb-bell balusters made in 1707 at Kedington, Suffolk. A group in Yorkshire have semi-circular projections, of which the earliest seems to be Wentworth, probably of 1684; others include Darton, St Michael-le-Belfrey, York, and St Martin-cum-Gregory, York, 1753, *(149)*. The rails at Coxwold, North Riding take this a stage further by having a long tongue curving westward in the middle of the west side of the rail. Semi-circular projections appear sometimes outside Yorkshire – at Holy Trinity, Sunderland, c.1735, and at West Wycombe, c.1760.

Piscinas

Piscinas always and sedilia usually form part of the architecture of the church as much as the furnishings, and will not be treated in detail here. A piscina is simply a drain to take away the water used to wash the communion vessels and the celebrant's hands during mass. The piscina for the high altar was always placed in the chancel south wall, except in great churches with chancel aisles where such a position was obviously impractical. Others were as near the altar they served as conveniently possible, usually in the south wall of the south aisle and the north or east wall of the north aisle. They were often richly carved, and were usually contrived in the thickness of the masonry. Above the drain, the arched recess may contain a shelf called a credence, though separate credences were sometimes installed.

Piscinas are usually only found in pre-Reformation churches. Saxon examples are now rare, though there is one at Sompting, Sussex. Such Norman ones as survive often have a bowl supported by a stone pillar,

and these are not uncommon, though rarely of more than local interest. At Swannington, Norfolk, the capital of the pillar has a carving of St George and the dragon, while at Tollerton, Nottinghamshire, the shaft is diapered, and the capital has scrolly volutes.

A fashion which began early in the thirteenth century and persisted until the fifteenth, especially in eastern England, was to extend the eastern jamb of the south chancel window to form a projection in which the drain was set. The piscina therefore had two arches, one facing north in the normal manner, the other facing west. These are known as angle piscinas, and early examples occur at Bapchild, Kent, made about 1200, Hartlip, Kent, and Blyford, Suffolk. Good later examples are frequently found in East Anglia, and there is a fine one much further west at St Mary, Cheltenham.

Later in the thirteenth century it became customary for piscinas to have two drains, one for the water used for washing the celebrant's hands, the other for the water used for rinsing the chalice and paten. This custom may have begun in Hertfordshire, for there are two here which are much earlier than the rest, at Great Wymondley and Graveley, where they date from the end of the twelfth century, but by far the majority belong to the late thirteenth and early fourteenth centuries. The practice of giving each drain a separate arch and enclosing these two arches in a containing arch encouraged the use of bar tracery. To begin with, as in the early example at Toddington, Bedfordshire, where the containing arch is round, the upper part is left plain, but in later ones, like Carlton Rode, Norfolk, beautiful designs were sometimes created. At Carlton Rode the lancets are trefoiled, and the superarch contains a diagonally placed quatrefoil with each of its lobes trefoiled, and the whole composition is richly moulded. At Baconsthorpe, Norfolk, there is a more conventional quatrefoil set in a circle, and the lancets are not trefoiled, but this combines the double with the angle form, though the single west-facing arch, which is trefoiled, is smaller than the others.

An alternative, very attractive form, was to set the piscinas in a rectangular surround, span the recess with a single round-headed arch, and interweave it with two demi-arches springing from a central column. One is found in the Chapel of Jesus College, Cambridge, *(162)*, there is another in the Chapel of St John's, and the rest are all found in Cambridgeshire and the adjoining East Anglian counties. At Brecon Cathedral, there is a thirteenth-century triple piscina, which may well be unique.

Quite early in the fourteenth century single piscinas

154 Above Wreay, Cumberland: sanctuary, 1842, by
Sara Losh

155 Right Elford, Staffordshire: communion rail,
Victorian, perhaps by G.E. Street

156 Top left Llantwit Major (Llanilltyd Fawr), Glamorgan: Jesse niche, mid-thirteenth century – possibly originally a reredos

157 Left Llandaff Cathedral: retable – The Seed of David, completed 1864, by D.G. Rossetti, in its original setting

158 Top right Metropolitan Cathedral of Christ the King, Liverpool: high altar, c. 1965, with crucifix by Elizabeth Frink and candlesticks by R.Y. Goodden

159 Right Durham Cathedral: high altar reredos, the 'Neville Screen', 1372–80 probably by Henry Yeveley

160 Left Westminster Abbey: St Peter – detail of retable, c.1280

161 Above Chichester Cathedral, Chapel of St Mary Magdalene: retable, '*Noli me Tangere*', 1961 by Graham Sutherland

162 Above left Jesus College Chapel, Cambridge: double piscina, mid-thirteenth century

163 Above right Swavesey, Cambridgeshire: piscina and sedilia, early fourteenth century

164 Left Lincoln Cathedral: Easter Sepulchre, c.1300

Opposite
165 Top Tarrant Hinton, Dorset: detail of Easter Sepulchre, c.1525

166 Right Hawton, Nottinghamshire: Easter Sepulchre, c.1330

167 Far right Coity, Glamorgan: probable Easter Sepulchre, c.1500

returned to fashion, and so remained until the Reformation. They often formed a single composition with the sedilia, like the fine example at Swavesey, Cambridgeshire, *(163)*. The most interesting single piscina is at Long Wittenham, Berkshire, where the head of the trefoiled recess consists of two small angels flying towards one another, with wings overlapping, and the front of the basin bears a tiny carved effigy of a knight, in whose memory it was presumably installed.

Credence shelves are usually plain, but in the thirteenth-century piscina at Ditchfield, Wiltshire, there are three separate projections. At Trelleck, Gwent, the piscina has a modern wooden shelf in the usual place about half way up the recess, but forming part of the same composition there is another triangular-headed recess above with two trefoiled shelf compartments, and, in the apex, an elongated quatrefoil containing a small pedestal, perhaps for an image. At Thorpe Arnold, Leicestershire, and other churches nearby, there are also piscinas with separate arched recesses above for the credence shelf.

Sedilia

Sedilia are seats for the celebrant, deacon and sub-deacon to use during the singing of the kyrie, credo and gloria. They are normally situated just to the west of the piscina on the chancel south wall, though the ones at Durham Cathedral, which are visually related to the Neville Screen, are on the north side. Continental practice was to provide free-standing wooden seats, but this is exceptional in England and Wales. At Beverley Minster, wooden sedilia of c.1345 stand opposite the Percy tomb, and Pevsner attributes both to the same designer.[82] The difference in material would not have been apparent when both were painted. There is a fifteenth-century wooden five-seater at Hexham Priory, and a two-seater with linenfold at St Oswald, Durham. In the south there is just one example, a standard fifteenth-century three-seater at Rodmersham, Kent.

The normal English custom was to carve sedilia of stone in a wall recess like piscinas, and the earliest examples we have belong to the late twelfth century, like the one at Avington, Berkshire, where there is simply a wide bench under a plain round-headed arch; but at the same period what was to become the normal type, with seats divided by shafts, each with its own arched canopy, were to be found at Earl's Barton, Northamptonshire, and St Mary de Castro, Leicester, where double columns are used, and in both cases the seats are stepped, giving the celebrant the most elevated and the subdeacon the

most lowly seat. Such stepped sedilia are quite common in the thirteenth century; a good example is at Haltwhistle, Northumberland.

Though most sedilia have three seats, there are exceptions as we have already seen. Sometimes a single sedile is provided, like the stone armchair at Compton Beauchamp, Berkshire, and two-seaters occur occasionally as at Kirkwhelpington, Northumberland, and Ryhall, Rutland. Four-seaters sometimes occur in large churches like Maidstone, Newark and Luton, and at Southwell Minster there is a free-standing stone five-seater.

Occasionally other features are included in a composition with the sedilia or piscina. At Chetwode, Buckinghamshire, c.1250, and Grafton Regis, Northamptonshire, c.1340, the sedilia are linked to the south chancel doorway, and at Longfield, Kent, piscina and aumbry are joined. Aumbries, incidentally, are simply cupboards for the plate, more often set in the north wall, which have long since given place to safes, and which, generally without their doors, now appear as dull recesses. The oldest is a seventh-century example at Jarrow. One at East Ilsley, Berkshire, is unusually elaborate, with dogtooth, and at Begbrooke, Oxfordshire, the fifteenth-century door is still in place.

The most elaborate sedilia belong to the early fourteenth century. The Southwell set, now heavily restored in plaster, were made by the same school of carvers who were responsible for the pulpitum, and those at Hawton, Nottinghamshire, and Heckington, Lincolnshire, share the elaboration of the rest of the chancel fittings there. At Wymondham Abbey, Norfolk, the sedilia were made of terracotta about 1525 by the same Italian craftsmen who did other work in East Anglia at the time. Traditionally they are also the memorial to the last Abbot, Elisha Ferrers, but as there is no inscription, and he was not elected until 1532, it seems unlikely. There are no gothic reminiscences in the composition and the canopy work in particular is completely different from contemporary English carving.

The need for piscinas and sedilia ceased with the introduction of the reformed liturgy, and they were only reintroduced in a few Anglo-Catholic and Roman Catholic churches in Victorian times. Victorian examples are pleasant enough but rarely memorable.

Easter Sepulchres

The liturgical drama of the Easter Sepulchre survived the reforms of Edward VI's reign, and was only discarded in 1560. Most Easter Sepulchres, that is, representations of the tomb of Christ, were made of wood, and were kept packed away in chests until Good Friday, when they were set up on the north side of the chancel. On that day, the Host was ceremonially interred in the breast of an image of Christ, which was then placed in the tomb. From then until Easter morning a candle burned before it, and a vigil was kept by a succession of watchers. Then the Host was triumphantly borne forth, sometimes to an acted paraphrase of the gospel record – the ritual used in Durham Cathedral has survived – but the sepulchre remained in place till the Friday of Easter week when it was dismantled and packed away until the following year.

Once redundant, their destruction in the later sixteenth century was thorough. Some were given to the poor as firewood; others were made into cupboards, steps, biers, even hencoops. Francis Bond, writing in 1916,[83] knew of the existence of two, one in Snetterfield Vicarage, Warwickshire; the other in a private house in Derbyshire. I do not know what has happened to these two, but there are two others whose identification as Easter Sepulchres seems plausible. The first, at Cowthorpe, West Riding, is a richly carved chest with a gable-roofed canopy above it. The second, at Coity, Glamorgan,*(167)*, made about 1500, is a chest with a saddleback top and crocketed gables, but without a separate canopy. The front panels of the chest have carvings of the instruments of the Passion, and this is what inclines one to think that it was indeed a sepulchre, rather than the alternative suggestion sometimes put forward, of a reliquary.

Many vanished examples doubtless also reflected the high standard of late medieval carpentry. In 1470 the church of St Mary Redcliffe, Bristol, purchased a new one 'well gilt with gold', from a Master Canynge. Bond records the specification: 'Item, an image of God almighty rising out of the same sepulchre; Item, thereto longeth Heaven, made of timber and stained clothes; Item, Hell, made of timber and ironwork thereto, with Devils to the number of 13; Item, 4 knights, armed, keeping the sepulchre with weapons in their hands; that is to say, 2 axes and 2 spears and 2 pavés; Item, 4 pairs of angels' wings for 4 angels, made of timber and well painted; Item, the Fadre, the Crown and Visage, the ball with a cross on it, well gilt with fine gold; Item, the Holy Ghost coming out of Heaven into the Sepulchre; Item, longeth to the 4 angels 4 chevelers.'

Often these wooden sepulchres were placed on a tomb chest, or a recessed canopied tomb with a flat upper slab, frequently that of the founder. The north

wall of the chancel was the standard place for the founder's tomb, and it is possible that some had movable effigies which could be temporarily taken out, though brasses were obviously more convenient. Brasses depicting the resurrection with the soldiers below are still to be found against the north wall of the chancels at Slaugham, Sussex, and Narborough, Norfolk. Elsewhere, plain low recesses may have been contrived solely as Easter Sepulchres, and occasionally elaborate permanent masonry sepulchres were built, among them some outstanding pieces of sculpture.

The origin of this fashion may well be traced to Lincoln Cathedral about 1300, *(164)*, where there is a six-bay composition of which the western three form a funeral monument, while the eastern three comprise the sepulchre. The base of this part shows three sleeping soldiers in relief. In the next 30 years or so, a series of more opulent examples appeared in the Lincoln neighbourhood. The finest of these is at Hawton, near Newark, made by the same carvers who produced the Southwell choir screen, *(166,* compare *104)*. Similar nearly complete ones are at Heckington and Irnham, Lincolnshire, and at Patrington, East Riding, but there are several others now badly damaged. In all cases the detail is intricate and beautiful. They all show the soldiers sleeping, but a century and a half later at Northwold, Norfolk, the soldiers are awake and alarmed. In addition to these elaborate examples, there are many simpler ones, like those at Swineshead, Bedfordshire, and Kelling, Norfolk.

At Twywell, Northamptonshire, there is an early example, combined with an aumbry, and covered with a pitched roof like that of a reliquary, or, indeed, the wooden sepulchres at Cowthorpe and Coity. It may also have served as a gospel desk. At East Bergholt, Suffolk, the wall at the back of the sepulchre bears a fifteenth-century painting of the resurrection.

Finally, at Tarrant Hinton, Dorset, there is a sepulchre given by Thomas Weaver, rector from 1514 to 1526, which, except for a four-centred arch, is in pure Early Renaissance style, a remarkably advanced piece for its date in England. It bears, in beautiful lettering, the inscription: *'Venite et videte locũ ubi posit erat Dñs.'* – 'Come and see the place where the Lord was laid.' *(165)*

Not every church had an Easter Sepulchre. In returns from 170 Lincolnshire churches quoted by Bond, 50 stated that they had one; two that they did not; while the rest made no mention of them. But the ceremony was one with a strong appeal to the medieval mind, and most parishes must have made provision for it somehow, however simply.

Miscellaneous Eucharistic Furniture

Vestments and Vestment Chests

The use of copes, of course, was not confined to the celebration of mass, but it is convenient to consider vestments and their storage here. Some old copes survive, almost alone of medieval vestments, sometimes now as altar frontals, sometimes in their original form. At Skenfrith, Gwent, for example, a medieval cope is displayed in a glass case. The best collection of vestments of different ages in a place of worship is in the Roman Catholic Chapel of Wardour Castle, Wiltshire.[84] Coventry Cathedral has a fine set of modern copes. Medieval cope chests remain in several cathedrals like York, Salisbury and Wells, shaped like a segment of a cylinder so that copes could be laid out flat, and sometimes enriched by scrolly ironwork. At Aylesbury, Buckinghamshire, and Bedwellty, Gwent, there are fifteenth-century vestment presses, and at Old Radnor the vestment chest is Elizabethan, a rare, if not unique period for such a piece of furniture.

Credence Tables

Credence tables, to hold the bread, wine and water used at the Eucharist, were occasionally made in the middle ages. By a curious coincidence two survive in villages called Fyfield. At Fyfield, Essex, it looks like one half of a double piscina, whereas at Fyfield, Berkshire, it takes the form of a carved pedestal. Credence tables have also been in use since the Reformation, being favoured especially by Archbishop Laud in the seventeenth century, and by followers of the Oxford Movement in the nineteenth. There is a fine example in Newcastle Cathedral, the gift of Henry and Elizabeth Maddison in 1604.

Sanctuary Panelling

Sanctuary walls were sometimes panelled to a height of several feet during the seventeenth and eighteenth centuries. At North Molton, Devon *(146)* the unusu-ally elaborate panelling is believed to date from Charles I's reign. Seventeenth-century panelling is also found at Northiam, Sussex, c.1638, and Barnby-in-the-Willows, Nottinghamshire. Eighteenth-century examples include Baginton, Warwickshire, 1723, St Mary-le-Bow, Durham, c.1731, Hatfield Broad Oak, Essex, and Gretton, Northamptonshire.

Sanctuary Carpets

A sanctuary carpet is a common sight, though rarely remarked upon in guide books. They are often good quality modern British pieces, though sometimes oriental rugs are used instead. Morris and Co. made some, like the one at Roker, Sunderland, and the one at Guildford Cathedral was designed by the architect, Sir Edward Maufe.

Houseling Tables

A few churches have low tables for communicants to kneel at. Three Warwickshire churches, Tredington, Whitchurch, and Willey, have simple seventeenth-century examples.

Pyxes and Corporals

Pyxes are receptacles made to contain the consecrated Host, whether for exposition, or for the communion of the sick. No medieval example survives in an English church, but Warkleigh, Devon, has a fifteenth-century pyx case, and there are pyx canopies at Dennington, Suffolk, Milton Abbey, Wells Cathedral and Tewkesbury Abbey. Sometimes the pyx was covered by a cloth, known as a Sindon Cloth. Hessett, Suffolk, possesses one, now on loan to the British Museum. Also on loan to the British Museum from Hessett is the burse, a case to hold the cloth called the corporal or corporas on which the bread and wine were placed for consecration. The only other, of thirteenth-century embroidered canvas, is at Wymondham Abbey, Norfolk.

Chapter 9
Wall-painting, Glass and Mosaics

Wall-painting

The record of wall-painting in England begins a generation after the Norman Conquest. The statement of the French monk, Raoul Glaber that the great rebuilding he had witnessed in the early years of the eleventh century made it seem 'as if the world, anxious to cast away its rags, wished to dress in a beautiful white robe of churches',[85] reminds us that at this time churches were plastered outside as well as inside. The mellow glow of Roman bricks that we find such an attractive feature of the eleventh-century tower of St Albans was no part of its designer's intentions: originally it would have gleamed white, and excavations at York Minster in the 1960s revealed that the church there built c.1070 was plastered white externally, with red lines painted on it to resemble the mortar between blocks of ashlar. Similar mock-ashlar painting is found internally in the cathedrals of St Albans, c.1080–90, and Norwich, c.1090–1100. The soffits of the arches at St Albans are painted in alternately red and white blocks, perhaps in imitation of polychrome masonry. Sometimes such painting was done over real ashlar, but at St Albans the plaster covers Roman bricks.

In contrast to contemporary fonts, where haphazard choice of subjects at the whim of the sculptor or his patron seems to have been standard practice, most twelfth-century figure painting belongs to a coherent iconographical scheme. This undoubtedly goes back to previous centuries, unless British practice was at variance with Continental custom, and it persisted in essentials, though with a widening repertoire, throughout the middle ages.

The search for symbolism in medieval churches has often been overdone, not least by pious contemporaries like the mystical thirteenth-century Bishop Durandus of Merde. But the idea that the people's part of the church, the nave, represented the Church Militant, while the priest's part, the chancel, where God was present in the form of the Sacrament, represented the Church Triumphant, seems to have been widely understood. In the nave, therefore, the paintings were designed to teach, and so such edifying subjects as the Lives of Christ and the Saints, the Seven Deadly Sins and the Seven Works of Mercy

and the Three Quick and the Three Dead were chosen.[86] In the late middle ages, St Christopher appears universally opposite the main entrance so that travellers could implore his protection before setting out. The Three Quick and the Three Dead apparently originated from a late thirteenth-century story told at the Flemish court of how three heedless young kings in the full vigour of life and manhood meet three corpses who remind them of the inevitability of death and the importance of preparing for it. In the fourteenth-century version at Widford, Oxfordshire, the story is depicted straightforwardly, but the story became more macabre with the telling, and details of the decay of the corpses are emphasized at Peakirk, near Peterborough, while finally at Belton, Suffolk, the dead leap out to attack the living.

The Christ of the Trades is a subject which has puzzled interpreters, probably because it was variously understood at the time. Here the risen Jesus is shown, complete with his wounds, surrounded by the tools of various occupations. At Fingringhoe, Essex, there is an inscription:'*In omnia opere memento finis*', perhaps meant to indicate that the purpose of work and the goal of life are alike truly comprehended through Christ, but Continental documentary evidence suggests that it could also mean that plying one's trade on the sabbath was hurtful to the Saviour.[87] It is not common in Britain, and the best preserved examples are probably those at Breage and St Just-in-Penwith, Cornwall, and Ampney Crucis, Gloucestershire. A similar subject is the warning to swearers found at Broughton, Buckinghamshire and Corby, Lincolnshire, where Christ's body is dismembered by those who swear by it, and at Peakirk there is also a warning to gossips, represented by two chattering women with a horned devil peering over their shoulders.

The boundary between the Church Militant and the Church Triumphant was the chancel arch, with its screen and the Great Rood. As we have seen in the chapter on screens, it was customary to paint a Last Judgement, or Doom, round the chancel arch. Christ the Redeemer died to enable mankind to enter the gate of the Heavenly Jerusalem; Christ the Judge, merciful but just, determined who had qualified to benefit from his sacrifice. According to the heed people had paid to the example of the faith of the saints, and to the moral precepts depicted in the nave, so they would be judged on the last day. These Dooms were based on the apocalyptic passages in Matthew, and show the darkness, the Son of Man coming in his glory, the angel with the trumpet, the gathering of the elect from the four winds, and the division of mankind into the saved and the damned.[88]

Here is inspiration indeed for painting, even without the awful conviction that it was literally true. The joys of the blessed and the pains of the damned are given equal space, but it is no use pretending that the joys were as interesting to paint. Freudian motivation apart, even though painters might leaven the horrors of hell with touches of macabre humour, the more vividly the appalling possibility was portrayed, the greater chance of persuading sinners to repent in time. Heaven, on the other hand, looks respectable but unexciting. Caiger-Smith describes the Heavenly Jerusalem at South Leigh, Oxfordshire, as 'very like a fifteenth-century Oxford College', on which, indeed, the painting was probably based.[89]

Our earliest remaining Doom, painted about the end of the eleventh century in the tiny church of Coombes, Sussex, is sadly incomplete. Christ is there in Majesty, and lower down he delivers the keys to St Peter and the book to St Paul, but not much else can be seen. About 1140 a similar version was painted at Clayton, Sussex, and here a great deal more has been preserved. As well as the same scenes that appear at Coombes, there are the blessed entering paradise and a group of the damned. Not far away at Hardham, there is a surprise. The mid-twelfth-century paintings above the chancel arch show scenes from Luke's infancy narrative, and the torments of the damned appear instead on the west wall. This seems to have been an alternative tradition, for there is a thirteenth-century Doom on the west wall at Wissington, Suffolk, and it is a subject also treated in glass, pre-eminently about 1500 in the great west window at Fairford, Gloucestershire.

A milder departure from the usual practice is found at Chaldon, Surrey, about 1200, where instead of a Doom above the chancel arch, there appears instead a painting of the purgatorial ladder, which teaches a similar lesson in a less scriptural way. Two famous late Dooms, neither of them great art, are at Wenhaston, Suffolk, on a boarded tympanum, and the heavily restored murals round the chancel arch at St Thomas, Salisbury (174). The one at Wenhaston was only discovered when the tympanum was turned out into the churchyard during a Victorian restoration, and exposure lifted the later paintwork to reveal it.

Through the barrier formed by screen, Rood, and Doom, lay the chancel. Originally attention was focused on the apse, which formed the sanctuary, the very place where Christ came down under the accidents of bread and wine, and here it was customary in the eastern and western church to portray Christ in Majesty, frequently with the symbols of the evangelists in mosaics. English artists did not aspire to wall-mosaics, but apse paintings of about 1140 of Christ in Majesty can be seen at Copford, Essex, and Kempley, Gloucestershire. At Copford the design has been repainted, thus giving an idea of what it looked like in its prime, while Kempley pleases by being in relatively good condition and virtually unrestored.

But the English did not care for apses. The Saxons used them occasionally in their more ambitious churches, and the Normans employed them in European fashion, but by the thirteenth century they were rapidly being torn down in favour of long, square-ended chancels, with increasingly large east windows which made it impossible for the old tradition to be followed. Thus the most moving east wall painting of the later middle ages, a fourteenth-century crucifixion at Brent Eleigh, Suffolk, is really only a reredos, and as such it is not even specifically a chancel subject. A similar crucifixion appears in the south aisle at Turvey, Bedfordshire.

So much for the subject matter: now the styles. Twelfth-century painting was robust, vigorously drawn and strongly coloured. In this it follows the style of contemporary manuscripts, and also tries to approach as closely as possible the effect of glass mosaic. Moreover, most twelfth-century churches were dark inside, and delicate, washy colours would have had little impact. The Majesty of c.1130 in St Gabriel's Chapel, Canterbury Cathedral, and the equally fine St Paul and the Viper (168) of c.1150 in St Anselm's Chapel there, show what the best painters of the time were aiming for. They also, particularly the Majesty, convey the impassivity so characteristic of twelfth-century art. It attracts the mind and elevates the spirit, but does not touch the emotions. The figures are remote, awesome, numinous, floating in space.

Fresco, the art of painting onto fresh plaster while it was still wet so that paint and plaster bonded together, was sometimes used at this period – the paintings at Coombes, Clayton and Kempley are examples – but the more usual method in England, now and later, was to paint the walls very soon after the plaster had dried. It was still porous enough to allow a very similar fusion of materials, but had the obvious advantage that timing was less critical. The pigments, mostly natural 'earths', were mixed with lime water or skimmed milk. The two expensive colours were malachite, to give a vivid green, and lapis lazuli, an unequalled blue. They were used only in the most important work, for example in Canterbury and Winchester Cathedrals.

A change of mood is discernible in the painting of the battle between the virtues and the vices on the north wall of the nave at Claverley, Shropshire, showing that already by about 1200 a more linear style was emerging. It can be more clearly seen in the Chapel of the Holy Sepulchre at Winchester Cathedral. Here the Deposition of about 1230 is still painted in the Romanesque manner, with broad underpainting followed by bold washes, the detail provided by pale highlights in the final stage,[90] but the slender figures are no longer static; they have the characteristic sway of early gothic art. The roundel of the Virgin and Child in the Bishop's Palace Chapel at Chichester shows the new style come to maturity about 1250. The Virgin's head leans forward to caress her child, and the colouring, using gold and silver leaf as well as lapis lazuli, has a new richness and glitter. It is beautifully drawn. The sequence of thirteenth-century painting, however, can be seen best in the nave at St Albans, where five crucifixions were painted on the piers between about 1215 *(170)* and 1275. Each is quite distinct and individual, and the mood of the interpretations shows an unexpectedly wide range.

Surviving late gothic murals are mostly poor stuff by comparison with the best of the earlier work. As windows grew in size, so glass took the place of wall-painting as the chief medium of visual teaching, until at Fairford, c.1500, the glass does it all, and the wall-paintings are simply ornamental. Besides, the arts do not all flourish at once. The late medieval English excelled in carpentry and stonemasonry, and, increasingly, in music. Their mural painting was a dying art, often poorly drawn and gaudily coloured. For example cinnabar, which gave a bright vermillion, became a popular pigment. Its tendency to blacken with prolonged exposure led to even more unfortunate effects. Popular impact was what counted, rather than the earlier ideal of the devotion of man's highest skill to the service of the Divine. As the fifteenth century wore on, moreover, woodcuts rather than manuscript illuminations provided much of the source material. Since even the best woodcuts were clumsy compared with the delicate, painstaking art of the illuminator, their enlargement to mural size makes their shortcomings blatant. Only the screen paintings at Ashton,

Devon, among woodcut-inspired church art show any real merit, and these, of course, are on a much smaller scale than murals. The best late gothic wall-paintings are respectable, if not inspiring, but only in three places, in what seems to be a deliberate rejection of popular fashion, has really first-class work survived.

The first of these paintings were executed in Eton College Chapel in a Netherlandish style by William Baker and Gilbert in the 1480s. Following tradition the narrative is shown in strips, and the theme is the Miracles of the Virgin. They are in monochrome, occasionally relieved by a little subdued colour, and the drawing is first class *(173)*. The same subject was chosen for a very similar set, in brown and grey, about 1500, in the Lady Chapel at Winchester. At Haddon Hall Chapel, Derbyshire, the paintings are also latest fifteenth century, also almost monochrome, and also good. But there the resemblance ends: both subject matter and style are different, the most notable feature being the quantity of flowers and foliage between each section of the figure work, the sort of thing that a late medieval Burne-Jones might have produced.

Medieval ceiling painting, as distinct from the painting of carvings like vault bosses or angels, has mostly disappeared, but among the little that has survived is some interesting work. The earliest is in the nave of Peterborough Cathedral, painted about 1220 *(171)*. The timber of the ceiling is set in patterns of lozenges, and the figures appear in the centre of each lozenge – kings, queens, saints, musicians, grotesques – and the colouring is original. Next comes the north aisle of St Helen, Abingdon, about 1390, with beautiful figure painting in panels reminiscent of the best East Anglian work of the time, and these two ceilings are by far the most valuable survivals.

At St Mary Beverley there is a remarkable chancel ceiling painted with English kings, ending with Henry VI, in whose reign in 1445, the work was originally done. Unfortunately it has twice been repainted. In St Albans Cathedral the thirteenth-century timber chancel vault has also been repainted twice, but it never was very ambitious work, perhaps because a stone vault was originally intended, and medieval abbots may have regarded it as temporary. The north and south chapels at East Dereham, Norfolk, have restored fifteenth-century ceilings. In the south chapel, the more elaborate of the two, there is a repeated, but not stencilled pattern in each panel of the Lamb of God inside a wreath, with tendrils and foliage surrounding it. Stencilled patterns were sometimes used, as in the fifteenth-century nave roof at Blythburgh, Suffolk.

The first post-Reformation church painting of any

significance was a vault decoration, at Boxgrove Priory, Sussex, by the same Lambert Bernard who about 1530 had painted the large panels at Chichester Cathedral for Bishop Sherbourne who 'steered a prudent course at the Reformation'.[91] Bernard steered an equally prudent course at Boxgrove: his painting has no suspicion of religious imagery, merely heraldry and foliage. It is pretty, and innocuous enough to have survived without ever having been overwashed.

By contrast almost every medieval painting on plaster to have survived has done so because it was limewashed at the Reformation and replaced in some cases by texts. It would be facile to suggest that the change marked the transition from an illiterate to a literate age, for medieval people were more literate than is commonly supposed, while later generations could by no means all read and write. At the same time, the invention of printing, and encouragement of education through the Renaissance had made the substitution of text for image more practicable than it would have been a century earlier.

The improving texts of the sixteenth-century reformers have in their turn almost entirely disappeared. In the days when every family came to have its Bible, as it did in the seventeenth century, they became obsolete in their turn. Hence the sixteenth-century texts in the walls at Puddletown, Dorset, have considerable historic interest, and nothing as complete survives elsewhere, though there are seventeenth-century ones at Abbey Dore, and others as late as 1711 at Hawkshead, Lancashire. Moses and Aaron, usually painted on commandment boards, occur occasionally on walls, as at St Clement, Hastings, where they were painted in 1721, and so do figures from secular legend, free from the taint of idolatry, like Father Time, who appears in a number of places like Spennithorne, North Riding, and Patricio, Brecon. Much more interesting is the work of 1626 at Passenham, Northamptonshire, already described in Chapter 1 (page 15). Seventeenth-century symbols of the Twelve Tribes of Israel exist at West Walton, Norfolk, Stoke Dry, Rutland, Burton Latimer, Northamptonshire, and Eyam, Derbyshire.[92]

Naive but vigorous ceiling paintings in a rustic vein are found at Staunton Harold, Leicestershire, 1655, by Samuel and Zachary Kyrk, and at Bromfield, Shropshire, of 1672 by Thomas Francis *(176)*. Here the Trinity Symbol is the centrepiece of the design, while angels, scrolls and clouds make up most of the surround.

The last years of the seventeenth century, however, witnessed the beginning of a much more sophisticated series of paintings which are among the finest in our churches. Among the earliest are those in the ceiling of Trinity College Chapel, Oxford, *(1)* painted about 1694 by Pierre Berchet. There are two small rectangular flanking panels, and a large centre panel depicting the Ascension, with the angels and gesticulating figures of attendants much beloved at this time. Quite a different style is exhibited by Giovanni Borgnis for the ceiling painting in the chancel at West Wycombe, 1765. There is far less chiaroscuro, far less dramatic highlighting – the whole picture is lighter in tone – and far less gesticulation by the figures, though their urgency has been vividly caught. Only the hovering cherubs show the continuity of the tradition. Between Trinity Chapel and West Wycombe in time are the ceiling paintings at Little Stanmore *(4)* and Great Witley *(177)*, which as we have seen in Chapter 1, were both originally commissioned by the Duke of Chandos. At Great Witley there are 23 paintings by Antonio Bellucci, of which three, the Nativity, the Deposition, and the Ascension, are large and important. At Little Stanmore the painted decoration on walls and ceiling form part of a single scheme, partly again by Bellucci, but mostly by Laguerre, and consisting largely of biblical scenes with a few figures of Virtues.

Another important work is the monochrome fresco series in the dome of St Paul's, showing scenes in the life of the cathedral's patron saint, and painted between 1716 and 1719 by Sir James Thornhill, who in 1724 also painted the walls of Wimpole Hall Chapel, Cambridgeshire. In both cases he used *trompe l'oeil* techniques: at St Paul's in the architectural setting for the figures, and at Wimpole Hall in the niches between pairs of Corinthian columns supporting an entablature in which the figures are set, a form reminiscent of the work at Passenham a century earlier. Thornhill also painted an Adoration of the Magi as an altarpiece at Wimpole Hall.

Coffering was a form of ceiling decoration much admired in Georgian England, but far too expensive for most churches. At Wimpole Hall Chapel, Thornhill painted the ceiling in *trompe l'oeil* coffering, and the same was done about 1746 at Mereworth, Kent, where the supporting Doric columns are painted to look like marble. The nave at West Wycombe also has painted coffering, surrounding a circle with a Greek-fret type of ornament in the centre of which is a circle of plaster feathers. The stucco work on the cornice and on the walls below, and the delicately carved Corinthian columns add to the beauty of this interior, the focal point of which is the large painted Royal Arms over the chancel arch.

For nearly a century after this there was little wall or ceiling painting of importance. About 1850 the late medieval wagon roof of the chancel at Carlisle Cathedral was painted blue with a pattern of gold stars, beautifully renewed in 1968, but the first major Victorian work was probably Thomas Gambier-Parry's at Highnam, Gloucestershire, a church which he commissioned himself. This was done about 1851; in 1865 he completed the nave ceiling at Ely Cathedral, begun in 1858 by H.S. LeStrange, who had painted the ceiling of the west tower in 1855. From Ely, Gambier-Parry moved to Gloucester Cathedral, where he painted the walls of St Andrew's Chapel between 1866 and 1868, returning to Ely to paint the west transept ceiling in 1878. His work is attractive, and shows a sympathy with its medieval setting as sensitive as that shown by such glass designers as Kempe. Several of these glass designers also did wall-paintings themselves: Kempe at Staplefield, Sussex, and his pupils at Castle Howard Chapel, North Riding; Clayton and Bell in several places like Ashley, Northamptonshire, North Nibley, Gloucestershire,

and Freeland, Oxfordshire; and the architect Bodley decorated Hemel Hempstead and Chigwell. But much Victorian work of this kind, like Street's painted and stencilled decorations at Luton, has been destroyed in the interests of mid-twentieth-century preference for plain surfaces and even lighting.

The pre-Raphaelite contribution includes some predictably good work, including ceilings at St Michael, Brighton and St Martin, Scarborough, by William Morris and Philip Webb, both of the early 1860s, and St Clement, Bradford, by Burne-Jones in the 1890s. There are four pre-Raphaelite ceilings in Jesus College Chapel, Cambridge, painted as part of Bodley's restoration between 1864 and 1867. The nave ceiling *(179)* is divided into rectangular panels with the sacred monogram alternating with the College arms and crest. The coving is painted to Burne-Jones designs, and consists largely of standing angels holding scrolls. The design is strong and the colours are gorgeous. One or two of Burne-Jones's cartoons for the angels are displayed on the walls below.

168 Canterbury Cathedral, St Anselm's Chapel: wall-painting, mid-twelfth century – St Paul and the Viper

169 Above Baunton, Gloucestershire: wall-painting, fourteenth century, St Christopher

170 St Albans Cathedral: wall-painting, thirteenth century, The Crucifixion

171 Above Peterborough Cathedral: detail of ceiling painting,
c.1220

172 Westminster Abbey: detail of sedilia painting, c.1308,
possibly by Thomas of Durham

173 Above Eton College Chapel, Buckinghamshire: detail of wall-painting, c.1479–88 by William Baker and Gilbert
174 Right St Thomas of Canterbury, Salisbury, Wiltshire: Doom, early sixteenth century, restored

175 Left Sandham Memorial Chapel, Burghclere, Hampshire: detail of painting, 1927–32 by Stanley Spencer

176 Above left Bromfield, Shropshire: ceiling painting, 1672 by Thomas Francis

177 Above right Great Witley, Worcestershire: ceiling painting, c.1720 by Antonio Bellucci; papier-mâché surround, c.1747, by James Gibbs

The twentieth century has produced little wall-painting.[93] The most important and the most controversial are Stanley Spencer's murals at the Sandham Memorial Chapel, Burghclere, Hampshire, painted between 1927 and 1932. These 19 paintings fall somewhere between conventional religious art and the interpretations of a war artist, but they are neither. If there is any glory in war, Spencer did not see it, and although he is more sensitive to its tragedy, he did not dwell on that either. He seems reluctant to draw morals, but, though the scenes are largely of everyday life at the front, they are certainly not merely factual reporting. Although the Chapel was a memorial to an officer, only one officer appears in the whole cycle, mounted, and reading a map (175). Many of the scenes are viewed from above, which foreshortens already pudgy, anonymous figures still further. The only explicit religious reference is on the east wall, where the resurrection of the dead soldiers is portrayed. Nothing could stand in greater contrast to the medieval Dooms. Christ is a small, humble figure, no more inclined to judge than Spencer himself, who stands receiving the crosses the soldiers hand in. The artist understood how inappropriate a judgement scene would have been in the context of a war which blurred morality to the point where the shared suffering of the combatants was far more significant than the individual merits of their lives. This is not an attractive series of paintings, and it was quite clearly never intended to be, but it compels far more attention than many more explicitly religious and more explicitly beautiful paintings. Rightly or wrongly, one feels that the spiritual dimension was so deeply felt, that it did not need to be assertively expressed.

Glass

However intrinsically interesting wall and ceiling paintings may be, there is no doubt that the contribution of glass to our churches is more important. Glass has the advantage of transmuting light instead of merely reflecting it, and at its best has a sparkle and vitality that no opaque surface can match. Its effect changes with the light, from one day to another and from one hour to the next, and there are moments when the whole interior of a church seems to take fire from it.

Glass does not have to be coloured to play its part. Some of the most attractively unrestored village churches are lit by a simple lattice work of plain, uneven crown glass of the eighteenth and early nineteenth centuries. The leading of these plain glass windows is sometimes more ambitious in the north.

Two memorable examples of patterned leading are in the chancel aisles at St John, Halifax, c.1650, and at Ponteland, Northumberland, attributed to the eighteenth century.

Fragments of coloured glass have recently been found during excavations at the seventh-century monastery at Jarrow, Co. Durham, but window glass was uncommon until centuries later, horn and canvas being frequent substitutes, and although further excavations may yield archaeologically interesting results, there is no enjoyable coloured glass in England earlier than the twelfth century.

The earliest glass we possess in quantity is in Canterbury Cathedral, where it was originally set in the new eastern parts built after the fire of 1174, and paid for by the already vast throng of pilgrims to the shrine of the murdered Becket. Some of it has now been moved to other parts of the cathedral, and some has been destroyed, but much is still in its original setting, where it was probably placed about 1200. Far more than we now have survived the Reformation unscathed, only to fall victim to Richard Culmer, rector of Chilham in the Puritan period, and nick-named, with more than necessary courtesy, 'Blue Dick'. He 'climbed to the top of the citie ladder, near 60 steps high, with a whole pike in his hand, ratling down proud Becket's glassy bones.'[94] It is fitting that the miracles of St Thomas form one of the themes. Others are biblical, including a set of types and antitypes, and enough remains to make the early glass of Canterbury one of the major treasuries of medieval art in the country (180). The windows are large for their date, and there is plenty of light glass round the figure subjects, so that the interior was never dark. The colours are wonderful, deep and glowing, with a great deal of ruby red and sapphire blue. The glass itself was made in France.

Obviously in many churches with smaller windows, such richly coloured glass would have made for dark interiors; moreover it was very expensive. So, in the thirteenth century, white glass with grey trails of foliage called grisaille was introduced, perhaps originally by the ascetic Cistercians. It looks best when it is relieved by vignettes of coloured figure glass, as in the best surviving example, the Five Sisters in the north transept of York Minster, glazed by 1250.[95]

At about the same time or a little earlier, the rose window in the north transept of Lincoln Cathedral, known as the Dean's Eye, was glazed. It has rich figure glass in the Canterbury tradition, with God in the centre, worshipped by angels, and Christ at the top of the outer circle, with more angels, saints and bishops. There are also contemporary scenes of other subjects inserted from other windows, which now confuse the scheme, but preserve the jewelled effect originally intended.

The colours in this early glass were produced by metallic oxides: copper for red, cobalt for blue, manganese for purple, and iron for green and yellow. The glass was coloured throughout and known as pot metal. Later, however, the advantages of lighter colours were realised, especially for the red which was sometimes almost opaque. So the technique of flashing was evolved, that is, annealing a sheet of white glass with a thin sheet of coloured glass. If the coloured glass was then scratched with a graver, patterns could be obtained that had not been possible before. Drawing outlines, features and folds was done in dark copper or iron-based pigment, spread on the surface with powdered glass, and wine or urine.

Templates were often made for figures, and the repetition of the same pose or its mirror-image show how they were used, and examples exist from the Canterbury glass onwards. The whole window was drawn in cartoon first, from which the designs were traced and the coloured glass then cut to shape. Next the details were painted by line-drawing, and finally any washes were done for highlights. Then the glass was fired to fix the designs, and the finished glass was pieced together with the lead 'calmes' and fixed into the window, supporting either by armatures following the shape of the panels, as in the early work at Canterbury, or, later, by a grid of iron bars called stanchions (vertical) and saddle-bars (horizontal), which prevented gale-damage. None of the actual glass was made in England during the middle ages – even now much of it is imported – and it was then usually brought either from Normandy or from the Rhineland. Generally speaking Norman glass was used in the south and Rhenish in the north.

Outside Canterbury, Lincoln and York there are few places where there is much glass made before 1300. The oldest is a twelfth-century window at Brabourne, Kent, and there are a number of interesting fragments elsewhere, some of them very beautiful.[96] Good glass of about 1300 exists at North Moreton, where there is a whole original window with scenes from the lives of Christ and the saints, and at Dorchester Abbey, Oxfordshire, where it is combined with sculpture in a unusual Jesse window. A much larger quantity of glass of this period survives in the chancel of Merton College Chapel, Oxford. There is some controversy about the exact date of the glazing, but it was probably just before the turn of the century. These windows anticipate standard fourteenth-century practice with richly coloured figures under canopies bordered by grisaille. The quality is not on a par with earlier work, and this, too, is prophetic, for, good though the best fourteenth-century glass is, it is not as good as the best of earlier generations.

However a major technical advance was made at this time. Early in the fourteenth century the process of staining was discovered, which consists of painting white glass with silver sulphide or chloride and then firing it. This produced a yellow colour, and if the process was repeated the colour darkened until a deep orange was produced. Staining was particularly useful in providing saints with haloes or kings with golden crowns without a great deal of leading small pieces of glass.

A compensation for the lower quality of some of the glass is the increase in the quantity that has survived. The best early fourteenth-century window left is the east window of the choir of Wells Cathedral, glazed about 1340. The subject is the popular Tree of Jesse, and the predominant colours are yellow and white, with a good deal of green and red, admirably suited to transmit the early morning sun. Merevale, Warwickshire, also has a fine Jesse window, taken from the nearby abbey, and there is a lovely quatrefoil of about 1316 at Kinwarton, Warwickshire, with the Virgin and Child with two donors. Stanford, Northamptonshire, has much more, including a crucifixion, a resurrection, and, more ominously, figures of saints.

Such rows of saints also appear in the great west window of York Minster – the 'Heart of Yorkshire' – glazed by 1338, and the great east window of Gloucester Cathedral, glazed probably about 1367.[97] The York window has flowing tracery, but the lower lights are transomed, while the Gloucester window is one of the earliest large-scale Perpendicular windows in existence. Although it is easy to exaggerate the extent to which the development of Perpendicular tracery was governed by glazing requirements, the convoluted upper lights of curvilinear windows must have been a nightmare to fill with a coherent design, while the prominent mullions and transoms in Perpendicular work, and the way in which the tracery bars often run right up into the head of the arch, were a glazier's dream. Each light thereby obtained was perfectly adapted for depicting a single figure *(181)*. At Gloucester the subject of the window is the Coronation of the Virgin, witnessed by a vast array of apostles and saints. Since light was all-important, there is a good deal of white and yellow glass, and only flashed red. The blue alone remained as rich and dark as the previous century liked it. The figures are finely drawn, well capable of standing up to careful scrutiny with field glasses, but such windows set the standard for the monotonous and stereotyped rows of saints which bedevil run-of-the-mill late medieval glass, and cast an even greater blight on the less inspired Victorian imitations. Soured by this knowledge, one's enjoyment of these two great windows is a good deal tempered.

At about the time of the Gloucester east window, marked changes were being made in some of the details of glass painting. Before about 1370, black lines were used for deep shadows, and light shadows were provided by means of a very thin enamel wash. Afterwards, lines were only used for outlining, and both light and dark shadows were indicated by stippling the surface of the glass with enamel brown.

The best place to enjoy fourteenth- and fifteenth-century glass in England is undoubtedly York, particularly of course the Minster, where it is basically fourteenth century in the nave and fifteenth in the chancel, but also the parish churches.[98] One of the reasons why so much survives is that when the city surrendered to Parliament in 1644, Sir Thomas Fairfax, the most moderate and civilized of the Puritan leaders, accepted the safety of the churches as one of the conditions. The names of many of the glaziers are known, showing it to have been very much a family craft; all the same, when the great east window needed glazing in 1405, the contract was given to John Thornton of Coventry, perhaps a recognition that the local industry needed revitalizing, and that Thornton was the man to do it. Among other changes, Thornton greatly expanded the quantity of narrative – a welcome revival – and used colour counterchange between figures and canopywork as contemporary screen painters did. He also increased the amount of painted white glass in the interests of luminosity.[99]

As the fifteenth century progressed, further changes took place, by no means only at York. Rectangular quarries became almost as common as lozenge-shapes for backgrounds, and quarries became complete in themselves, the pattern no longer continuing from one to another. More important changes took place in the figures. Up until about this time they were designed, very sensibly, to be seen at a distance, so that outlines were bold, and detail minimized. Now glass painters began to take less account of impact and more of the quantity of subject matter that could be fitted in. Much more detailed drawing was employed, the subtleties of which are often only visible through field glasses or a telephoto lens. Renaissance influence led to less conventionalized, more three-dimensional representations such as had become normal in easel painting. Together with a decline in the importance of the leading in the design, these were the first steps on the slippery slope of pictorialism which was not reversed until well into the nineteenth century. For all this incipient decline, the best works at the beginning of the period are still exquisite, none more so than some figures now in the east window of Merton College Chapel, Oxford, but made originally for one of the transept windows about 1425 (182).

However, the best impression of fifteenth-century glass can be obtained at Great Malvern Priory, glazed between about 1440 and 1506, and it is possible to trace the development from the old-fashioned conventionalism of the early work to the new-fangled three-dimensional realism of the later. There are plenty of narrative scenes in the York tradition as well as the less interesting single figures, and the west window once had a Doom like the one that still exists at Fairford. It is quite clear at Malvern, as it is in the earlier glass at Tewkesbury, that the glass in the monastic choir is just as didactic as in the parochial nave, underlining the point that visual representations were no more the prerogative of the illiterate then than they are now. Much white glass is used at Malvern, and yellows, browns and blues are more dominant than red and green. Even the latest windows are still leaded in medieval fashion and brilliantly coloured in pot metal.

From the fourteenth century it had become customary for about half the glass to be uncoloured, and at Doddiscombsleigh, near Exeter, there are five fifteenth-century windows where perhaps 60%–70% of the glass is white, and yellow is the dominant colour. This tendency is general, even though there are marked regional variations in style: Norwich glass, (183), is quite different from York or Exeter glass in other respects, but not in this. But this was a high point in illumination, and the sixteenth century was moving back to a higher proportion of colour before the Reformation interrupted development.

By about 1500, the influence of easel painting had grown considerably. Beforehand, the discipline of the glazier was to fit his subjects into the tracery of a window, but now the confines of a single subject to a single light were broken, and scenes sometimes occupied whole windows, the effect being that of a picture standing behind the window rather than in it. Purists deplore the tendency, but although some of its effects were baleful, an uncensorious mind can still derive much pleasure from examples.

At Fairford, Gloucestershire, where the glass of about 1500 is still miraculously almost complete, the work is most probably by the firm of Bernard Flower, a Fleming who became Master Glass Painter to

178 Top St Paul's Cathedral: dome frescoes: scenes from the Life of St Paul, 1716–19 by Sir James Thornhill

179 Bottom Jesus College Chapel, Cambridge: antechapel ceiling, 1864–67 by William Morris and Sir Edward Burne-Jones

180 Left Canterbury Cathedral: glass, c.1200

181 Below left Edgeworth, Gloucestershire: glass, fourteenth century; St Thomas of Canterbury

182 Below right Merton College Chapel, Oxford: glass, early fifteenth century. Virgin and Child, possibly by Thomas Glazier

183 Top St Peter Hungate Museum, Norwich: glass, mid-fifteenth century

184 Left Northill, Bedfordshire: glass, 1664, by John Oliver

185 Right New College Chapel, Oxford: detail of the great west window, 1778–85, designed by Sir Joshua Reynolds, made by Thomas Jervais

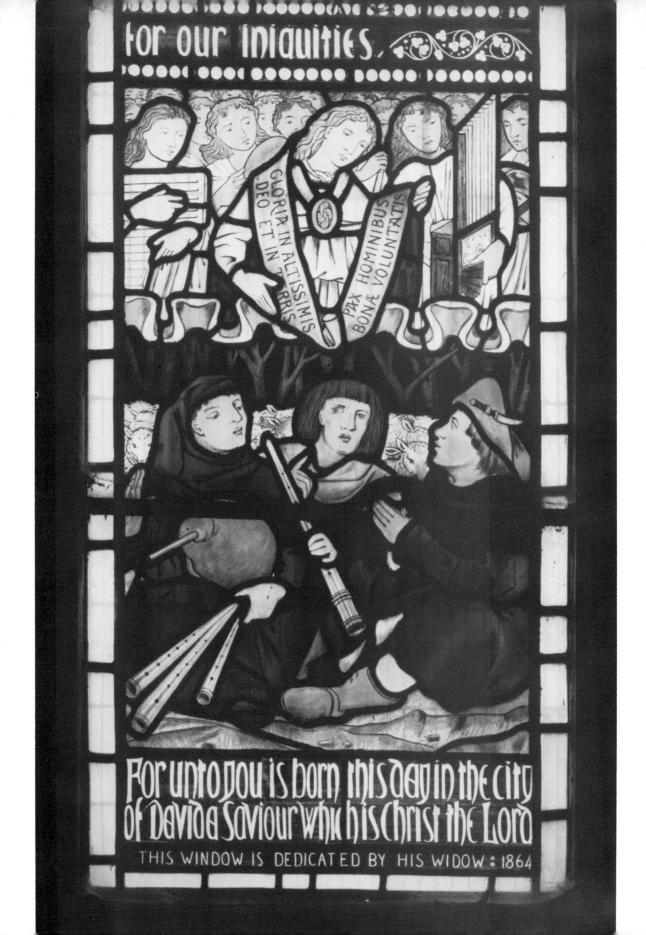

for our iniquities.

GLORIA IN ALTISSIMIS DEO ET IN TERRIS

PAX HOMINIBUS BONÆ VOLUNTATIS

For unto you is born this day in the city of David a Saviour which is Christ the Lord

THIS WINDOW IS DEDICATED BY HIS WIDOW : 1864

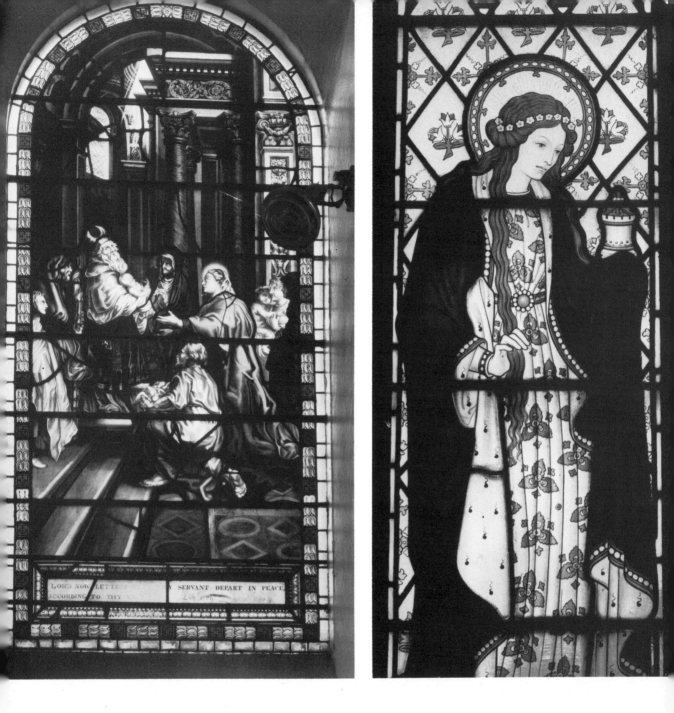

186 Left Amington, Warwickshire: glass, 1864, angels and shepherds, designed by Sir Edward Burne-Jones, made by William Morris

187 Above St Michael, Shrewsbury: glass, The Presentation in the Temple, 1830, by David Evans

188 Above right Glandford, Norfolk: glass, Head of St Mary Magdalene, c.1900, by Ernest Heasman

189 Birmingham Cathedral: glass, the Last Judgement, c.1887, designed by Sir Edward Burne-Jones, made by Morris and Co

190 Eton College Chapel, Buckinghamshire: east window, 1948 by Evie Hone

191 Oundle School Chapel, Northamptonshire: glass, 1955, designed by John Piper, made by Patrick Reyntiens

192 Bishop's Palace Chapel, Peterborough: Trinity window, 1958, designed and made by Patrick Reyntiens

193 Moreton, Dorset: glass, The Four Seasons as Bubbles round the Sun, engraved by Lawrence Whistler, c. 1973

194 Westminster Cathedral,
Lady Chapel: marble and
mosaic decoration. Retable by
Anning Bell; vault mosaic
1931–2 by G.A. Pownall

195 Below St Aidan, Leeds:
apse mosaic, the Life of St
Aidan, 1916, by Sir Frank
Brangwyn

Henry VII. Compared with Thomas Glazier's figures at Merton College, Oxford, and John Thornton's at York, the draughtsmanship is pedestrian, and many of the designs are unfortunately taken from woodcuts in the *Biblia Pauperum*, but the overall effect is still stunning, and not just because of its rarity. The great west window is a fine example of the new technique, and takes the form of a highly dramatic Doom. It was badly damaged by a gale in 1703, but luckily full repair was delayed until the nineteenth century, when it was wisely entrusted to Hardman of Birmingham who reproduced as accurately as possible what he could not restore. However much standards declined around 1500, the impact of this window is far greater than that of the technically superior west window of York or east window of Gloucester. The aisle windows are more completely original. Though still basically medieval in style, renaissance influence is particularly clear in the landscape perspectives.

From 1515 to 1517, the last two years of his life, Flower was working on windows for King's College Chapel, Cambridge, where the style more closely follows renaissance ideals. After his death, work stopped until 1526, when Flemish, German and English contractors were all employed, among them the Fleming Galyon Hone, the new King's Glazier. The designs, all apparently Flemish, are crowded, and, from ground level, often obscure. Much of the design was now merely painted on the glass, and the calmes no longer strengthen the composition. In other words, the art of the glazier has been subordinated to that of the painter, and there is no clear outline to help the eye. There is much modelling in light and shade, and realism in the figures. Magnified details are attractive, but in spite of a medieval iconographical scheme, the main purpose of the windows seems to be to soften white sunlight into gentle kaleidoscopic colour.

For a hundred years and more after this, there are more records of the destruction of glass than of its manufacture. A few heraldic windows were made, a form of display generally unobjectionable to Protestant humanism, and some survive: at Bishopbourne, Kent, of 1550, at Sywell, Northamptonshire, of 1580, and at Northill, Bedfordshire, of 1664, *(184)*. By the time of the Northill windows, made by John Oliver, the grid pattern of glazing bars had become entirely regular. Only at the top of the design is there a variation, to form an arch, and to indicate the sun's rays. Enamelling, too, had become standard practice, another good example being the heraldic window of 1676 by Henry Giles at Staveley, Derbyshire.

One of the last windows in the old tradition was made about 1633, probably by Flemings, at Lydiard Tregoze, Wiltshire, and the date is significant, since one reason for the excessive use of enamelling was the unavailability of pot metal after Louis XIII's destruction of the Lorraine glassworks in 1636 as an accident of war. After this, white glass was used and painted. Windows made entirely of painted white glass are first seen in England in the work of Abraham and Bernard van Linge at Oxford. Abraham, who made the 'Jonah' window at the cathedral in the 1630s, and most of the glass in University College Chapel in 1641, was the more talented brother. His colours are rich, his settings attractive, and his sense of animation and composition strong.[100]

New College, Oxford, is as good a place as any to get an idea of eighteenth-century glass, alongside late fourteenth-century glass for contrast. The glaziers include William Peckitt of York, William Price, Junior, and Thomas Jervaise. Jervaise made the west window of 1779, designed by Sir Joshua Reynolds. Reynolds was deeply disappointed with it, and Horace Walpole called it 'washy'. Most modern critics have dismissed it out of hand, especially as the enamel, used very freely, has shown an unfortunate tendency to flake. Nevertheless, Parson Woodforde, who saw the first three figures when they were brand new, described them as 'most beautiful . . . No Painting can exceed them I think on glass', and the College authorities at least have shown enough liking for the window not to replace it in spite of two centuries of criticism. It has indeed, a fragile, period charm, *(185)* and one has to remember first that pot metal was unavailable and second that two centuries of tradition had taught glaziers to use glass as though it were canvas. It is certainly possible to be too censorious.[101] However, enamelling was a blind alley, and it was left to the nineteenth century to return to the sounder principles of earlier generations.

To see the transition one should visit Shrewsbury. The east window of St Alkmund, by Francis Eginton, 1795, is still in the painterly tradition at its purest, a grid of glass tinted so delicately (and not with enamels) that it is like a watercolour. David Evans made glass for several Shrewsbury churches, much of it rather garish and in the painterly style, *(187)*. But his colours come into their own when he designs in the gothic style at St George c. 1830. Here the glazing bars and the attitudes and modelling of the figures are still in the Georgian tradition, but the dark backgrounds of the figures and the canopy work are clear signs of a return to medieval ideas, and the best glaziers of the following years, men like Wailes of Newcastle and

Willement, tried with some success to revive medieval techniques without the advantage of pot metal.

The recovery of pot metal enabled the real breakthrough to be made. It was first used by Hardman in 1863, and with the gothic revival in full swing, great efforts were made to emulate the excellence of the best medieval glass. It never quite came off. Victorian glass is at its best when it is at its least medieval and its most honestly Victorian, and the sheer volume of indifferent and downright bad Victorian glass still in our churches makes it difficult even now to appreciate how good the best was.

One has to remember that names like Kempe, Morris, Hardman and Powell are firms as well as individuals, just as Bernard Flower was. Consequently the standard of their work varies, though in the case of Kempe and Morris, their best work was generally their earliest, when their ideas were fresh, their firms small, their degree of personal involvement correspondingly great, and the temptation to repeat a successful formula for undemanding clients scarcely felt.

The main Victorian tradition was certainly gothic. To see Hardman's best glass in quantity one should go to Worcester Cathedral, where, among others, the east window, designed by John Hardman Powell, and the west, designed by Scott, are particularly pleasing. Glass by Hardman and designed by Pugin is a real asset to the thirteenth-century lancets in Jesus College Chapel, Cambridge, and very instructive to compare with the Morris glass in all the late medieval windows. Excellent Pugin glass can also be seen in Ushaw College Chapel, Co. Durham, and at St Marie, Sheffield. The Powells, father and son, did much fine work, none better than the jewel-like windows in the Roman Catholic Cathedral in Norwich, while Henry Holiday's finest work appears at Alrewas, Staffordshire, 1877, and Worcester College, Oxford, rather pre-Raphaelitish, finely drawn, and without irrelevant details, though also without the delicacy of the best Morris glass.

But the giants of Victorian glass are Charles Kempe and William Morris. Not all their work is good, and Kempe's especially can be rather anonymous, but at its best the draughtsmanship is excellent, and complete sets of his work can be very impressive.[102] Kempe's pupil Ernest Heasman worked alongside him at Glandford, Norfolk, glazed between 1896 and 1906. His draughtmanship is as good as his master's, and his portrait of St Mary Magdalene *(188)*, is exceptionally beautiful, a pleasing change from the repetitive over-chinned pre-Raphaelite women.

All the same, Morris in general had the advantage over Kempe of better designers, especially Burne-Jones and Ford Madox Brown, but also Rossetti, Solomon, Webb, and Morris himself. Burne-Jones's earliest work was done for Powell and Co, and his Latin Chapel window in Oxford Cathedral, 1859, is in some ways the first modern stained glass window in England, vigorously designed and strongly coloured, and there is another fine Burne-Jones-Powell window at Waltham Abbey made in 1861. But 1861 was the year Morris and Co. started in business, and Burne-Jones henceforth designed for them. Morris glass uses the calmes effectively to strengthen the designs, and the colours are excellent, with especially strong browns, blues and yellows. The detail of the east window at Amington, Warwickshire, made in 1864, shows the quality of their best work, *(186)*, and the general effect of large windows, like those in Birmingham Cathedral *(189)*, is even more telling. There is not the delicacy of draughtsmanship associated with Kempe and Heasman, but inspiration is wisely drawn from the earlier middle ages rather than from the fifteenth century. If Kempe could be over fussy, Burne-Jones could be sentimental, and not all pre-Raphaelite glass is good either in design or in technical quality. Indeed, after 1880, the general level starts to decline, and after the deaths of Morris and Burne-Jones becomes thoroughly pedestrian. Morris, however, more than other Victorian glaziers, escaped from the tyranny of the easel, back to a genuine appreciation of the nature of glass.[103]

The recovery of the use of leading in the design of windows was sometimes taken to extremes in the early twentieth century, as in the window by Parsons at Eastchurch, Isle of Sheppey. The desire for light, and the need for economy often led early twentieth-century designers to place their subjects in white glass surrounds, which could, of course, be leaded in rectangular quarries. Martin Travers's window at Cricklade, Wiltshire, is a good example, but, sadly, it is also a good example of how the grey characterless faces of much Victorian glass persisted into the following period. His best work, though, had great charm, witness the pretty Madonna and Child with a willow tree made for the east window at Tyneham, Dorset.[104]

An acute problem for glass designers at this period was to try to satisfy clients and at the same time work in a modern idiom. Expressionism at its best does just this, like Erwin Bossanyi's windows of 1956 in Canterbury Cathedral. The trouble with most expressionist work, however, is that it is a compromise. It goes well enough with the compromise architecture of the time, but looks uneasy in great buildings. Even

Evie Hone's great window at Eton, of 1949–50, *(190)*, which shows the emergence of a more vital style, clashes with the architecture. The surprising thing is that sensitive abstract designs such as can be seen in the cathedrals of Bristol, Chichester and Derby, blend very much better with venerable surroundings.

The breakthrough came, as in other respects, with Coventry Cathedral, where glass by almost every major practitioner in England was used.[105] No disrespect to other artists is intended if John Piper's baptistry window, made by Patrick Reyntiens, is singled out, both for sheer size and for a new tranquility in its abstraction, The other glass in the cathedral is busy, in part a hangover from the expressionist tradition. Piper and Reyntiens were also commissioned to glaze the huge lantern at Liverpool Metropolitan Cathedral a few years later, the largest glass composition in the world, and a tremendously dramatic one. Unforgettably simple is the abstract glass which forms part of an ensemble in the Blessed Sacrament Chapel in the same cathedral by Ceri Richards. Henry Haig's glass near the baptistry in Clifton Cathedral, 1973, the only coloured glass in the cathedral, is also abstract, but gets away from the angular, geometrical shapes of the 'sixties to a mobile, liquid, bubbliness which in this country at least, is something new.

But not all good modern glass is abstract. The Piper-Reyntiens windows at Oundle School Chapel, 1955 *(191)*, and Patrick Reyntiens's window in the Bishop's Palace Chapel at Peterborough, 1958 *(192)*, show that figure glass is perfectly possible in a contemporary idiom, and since these reproduce more effectively in half-tones than abstract work, which is nothing without its colour, I have chosen these as illustrations.[106]

The other technique which has gained in popularity is engraving, whose two chief practitioners have been John Hutton and Lawrence Whistler. Hutton's glass at Guildford, and more especially at Coventry Cathedral, has vigorously drawn, animated figures. Whistler's style is quite different, exquisite in the manner of a miniaturist of exceptional skill. His best church work is at Moreton, Dorset, *(193)*. Engraving glass is not necessarily confined to windows: Warwick Hutton engraved a vestry screen for Pott Shrigley, Cheshire, in 1975, depicting the Agony in the Garden.

Mosaics

In the middle ages, mosaics were only used in England for pavements, and these will be considered under 'Tiles' in the final chapter. Here, wall-mosaics were a product of the catholic revival of the nineteenth century. Bentley's Roman Catholic Cathedral at Westminster was designed to have marble panelling and mosaics on the walls from the beginning in 1894, but so expensive has this proved that, though work continued into the 1960s, the scheme is still far from complete. Nevertheless, the interior is unique in England, and the contrast between the plain surfaces of beautiful marble and the complex designs of the mosaics makes for a splendid overall effect *(194)*, even if the mosaics themselves are uneven in quality. The mosaics in St Paul's, by Richmond and Watts, were made in the 1890s, and though they are out of keeping with the architecture, they give a glittering opulence to the chancel which makes this the one successful feature of a generally disastrous restoration.

Much minor work was done about this time, and some a good deal earlier: Sharnbrook, Bedfordshire, has a mosaic reredos of 1855. Some was imported work by Salviati of Venice, but English firms like Powell and Clayton & Bell also contributed, if not very memorably.

St Aidan, Leeds, has an outstanding series of mosaics made in 1916 by Sir Frank Brangwyn *(195)*. The main composition is in the apse, and shows scenes from St Aidan's life, but there are also mosaics on the cancelli which takes the place of a chancel screen. Not much has been done since, outside Westminster, and it is doubtful whether there is much future for such an expensive form of decoration in our churches.

An entirely different technique which produces a broadly similar effect to mosaic is sgraffito, which consists of incising lines in fresh damp plaster of different colours. A very fine example exists in the disused church of St Agatha, Portsmouth, carried out by Heywood Sumner in 1901 in a style reminiscent of his friend William Morris, and imparting a strongly Byzantine flavour to the apse.

Chapter 10
Memorials to the Dead

Introduction

Tombstones with Christian symbols, some as early as the fifth century, are among the oldest tangible remains of Christianity in Britain. They are usually simple, with a straightforward inscription: one of c.550 from Castell Dwyran, Carmarthenshire, has a Latin inscription reading: 'In memory of Vorteporix the Protector', and has a small equal-armed cross in a circle inscribed above. One of several functions of standing crosses, mostly made between the seventh and eleventh centuries, was also to commemorate the dead. Thus an inscription on a wheel cross in the church of Llantwit Major, Glamorgan, is translated: 'In the Name of the Father, and of the Son, and of the Holy Spirit. Hywel prepared this cross for the soul of Rhys his father.' Recording the name of the donor as well as the departed is a very ancient custom, and is found on the Latinus stone of c.450 at Whithorn, in south west Scotland, one of the oldest Christian memorials in Britain.

But these early monuments, together with the later 'hogback' coffin lids found in northern England and southern Scotland during the Viking period, were made to stand out of doors, and even though many have found their way into churches or museums for protection, they fall outside the scope of this book.[107]

Intermural burial was not permitted until the Council of Nantes in 658, and even then was restricted to porches, and the surviving evidence suggests that in Britain outside burial continued to be the standard practice, even for the great, until long afterwards. St Swithun of Winchester specifically desired to be buried in the Minster churchyard, and the Kings of Scotland were buried in the open air at Iona until the end of the middle ages. Among the very few surviving Saxon monuments which were probably always meant to stand inside is the splendid coffin at Wirksworth, Derbyshire, made about 800, and decorated with sculptured scenes from the Life of Christ. It must have been made for someone important, and it is only when it is compared with such masterworks as the St Andrews sarcophagus that its provincial quality becomes apparent.

Later coffin lids of local freestone, especially those of the twelfth and thirteenth centuries, survive in great numbers. Some of them may always have been inside the church; others have undoubtedly been dug up in the graveyard. The commonest motif is a foliated cross, which sometimes grows out of a beast. At Penshurst, Kent, the expressive praying figure seems to be trapped in the slab by the weight of the cross. Effigies in fact are not very common on coffin lids of this type; when they do occur, often just the bust and sometimes the feet can be seen, the rest of the body lying, as it were, under the surface of the stone. At Newton Regis, Warwickshire, there are kneeling acolytes, and the soul of the deceased in a napkin, an idea probably taken from one of the Tournai marble slabs favoured by the great.

It is with these Tournai slabs that the story of our intermural monuments effectively begins. The earliest ones, like that of St Osmund, 1099, in Salisbury Cathedral, are very plain. Much more interesting is the slab, probably commemorating Bishop Nigellus, 1169, at Ely, which bears the large figure of an angel carrying the bishop's tiny soul heavenwards, an awe-inspiring angel in line with the general theological outlook of the time, very different from the angels of even two centuries later, let alone the gentle, pretty creatures of Georgian and Victorian imagination.

Effigies

The twelfth century, too, is the time when the first effigies appear in Britain, the earliest survivor being the one attributed to Bishop Losinga, c.1120, in the cathedral at Norwich which he built, and which still bears traces of colour.[108] He is in low relief, carved out of the stone of the surround, above which he does not project; nor does Bishop Bartolomeus Iscanus of Exeter, 1184, but from about 1200 to 1275 effigies gradually develop into pieces of sculpture in their own right, apart from the rest of the tomb. Bishop Marshall of Exeter, 1206, is in much higher relief than Iscanus, and the same development can be traced in the fine Alwalton marble tombs of Abbots of Peterborough from about 1190 to 1225, and in the series of Bishops of Wells from about 1220 to 1240. Some of these early effigies are impressive, and with their original gesso detail and paintwork they would have been more impressive still. The outstanding effigy of this period is King John in Worcester Cathedral, made about 1230 of Purbeck marble, which remained a popular material for effigies until the fourteenth century. By the end of the thirteenth century some effigies were made completely separately from the tomb chest, among them William Torel's bronze-gilt representations of Edward I's beloved Queen Eleanor and his father Henry III, both in Westminster Abbey and made in 1291. Long, slim, elegant, and beautifully stylized, they are every inch royal, though they probably bear no resemblance to the living appearance of those whom they commemorate.

Portraiture, indeed, was very rare in the middle ages and for some time afterwards, and as late as the fifteenth century it was virtually confined to royalty like Richard II and Henry IV and their Queens. Even effigies commissioned during the lifetime of those they were to represent made no attempt to show likenesses. Sculptor and patron rarely met, and surviving contracts, though meticulous in the most minor details, merely stipulated some such generalization as a 'counterfeit' of a lady or an esquire. Identity was indicated by inscriptions and heraldry. So full of character are some effigies that portraiture seems certain until one discovers, say, that William of Wykeham, 1404, in Winchester Cathedral, whose fleshy, worldly, but intelligent face is exactly as one might expect him to have looked, has the same features which had already served, equally suitably, for Archbishop Courtenay of Canterbury in 1396. Only in the second half of the seventeenth century can we be sure that in all cases a portrait, realistic or idealized, is intended.

Costume was portrayed with great care and attention to detail; indeed the history of medieval dress and armour would be difficult to write without funerary sculpture as a guide. The custom of dressing an effigy fashionably persisted until the nineteenth century, but not invariably. The chief departure from this tradition took place between about 1680 and 1760 when people were quite frequently shown in something approaching Roman dress. Thus in 1684 Grinling Gibbons attired the 7th and 8th Earls of Rutland at Edmondsthorpe, Leicestershire, and in 1686 the 3rd Viscount Campden and his family nearby at Exton, Rutland. Such figures sometimes came dangerously close to absurdity. John Nost portrayed Sir John Banks, 1699, at Aylesford, Kent, in Roman robes but with wig and cravat. However, this probably did not seem strange to an age which could accept an operatic Julius Caesar singing soprano in a full-bottomed wig. In the eighteenth century Roman dress was sometimes used by such great sculptors as Roubiliac, Rysbrack and the Scheemakers, but with the movement away from the baroque towards a 'chaste' classicism the custom died out, a fact which tends to be obscured by the popularity of Grecian fashions for women in real life in the early nineteenth century. Grecian dress has given us a number of charming female figures, both effigies and allegories, some with one breast bare, including even royalty in the person of Princess Charlotte *(222)*.

Medieval effigies are nearly always recumbent, but the actual posture varies a good deal in detail. Early bishops like Roger of Sarum, 1139, in Salisbury Cathedral, hold their crozier in one hand and raise the other in blessing, a form which, though obviously without the crozier, was revived for the low-relief effigy of the priest Henry of Middleton at Scarborough early in the sixteenth century. In such effigies the posture is thought of as a standing one, translated into a horizontal position.

Military effigies start with William Longespée the elder, 1226, at Salisbury *(196)*. He, however, like the almost contemporary King John, is thought of as lying down, head on a pillow, though, unlike the king, his head is turned slightly to one side, and his left arm carries a long shield. Not long afterwards the fashion for depicting knights cross-legged begins. Longespée the younger, 1250, also at Salisbury, must be one of the first. This posture remained fashionable until about 1350, and persisted till towards the end of the century judging by the armour of the knight at Alvechurch, Worcestershire. On the other hand, Madoc ap Llywelyn ap Gruffydd, c.1331, at Gresford, Denbighshire, Sir Richard Pembrugge at Clehonger, Herefordshire, c.1345 and Sir John de Sutton of Sutton, near Hull, 1347, already have their legs uncrossed. But, while it lasted, the cross-legged fashion gave rise to some remarkable effigies, justly the most famous of which is the unknown knight of c.1280 at Dorchester-on-Thames, Oxfordshire *(197)*, who is shown drawing his sword with an expression of vigorous, almost snarling determination, and in a pose so animated that he appears about to leap to his feet. The swirling drapery of his surcoat emphasizes the impression of writhing movement, and the whole composition has a tension unique in English medieval sculpture. Other knights lie more quietly, and seem to be sheathing rather than drawing their swords, while Sir William Hastings, c.1340, at Abergavenny Priory, Gwent, lies peacefully asleep.

Later in the middle ages the pose with hands pressed together in prayer becomes common for all types of effigy from royalty downwards. It can give an expression of serene faith in the hands of a master like Torel, whose work perhaps did much to popularize it, but its repetition in the hands of less gifted sculptors too often gives a tedious impression of conventional piety. One way of escaping from the cliché was to show the deceased holding a book, like the late thirteenth-century deacon at Ryton, Co. Durham, a priest of about the same time at Rippingale, Lincolnshire, and a civilian of c.1350 at Gresford. Stone effigies of civilians are rare in the middle ages: they are more often commemorated in brass.

Few medieval effigies record human emotion. Rare and touching even are the couples who hold hands, however expressionlessly. This seems to have been a convention introduced by the brass engravers, and so appear Richard Torrington and his wife, 1356, at Berkhamsted, Hertfordshire, and so once appeared Sir Miles and Lady Stapleton, 1364, on a brass now destroyed, at Ingham, Norfolk. Later the alabasterers took up the theme with the Earl and Countess of Warwick, 1370, at St Mary, Warwick *(202)*, Sir Thomas and Lady Arderne, 1391, at Elford, Staffordshire, and Sir Ralph and Lady Green, 1419, at Lowick, Northamptonshire.[109] The exceptional effigy of Richard Beauchamp, Earl of Warwick, c.1450 in St Mary, Warwick, has his hands expressively apart, while his eyes gaze with rapt intensity at a boss of the Assumption. Like the Dorchester knight, it seems that here the veil of impassivity has been drawn aside, and that a human being capable of emotion has been portrayed.

It was customary in the middle ages to show the deceased alive. About 1400, however, some French tombs emphasized physical dissolution by depicting a cadaver or skeleton below the effigy. The oldest example in England is the tomb of Bishop Fleming, 1431, at Lincoln, but it was soon taken up, especially by other bishops, like Bekynton at Wells. The idea persists as late as 1608 at Gawsworth, Cheshire, where Francis Fitton's effigy lies above, and his skeleton below, exactly as Bishop Fleming's had done nearly two centuries earlier, in Robert Cecil's tomb, 1612, at Hatfield, Hertfordshire, *(212)* and even 1689 in the monument to Sir John Hotham at South Dalton, East Riding.

An alternative way of portraying death was to show the effigy in a shroud, a form which first appears in brasses like those to Thomas Humphre, c.1470, at Berkhamsted, and Robert Lockton and his wife, c.1500 at Sawston, Cambridgeshire. The Locktons are completely parcelled up with the shrouds tied over their heads, and the same unattractive, morbidly

comic idea is found at Chesterfield, Derbyshire, c.1580, in relief, and at Fenny Bentley, in the same county and at about the same time, in the round. At Spixworth, Norfolk, Edward Marshall, though not covering the heads of his subjects, William Peck and his wife, 1635, nevertheless shows them as uncompromisingly dead, but John Donne, Dean of St Paul's, posed in a shroud before his death for his effigy which shows him rising from it, an emphasis on resurrection characteristic of his age and of his own faith. This popular and influential figure began something of a fashion for similar memorials. Here we need only notice two variants. At Steane, Northamptonshire, John and Mathias Christmas, usually rather conservative sculptors, show Temperance Browne, sitting up in her coffin, awakened by the last trump, and at Stratton Strawless, Norfolk, an unknown sculptor has shown Thomas Marsham, 1638, in his shroud but reclining comfortably – a very odd idea. But the most dramatic expression of faith in the resurrection is to be found on Roubiliac's memorial to Mary Middleton at Wrexham, where she is shown rising eagerly from her coffin, her faculties vigorously renewed.

Recumbent effigies did not quite die out in England, though they never recovered their earlier popularity after about 1580. Once varying poses had been introduced, it seems that all original thinking went into them, and recumbent effigies, however finely carved, usually lack inspiration *(213)*. An outstanding exception is Nicholas Stone's memorial of 1617–20 to Lady Elizabeth Carey at Stowe-Nine-Churches, Northamptonshire *(207)*. But when recumbent effigies are used in the seventeenth and eighteenth centuries it is often the other figures on the monuments that engage our attention.

One variation on the theme of recumbence is the use of a rolled-up mat as a pillow, a Netherlandish idea, first used in the Nassau tomb at Breda c.1535, which reached England some time during Elizabeth I's reign, and which appears in the Petre monument of c.1572 at Ingatestone, Essex. By 1590 it had become popular, and a good example of this time is the monument to the Earl of Shrewsbury in Sheffield Cathedral. It was used in some of the more conservative Jacobean monuments, and still appears as late as 1677 for 13-year-old Thomas Sackville at Withyham, Sussex, and 1689 for the tomb of Richard Winwood and his wife by Thomas Stayner at Quainton, Buckinghamshire. It even enjoyed a minor revival after 1800: for example, Westmacott used it in 1816 for his monument to the assassinated Prime Minister Spencer Perceval in Westminster Abbey, and Chantrey in 1832 for Sir Hugh Inglis at Milton Bryan, Bedfordshire.

An obvious step from representing someone lying down praying is to show him kneeling in prayer. A striking but isolated example is Edward Despencer, c.1380, in Tewkesbury Abbey, where he kneels under a canopy on the roof of his chantry, facing the high altar. The fashion seems rather to have been started in brasses, like that to Robert de Paris and his wife, c.1408, at Hildersham, Cambridgeshire, where they kneel at the foot of a cross. Again the idea was taken up by the alabasterers, in the very remarkable monument to Robert Gylbert, his wife, and their 17 children, c.1492, at Youlgreave, Derbyshire. This is a wall-tablet, that is, it is fixed to a wall above ground level, a memorial, not a tomb, and a form which again may owe its origin to brasses, in this case the less ambitious ones, but which did not become common until well into the seventeenth century. The figures kneel in profile either side of a frontal figure of the Virgin Mary, and the whole composition is in low relief. Similar, but smaller, is the memorial to Trustram Fauntleroy, 1538, at Michelmersh, Hampshire, but there is no central figure of the Virgin. Roger Legh, 1506, at Macclesfield, Cheshire, kneels with his children, but his wife and her share of the children are missing. Between them is the assurance, written in English, that the pardon for saying five Paternosters, five Aves and a Creed is 26,000 years and 26 days. At Whalley, Lancashire, Raffe Catterall and his wife, 1515, kneel either side of the indent for a shield-shaped plate which presumably contained an image. Missing, too, is the statuette which undoubtedly once stood on the bracket between the effigies of John Dawtry and his wife, 1527, at Petworth, Sussex. Here at last the kneeling figures have been carved in a fully three-dimensional form, and here, as on the Catterall brass, appear the prayer desks of Flemish origin that remain after the Reformation when such effigies merely face one another without the *raison d'être* of a religious symbol between them.

A startling variation on this rather dull theme is the monument to Blanche Parry, maid of honour to Elizabeth I, at Bacton, Herefordshire, where she is shown in profile kneeling before her mistress who appears frontally – a composition which is narrowly saved from blasphemy by the presumption that the somewhat ambiguous posture of the Queen is also supposed to be a kneeling one. The kneeling posture remained popular during the first quarter of the seventeenth century *(209)*, and survived as late as 1711 for Sir William and Lady Coryton at St Mellion, Cornwall, and 1713 for Luke and Elizabeth Lillingston

at North Ferriby, East Riding.

Semi-reclining effigies, propped up on one elbow, began as an Italian fashion about 1500, and reached England by 1570, where one of the first examples must be the remarkably innovative monument to Sir John Jefferay at Chiddingly, Sussex. Once here it soon became popular, but the posture, in the hands of all but the best sculptors, scarcely suggested the repose that was intended. The Seymours at Berry Pomeroy, Devon, and the first of the Fettiplaces at Swinbrook, Oxfordshire, *(211)* lie in three shelf-like tiers apiece, desperately uncomfortable in spite of cushions to support their elbows. John Webster, in *The Duchess of Malfi*, published in 1623, shows that the temptation to make fun of such memorials is not new:

Princes' images on their tombs
Do not lie as they were wont, gazing on Heaven,
But with their hands under their head, as if
They died o' the toothache . . .

By 1686, when William Bird designed a companion monument at Swinbrook to three later Fettiplaces, he kept the three shelves, but their occupants are far more relaxed. It was a change in emphasis noticeable in other poses over the same period, and which continued into the Georgian age, where comfort blossomed into unashamed luxury, a luxury already apparent in William Stanton's monument to the first Earl of Coventry at Elmley Castle, Worcestershire, as early as 1699 *(214)*.

Demi-figures and busts have an early origin, though they were not at all common during the middle ages. They seem to have been used first for heart-shrines, that is, where the heart was buried separately from the rest of the body. As early as 1261 a frontal demi-figure appears on the heart-shrine of Bishop Aymer de Valence in Winchester Cathedral, and only a little later, c.1280, is William d'Albini in his knight's armour at Bottesford, Leicestershire, though it is possible that this effigy was originally complete and recumbent. The most remarkable medieval demi-figures are those of Sir Godfrey and Lady Foljambe, 1377, at Bakewell, Derbyshire, made of alabaster under a canopy that makes them look as though they were in a theatre box.

At Tong, Shropshire, the priest Arthur Vernon, 1515, is also represented by a frontal demi-figure, on a bracket, with a book in his hand, almost as though he were standing in a pulpit preaching. He too has a canopy over his head, but more significantly this memorial is prophetic of the tradition which began towards the end of the century of representing churchmen and scholars in particular by such figures.

196 Above left Salisbury
Cathedral: William Longespée,
d. 1226

197 Right Dorchester-on-
Thames, Oxfordshire: knight,
c. 1280

198 Far right Stoke d'Abernon,
Surrey: Sir John d'Abernon,
d. 1277

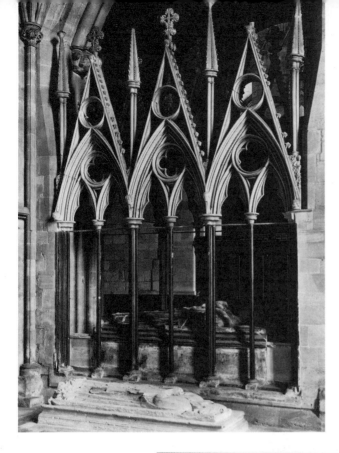

199 Above left Hereford
Cathedral: Bishop
Aquablanca, d. 1268

200 Above right Gloucester
Cathedral: Edward II, d. 1327

201 Right Westminster
Abbey: grille for the tomb of
Queen Eleanor of Castille,
d. 1294, by Thomas of Leighton

202 Left St Mary, Warwick: Thomas Beauchamp, Earl of Warwick, d. 1369, and his wife, Catherine Mortimer

203 Below left Bristol Cathedral: Abbot Newbery, d. 1473; surround c. 1300

204 Right Beverley Minster, Yorkshire: detail of the Percy Tomb, c. 1340

205 Below right Worcester Cathedral: Prince Arthur's Chantry, begun 1504

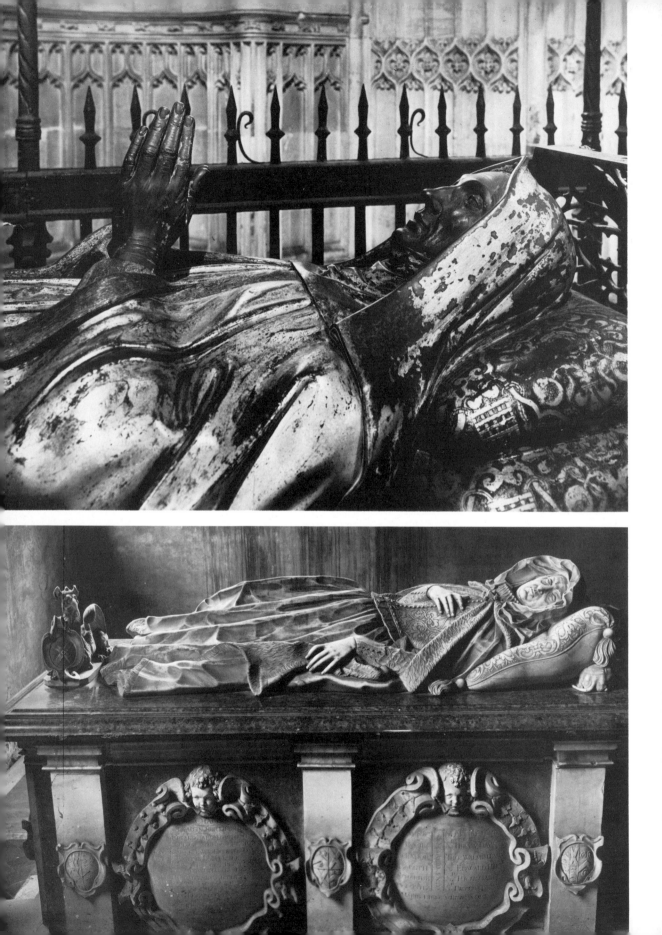

206 Above left Westminster Abbey: Lady Margaret Beaufort, by Pietro Torrigiani, 1511–13
207 Left Stowe-Nine-Churches, Northamptonshire: Lady Elizabeth Carey, d.1630, by Nicholas Stone, 1617–20
208 Above Wing, Buckinghamshire: Sir Robert Dormer, d.1552

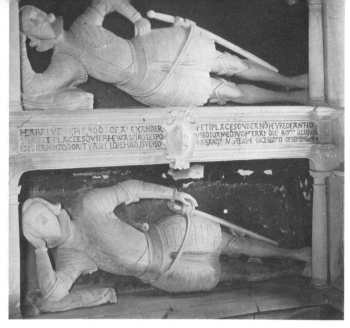

209 Left Bisham, Berkshire: Lady Elizabeth Hoby,
d. 1609

210 Below left Framlingham, Suffolk: Thomas
Howard, 3rd Duke of Norfolk, d. 1554

211 Right Swinbrook Oxfordshire: Fettiplace
monument, detail, c. 1613

212 Below right Hatfield, Hertfordshire: Robert
Cecil, 1st Earl of Salisbury, d. 1612, by
Maximilian Colt and Simon Basyll

Early busts of this sort are found at Braughing, Hertfordshire, 1587, and Burnham, Buckinghamshire, 1594, and the fashion seems to have reached its height about 1630. Oxford has a fittingly large number of such memorials in its churches, and there they span the period 1590 to 1703.   Portrait medallions, which consist of a bust, usually in profile or three-quarter face in a round or oval surround, seem to have been introduced by Torrigiani for Sir Thomas Lovell, 1524, in Westminster Abbey. This, in bronze, was well ahead of its time in England, and it seems to have had no successors until Thomas Wotton, 1587, at Boughton Malherbe, Kent. Indeed, real popularity only came in the eighteenth century when it was taken up by such sculptors as Roubiliac and Cheere.

The earliest standing effigies in England seem to be those on the remarkable Jefferay tomb at Chiddingly already referred to. Lady Jefferay is recumbent, Sir John is reclining on one elbow, and his son-in-law and daughter, Sir Edward and Lady Montagu, stand in niches on either flank. After this one has to wait until the 1630s with Nicholas Stone's John Donne, 1631, Hubert le Sueur's Admiral Sir Richard Leveson, 1634 at Wolverhampton, and Epiphanius Evesham's Sir William Slingsby, also 1634, at Knaresborough, West Riding. It is not surprising that these three should be by the leading sculptors of their generation, a generation anxious to escape from the trite formulas of the Elizabethan period. At St John, Hackney, Thomas Wood and his wife, 1649, stand facing one another across a prayer desk, in a variation of the old kneeling theme, but until about 1680, standing effigies remain somewhat daring, and though fine examples exist from the previous 30 years,[110] it is after this date, and on into the eighteenth century that standing figures come into their own, inspiring some of the finest memorials of any age.

It was the same restless decades of the early seventeenth century that introduced the seated effigy. One of the first must be Margaret Legh, 1605 at All Saints, Fulham, who sits stiffly frontally with two babies; then a much more remarkable piece, Sir Francis Bacon, 1626, at St Michael, St Albans, fast asleep in his chair. Such naturalism was to be rare for a while yet, but Sir Giles and Lady Mompesson, 1633, at Lydiard Tregoze. Wiltshire, seem relaxed enough as they sit facing one another, though, being in separate niches, they are unable to see one another. Maria Wentworth at Toddington, Bedfordshire, died in 1632, but her monument was probably not made until about 20 years later. She sits frontally with considerable dignity under a baldacchino, the curtains of which are held back by two *putti*. The last of the early seated effigies which must be mentioned is Lady Tyrril, 1671, at Castlethorpe, Leicestershire, for her husband is shown semi-reclining with his head in her lap.

Materials

Mention has already been made of Tournai marble, and its replacement near the end of the twelfth century by English shelly limestones from Purbeck, Teesdale and Alwalton. Although these 'marbles' did not go entirely out of fashion for tomb chests until well into the sixteenth century, they, like wood, were replaced for effigies by a gradually increasing use of local freestones, and, especially from the fourteenth century onwards, by alabaster.

Wooden effigies are usually of oak, and can be very fine, like Robert, Duke of Normandy in Gloucester Cathedral. The eldest son of William I, he died in 1134, but his effigy, showing him as a cross-legged knight, was not made till near the end of the thirteenth century, and his tomb chest, also of wood, is later still. Wooden effigies are found particularly in counties like Essex where stone was scarce, but also in good stone counties, like Northamptonshire, which contained large tracts of forest. Very few are found after 1360, though there are Elizabethan examples at Boxted, Suffolk, and Brecon Cathedral, and Stuart ones at Brading, Isle of Wight, for Sir William Oglander, 1608, and Sir John Oglander, 1655. At Therfield, Hertfordshire, there is an effigyless baroque wooden hanging memorial to Ann Turner, 1677, with figures of a skeleton and Father Time, whose general design shows kinship with the wooden reredoses of the period.

Wood was also used for the lozenge-shaped frames of hatchments, armorial bearings painted on canvas in the seventeenth and eighteenth centuries, and hung up outside the home of the corpse, and then, up to a year later, transferred to the church. In Cheshire, four generations of the Randle Holme family specialised in painting heraldic memorials not unlike hatchments between 1611 and 1708, and their work can be seen in a number of churches. The most ambitious painted monuments however, are the triptychs found occasionally like the one at Lydiard Tregoze, originally erected in 1615 to Sir John St John, but with additions in 1699 and the eighteenth century.[111]

The quality of freestone monuments varies with the quality of the stone. As in architecture, some of the best work is made of oolitic limestone, and some of the least satisfactory from the coarsest sandstones, but in the middle ages these were finished with gesso before painting. Freestone is not very common in post-

Reformation monuments, alabaster, and later marble being preferred.

As we have seen, alabaster is one of the softest and easiest of stones to carve. Its use for monuments began about 1300, and the earliest survivor is Sir John de Hanbury, 1303, at Hanbury, Staffordshire, not far from the Chellaston quarries. It was not long before it was sent to London to be carved, and Edward II, c.1330 in Gloucester Cathedral, and his son John of Eltham, 1337, in Westminster Abbey, have London-made effigies. Edward II's tomb chest, incidentally, was made of Purbeck marble, and the canopy above of Caen stone, making one of the finest medieval tombs in England (200). Early London alabaster work was confined to very special clients, like Archbishop Stratford, 1348, at Canterbury, and Prince William of Hatfield, 1344. But, whether carved in London, in Nottingham or at Chellaston, it soon became very popular, probably because it carved so finely that no gesso was needed before painting.

The Chellaston quarries continued to supply the bulk of the stone, but there is a series of sixteenth-century tombs in Margam Abbey, Glamorgan, made of local alabaster. By the end of the century the fashion was changing and by about 1650 the use of alabaster and touchstone for black and white memorials had finally given way to marble, though there is a late example of 1656 at Morley, Derbyshire, and the last, before a minor Victorian revival, was made for Dame Abigail Poley at Boxted, Suffolk, in 1725.

True marble was hardly ever used in England for tombs in the middle ages, though it was imported for flooring in Durham Cathedral, for example. Torrigiani used it for the tomb of Henry VII and Elizabeth of York about 1512, and for Lady Margaret Beaufort perhaps a year earlier. It was used again for Lord Audley, 1544, at Saffron Walden, and then with increasing frequency in the early seventeenth century, no doubt made fashionable by the tombs raised by James I in Westminster Abbey for his mother, Mary Queen of Scots, and his predecessor, Elizabeth I. In the first half of the seventeenth century the sculptor Edward Marshall in particular did a good deal to popularize it, and after his time it became the standard material. Most ledger stones set into church floors were made of black marble in these later days, and local freestone was more or less banished to the churchyard for the tombs of lesser folk. The careful heraldry on ledger stones, and the beautiful lettering on them, and on churchyard stones in the seventeenth, eighteenth and early nineteenth centuries, incidentally, can easily be overlooked by visitors intent on a church's more spectacular charms.

A Cornish speciality was the use of slate, both inside and outside churches. Many of these monuments are pleasingly naive, but some are quite ambitious in an unsophisticated way. The bedding of the slate precludes deep carving, and so most appear in quite shallow relief, like John and Richard Courtenay at Lanivet, 1632, (228). Metals, other than brass, were rarely used in the middle ages, and only in the costliest monuments like those to Henry III, the Black Prince, and Richard Beauchamp, Earl of Warwick. Subsequent pillage makes them even rarer now than they were originally. Later they were still uncommon and only appear in such tombs as those of Lord Portland, 1634, in Winchester Cathedral, and the Duke and Duchess of Richmond and Lennox, 1639, in Westminster Abbey, where bronze was in both cases used in combination with marble by the Frenchman Hubert Le Sueur. The baroque, rococo and Grecian sculptors avoided metal, and bronze was only revived by Alfred Gilbert in the 1890s. At a humbler level, cast-iron gravestones are not uncommon in various parts of England, and are often considerable masterpieces of folk art.

Iron had a subsidiary part to play in many tombs in the form of railings. These for the most part have been done away with by well-meaning restorers, but are still not uncommon (209). Sometimes this ironwork was an ambitious piece of craftsmanship, and the grille surrounding Queen Eleanor of Castille's tomb in Westminster Abbey is a fine piece of late thirteenth-century work by Thomas of Leighton, (201).

But metalwork in memorials means, first and foremost, brasses, which often originated fashions later taken over by the stone carvers. The earliest brass of which we have knowledge was the one to Simon de Beauchamp, 1208, at St Paul, Bedford, now, alas, only represented by its matrix. Surviving English brasses begin a little before 1300, and the earliest all represent knights. Sir John d'Abernon, 1277, at Stoke d'Abernon, Surrey, is straight-legged, (198), but the next three, Sir Roger de Trumpington, 1289, at Trumpington, just outside Cambridge, Sir Robert de Bures, 1302, at Acton, Suffolk, and Sir Robert de Septvans, c.1306, at Chartham, Kent, are all cross-legged. Originally their shields bore their heraldic colours, and Sir John d'Abernon's still bears traces of blue enamel. The Septvans brass is rather different in style from the others – for example, both head and hands are bare – and it is thought that it was made in France. The oldest existing female brass is to Lady Camoys, 1310, at Trotton, Sussex.

All these early brasses are superb, but the general quality declined sharply later, especially with the proliferation of cheap, small ones for the less well-to-do. There are, however, exceptions of both English and Flemish manufacture. Broadly speaking the English custom was to cut figures and architectural surrounds out of sheets of latten and fix them separately to the matrix slab, leaving areas of stone visible between. The Flemish custom was to engrave rectangular sheets of brass with figures and background, usually with a mass of ornament. A good example of English technique is Sir Peter Courtenay, 1409, in Exeter Cathedral. Flemish technique is naturally commoner further east, witness the fine memorials to Adam de Walsoken, 1349, and his wife, and to Robert Braunche, 1364, and his two wives, both at St Margaret, King's Lynn. All the same, in view of the quality of the best English work, it is surprising how many were imported, often with their Tournai marble matrix slabs, which must have added a good deal to carriage costs.

The smaller medieval brasses, uninteresting though they may be as works of art, are not without social significance, for they mark the beginning of the emergence of civilians from anonymity in death. Indeed, after the Reformation they seem to have been used principally for civilians, and, if there is not much work to bring honour to the medium after the outstandingly good monument to Sir Thomas Boleyn, 1538, at Hever, Kent, the last hundred years or so of brass-making help to chronicle the emergence of the middle class.[112]

Few other materials need mentioning. Terracotta enjoyed a very brief and restricted vogue. Torrigiani used it for the effigy of Dr Yonge, 1516, now in the Public Record Office which stands on the site of the Rolls Chapel where it belonged. One or more Italian craftsmen worked in terracotta in East Anglia, and among their work is a series of spectacular tombs at Layer Marney, Essex, St George Colegate, Norwich, and Bracon Ash, and Oxborough, Norfolk. None of these tombs has an effigy. Peter Scheemakers used terracotta for a bust of Alexander Small, 1752, at Clifton Reynes, Buckinghamshire, but these are all isolated instances, and it never became popular.

Coade stone, an artificial stone marketed effectively by Mrs Coade after the death of her husband who invented it, was quite popular for tombs in the late eighteenth century, but though a number of pleasing memorials were made in this material, it produced no masterpiece. Plaster was used occasionally, but only one memorial is worth recording, a fine baroque piece, perhaps by Bacon, to Thomas Langton Freke, 1769, at King's Sutton, Northamptonshire.

Tomb Chests and Surrounds

Medieval tomb chests follow the architectural fashions of the day, and frequently contain carved quatrefoils or heraldry. Even in the thirteenth century, figure sculpture was used as well, and apostles and saints appear as early as 1210 in Henry Marshall's monument in Exeter Cathedral. Figures under arches are found in Bishop Cantilupe's shrine in Hereford Cathedral about 1287, but the first surviving English use of what became the popular custom of depicting mourning relatives may be the tomb chest of Lady FitzAlan at Chichester, 1275. This custom was of French origin, but an English innovation was the use of angel weepers, seemingly pioneered by the Chellaston alabasterers, but also used in stone.

Angels were also sometimes used at the heads of effigies, and the contract for the Green tomb at Lowick specifies their use to hold the lady's pillow, as it also specifies the small dogs at her feet.

About 1450 weepers came back into fashion, and though they eventually evolved into forms undreamed of by medieval carvers, they never again fell out of fashion until funerary sculpture itself did so. Some of the best late medieval examples are on Richard Beauchamp's tomb at Warwick, the two Fitzherbert tombs of 1473 and 1483 at Norbury, Derbyshire, and the Matthews tomb of 1520 in Llandaff Cathedral. Sometimes, for benefactors of almshouses, standing or sitting bedesmen are used instead; occasionally they escape from the tomb chest, like the amusing little garden gnome-like creature who sits casually on the back of a lion at the feet of Sir Nicholas Fitzherbert at Norbury, elbow resting on his knee, and chin resting on his hand. By comparison the three monks at the feet of William of Wykeham at Winchester, though grouped with unusual informality for their date, are solemn indeed. The stiff rows of kneeling children in Elizabethan and Jacobean monuments show a sad falling away from medieval standards, but the liberation which made them figures in their own right leads to some marvellous compositions later.

The Italian Cosmati work by Odericus and his son Petrus for the shrine of Edward the Confessor and the tomb of Henry III is exceptional in England. These tombs are made of red and green porphyry and white and gold glass mosaic, and the style is classical, not gothic. After this there is a gap of over two centuries until Italian work is used again, also in Westminster Abbey, when Torrigiani was commissioned to make his royal tombs. Here medallions take the place of gothic niches, and the angels and *putti* are eloquent of the new tradition.

But gothic survived in tombs as in architecture until well into the second half of the sixteenth century, as the monument to William Thorolds, 1569, at Marston, Lincolnshire, shows. But from the 1520s onwards many tombs show mixed motifs, often achieving a charming harmony of apparent irreconcilables, as in the de la Warr chantry at Boxgrove, Sussex c.1530, and Bishop Gardener's chantry of c.1555 in Winchester Cathedral, where shell-headed niches and fan-vaults occur side by side. The transition can be closely observed at Framlingham, Suffolk. The tomb of Henry Fitzroy, Duke of Richmond, 1536, shows a mixture of late gothic and Flemish renaissance motifs. Thomas Howard, 3rd Duke of Norfolk, 1554, has a beautiful early renaissance tomb chest, with figures of the apostles in the position of weepers under shell-headed niches, *(210)* while the wives of the 4th Duke, who died in 1557 and 1563 share a high renaissance tomb chest, with Corinthian columns, egg-and-dart ornament, and arabesques.

Important monuments were often surmounted by canopies. They first appear in the thirteenth century, like the very beautiful ones over Archbishop Grey, 1255, in York Minster, and Bishop Aquablanca, 1268, at Hereford *(199)* where the canopies are gabled, Aquablanca's with Purbeck shafts and bar-tracery in the arches. The best fourteenth-century ones are full of spiky tabernacle work, like the one over Edward II at Gloucester *(200)*. At about the same time in Beverley Minster there arose another canopy, quite different in form, but in its own way at least as beautiful *(204)*. It was designed after 1339, but in all probability commemorates Lady Eleanor Percy who died in 1328. It uses a single nodding ogee arch under a gable as its main feature, but the joy is in the delicacy of the carving.

Canopies are closely connected with the development of chantries, forming an enclosure which acted as a miniature chapel for the celebration of masses for the donors' souls. Consequently they grow commoner towards the end of the middle ages when they are often flat-topped and vaulted inside. A surprising number of these survived the Reformation, especially in cathedrals, and there is also an exceptionally good set in Tewkesbury Abbey. Most of these chantries are free-standing, but more medieval tombs are found in wall-recesses, where the canopy work can be equally good. The most remarkable ones are at Bristol Cathedral *(203)* where the recesses of a unique design were put in when the church was first built about 1300, and filled by various abbots and benefactors over the years. Another fine set is at Aldworth,

Berkshire. Just occasionally a tomb was set in a screen. Bishop Gower, 1347, lies in the pulpitum at St Davids which he had built, and the Wenlock tombs, 1392, at Luton, and the Kirkham Chantry at Paignton, Devon, are of this type; so probably was the Harrington tomb at Cartmel Priory, 1347, though it has been moved from its original position.

Later, standing wall monuments became standard, though Lord Cobham, 1561, lies in the middle of the chancel at Cobham, Kent, and a few freestanding tombs can be found from the seventeenth, eighteenth and nineteenth centuries. Elizabethan monuments can be huge and spectacular, and Lord and Lady Hunsdon's, 1596, in Westminster Abbey, is 36 feet high. Not that vast size was an Elizabethan prerogative as the most elaborate late medieval chantries, like Bishops Alcock's and West's in Ely Cathedral, and not a few Stuart and Georgian monuments, show. Unfortunately the largest Elizabethan monuments were rarely the best, and are often cuckoos in the nests of small parish churches.

However, the second half of the sixteenth century saw some work which can hold its own with the best of any other period. Some have no effigies, like the tombs of Gregory Cromwell, 1551, at Launde, Leicestershire, Sir Robert Dormer, 1552, at Wing, Buckinghamshire, *(208)* Sir William Compton, 1566, at Lacock, Wiltshire, and Richard Neeld, 1574, at Tugby, Leicestershire. Outstanding monuments with effigies include those to Lord Chief Justice Bromley, 1555, at Wroxeter, Shropshire, Lord Mordaunt, 1560, at Turvey, Bedfordshire, Sir John St John, 1559, at Bletsoe, Bedfordshire, and Bridget Coke, 1598, at Tittleshall, Norfolk.

Surrounds still followed the architectural styles of the day. Coffered arches are common in Elizabethan and Jacobean monuments, and pediments, sometimes broken, occur frequently in the succeeding age. Later it became usual not to have a canopy, but to place the figures against an obelisk or pyramid, a typically baroque fashion, but one which survived into the beginning of the ninteenth century.

Hanging wall memorials became common from the seventeenth century onwards, but reached the height of their popularity from about 1760 to 1840. Many of them were modest, the inexpensive work of local men, commemorating comparatively modest people, but, like the ledger stones and churchyard headstones of the same age, these small memorials are often very effective in their simplicity. They gave way finally to the brass plate, but in modern times there has been a revival of very simple small stone wall plaques.

Mich? Ryſbrack Fecit

Here Lyeth

The Body of THOMAS Lord WYNDHAM Baron WYNDHAM of *Finglaſs* in the Kingdom of *Ireland*, Youngeſt Son of JOHN WYNDHAM of *Norrington* in this County Esq?

He was educated in the *School* of the *Canons* of this *Cloſe*, from whence He went in 1698. to *Wadham College* in the *Univerſity* of *Oxford*. He removed from thence to *Lincoln's Inn* in 1701, and was there called to the Degree of *Barriſter* at *Law* in 1705.

In the Year 1724. His Majeſty King GEORGE the Firſt was pleaſed to appoint him *Chief Juſtice* of the Court of *Common Pleas* in *Ireland*, where He ſat two Years.

In December 1726. He was advanced to the *Office* of Lord High *Chancellor* of *Ireland*, and conſtituted One of the Lords *Juſtices* of that Kingdom; into which laſt *Office* He was ſworn eight ſeveral Times.

On the Demiſe of King GEORGE the Firſt, His Majeſty King GEORGE the Second renewed his Commiſſion of Lord High *Chancellor*; and, in September 1731. in Conſideration of his diligent and faithfull Services, was pleaſed to create Him a Baron of the Kingdom of *Ireland*.

He preſided in ſix Seſsions of Parliament as Speaker of the Houſe of Lords of *Ireland*, where there is a Seſsion, but once in two Years.

In April 1739. He ſat as Lord High Steward of *Ireland* on the Trial of the Lord BARRY of *Santry*, being the firſt Lord High Steward that ever was appointed in that Kingdom.

In September 1739. He reſigned his *Offices* at his own Requeſt, on account of an ill State of Health, contracted by a too intent and too long application to the great Variety of Buſineſs He had been engaged in.

He was a Member of the Eſtabliſhed Church, a ſtrenuous Aſſertor of Lawfull Liberty, a zealous Promoter of *Juſtice*, a dutifull Subject, and a kind Relation
He was born on the 27ᵗʰ Day of December 1681.
He died on the 24ᵗʰ Day of November 1745

213 Above left Miserden, Gloucestershire: Sir William Sandys, d.1640, and his wife Margaret Culpeper, d.1644, possibly by Edward Marshall

214 Left Elmley Castle, Worcestershire: 1st Earl of Coventry, c.1700, by William Stanton

215 Above centre Salisbury Cathedral: Thomas, Lord Wyndham, d.1745, by J.M. Rysbrack

216 Above right Westminster Abbey: Mr and Mrs J.G. Nightingale, 1761, by L-F. Roubiliac

GEORGE FREDERICK HANDEL Esqr
born February XXIII. MDCLXXXIV.
died April XIV. MDCCLIX. L.F.Roubiliac inv. et sc

217 Left Westminster Abbey: George Frederick Handel, detail, 1761, by L-F. Roubiliac

218 Below left Warkton, Northamptonshire: Mary, Duchess of Montagu, d.1753, detail, by L-F. Roubiliac

219 Centre right Powick, Worcestershire: Mrs Russell, d.1786, by Thomas Scheemakers

220 Far right Powick, Worcestershire: Mrs Russell, d.1786, detail, by Thomas Scheemakers

221 Below right Warkton, Northamptonshire: Mary, Duchess of Montagu, d.1775, by Robert Adam and P.M. van Gelder

222 Left St George's Chapel, Windsor: Princess Charlotte, d.1817, by M.C. Wyatt

223 Right Hafod Church, Aberystwyth: Mariamne Johnes, d.1811, by Sir Francis Chantrey. Destroyed by fire, 1932

224 Below right Gloucester Cathedral: Sarah Morley, d.1784, by John Flaxman

225 Condover, Shropshire: Sir Thomas Cholmondeley, d.1864, by G.F. Watts

227 Newland, Gloucestershire: brass, Free Miner of the Forest of Dean, late medieval

226 Chenies, Buckinghamshire: Lord Arthur Russell, d.1892, by Alfred Gilbert

228 Lanivet, Cornwall: John and Richard Courtenay, 1632, slate

Designers and Sculptors

All too few names of the makers of medieval tombs are known, though sometimes the chance survival of contracts draws aside the veil of anonymity. In the contract for Richard Beauchamp's tomb at Warwick, no fewer than six craftsmen are mentioned by name, as well as the name of the supplier of the Purbeck marble. This, of course, was an exceptional tomb, but one wonders how many men worked on Edward II's, or on Torrigiani's royal tombs. Even in the late sixteenth century, few names are known for certain, but among those that are, Dutchmen and Flemings occur frequently, like Hollemans, who worked at Burton-on-Trent, and the Johnson family, who were Janssens when they crossed the Channel. The Netherlandish influence, indeed, can be said to have begun with the earliest Tournai slabs at the end of the eleventh century, and not to have ceased until after the death of Peter Scheemakers in the late eighteenth.

Nicholas Johnson was one of the first sculptors to move away from the clichés of the Elizabethan style. His Robert Kelway, 1580, at Exton, Rutland, shows him recumbent, while his daughter, son-in-law, and grandchild kneel by the tomb chest, no longer small conventional weepers, but characters in their own right.

The most important links between the late Tudor and the early Stuart period are Epiphanius Evesham and Maximilian Colt. Evesham was not a radical innovator, but a fine sculptor who showed a welcome freshness in the details of his work. He was probably responsible for the splendid battle relief on the monument to John Farnham, 1587, at Quorndon, Leicestershire. At Felsted, Essex, the first Lord Rich reclines while his son kneels, and three reliefs show him with allegorical virtues, to which in life this unscrupulously ambitious man paid little regard. The monument was not erected until 1602, many years after his death, by which time his faults might have become blurred in the memory; besides, Dr Johnson's remark about a man not being on oath when composing lapidary inscriptions can equally well apply to the whole design of memorials. The representation of the deceased as the embodiment of all the virtues seems, indeed, to be a typically Pelagian English protestant substitute for the medieval orates to speed a soul's course to heaven, replacing a superstition by a lie. At Boughton-under-Blean, Kent, Evesham depicts the children of Thomas Hawkins and his wife, 1617, as weepers, standing in informal groups, with one little girl in tears. Sorrow could at last be naturally expressed.

At about the same time, Maximilian Colt, a refugee from Arras, and designer of the unoriginal tomb of Elizabeth I, was introducing far more radical ideas, chief among them the Dutch-style monument to Robert Cecil, 1st Earl of Salisbury, 1612, at Hatfield, *(212)*. Although, as we have seen, with its cadaver below the effigy, it is a variation on an old theme, its openness and bold use of allegories break new ground in England. It inspired a few other monuments, like Francis Grigs' Sir Robert Hitcham, 1638, at Framlingham, where there is no effigy, but a slab carried by four angels. A much stranger memorial is Colt's Princess Sophia in Westminster Abbey. She died in 1606 aged three days, and is shown as a rather older baby, realistically coloured, asleep in her cradle.

A visiting sculptor of great distinction was the Frenchman, Hubert le Sueur. His tomb of the Duke and Duchess of Lennox and Richmond in Westminster Abbey has gilt-bronze effigies, and a canopy supported by caryatids. He used bronze, too, in 1634, for the standing effigy of Admiral Sir Richard Leveson at Wolverhampton; and the bronze bust of William Godolphin, 1636, at Bruton, Somerset, is also attributed to him, as is the bronze effigy of Lord Portland, 1634, in Winchester Cathedral. The surround of this last tomb, in coloured marble, has a classic serenity unexpected in England quite as early as this, and was perhaps also his design.

Among Englishmen of this era, the best monumental sculptor by far was Nicholas Stone, who trained in Amsterdam under Hendrik de Kayser, returning home in 1613 well versed in Dutch fashions. He rapidly made a name for himself, and was able to charge as much as Le Sueur for one of his larger compositions – up to £600 for Lord and Lady Spencer at Great Brington, which was two or three times as much as most of his contemporaries could expect. His inventiveness was unrivalled, and he was an accomplished craftsman *(207)*. Later, it seems that he came under the influence of Inigo Jones, and was also inspired by Charles I's acquisitions from the Duke of Mantua's collection, in both cases to the great benefit of his work. In Norfolk alone he used the traditional recumbent effigy at Emneth, c.1625, a kneeling effigy at Holkham, 1639, a semi-reclining effigy at Paston, 1629, a bust at Oxnead, 1636, and no effigy at all at Paston, 1632. The two Paston monuments are particularly instructive, standing as they do, side by side. The earlier is of alabaster, and completely in the Jacobean tradition; the later is of marble in the fashion of Inigo Jones. He also used upright effigies, in the Donne monument in St Paul's and the Holles monument of 1626 in Westminster Abbey.

The work of Stone and his contemporaries led in

the second half of the seventeenth century to some of the finest tombs to be found in English churches. Foreign influence, however, remained strong. Jan van Ost, anglicised as John Nost, made a number of sumptuous tombs, among then the splendid Earl of Bristol, 1698, who stands in Sherborne Abbey, flanked by his two wives. Though his father was English, Grinling Gibbons was born in Rotterdam, and while his stone carving is not as exceptional as his work in wood, his best tombs, like the 7th and 8th Earls of Rutland at Exton are highly accomplished.

Caius Gabriel Cibber, father of Colley Cibber the Poet Laureate, came from Holstein. His monument to Thomas Sackville at Withyham has been mentioned before because of its revival of the old motif of the half rolled-up mat. In other respects it breaks new ground, for the boy's parents, the Earl and Countess of Bristol, kneel on either side of his tomb chest gazing into the loved face of their son, and obscuring part of the reliefs of other children along the sides of the sarcophagus as if, as Pevsner puts it, they had only that moment decided to kneel there.[113] Not since the Dorchester knight nearly four centuries earlier had such spontaneity appeared in English funerary sculpture, and the poignancy of the composition is something quite new.

Bushnell, who was Italian trained, was another sculptor capable of conveying emotion, as where William Ashburnham kneels before the recumbent body of his wife at Ashburnham, Sussex. He could also carve magnificent busts, as can be seen in the monument to Sir Thomas and Lady Broderick at Peper Harow, Surrey.

But it was an age of great talent in general, and the work of men like Francis Bird and Richard Crutcher is as good as anything by Gibbons or Bushnell. So far as we know, Crutcher only designed one memorial, a mighty piece of architecture with standing figures commemorating Sir Robert and Lady Clayton, 1707, at Bletchingley, Surrey. Francis Bird is well represented in Westminster Abbey, and if one had to choose one example of his work, it would perhaps be Dr Busby, 1703, with his scholar's cap, rather than some of his larger and more pretentious pieces.[114]

The next generation saw a new freedom of composition and a significant change in conventions. Now the principal figures are often no longer the deceased, or mourning relatives, but allegories. This convention hardens as the century progresses, and tends to become mechanical, but in the early days it brought vigorous new life to the memorialists' art. Thus one finds Field-Marshal Wade, 1750, in Westminster Abbey, his portrait in a medallion, while Fame struggles with Time as the main feature of the composition.

Wade's tomb is by Roubiliac. Louis François Roubiliac was born in Lyons and settled in England about 1730. Sometimes attributed to him is the monument to Mr Justice Dormer at Quainton, Buckinghamshire, where the expiring young man is flanked by his standing parents, his mother weeping.[115] This early work is something of a transitional piece in the tradition of Cibber and Bushnell, and, good though it is, it is not in the same league as his best mature works. Appropriately he was chosen to make Handel's tomb in Westminster Abbey, showing the great composer, whom he had known well, holding the score of 'I know that my Redeemer Liveth', *(217)*. This then, is a Christian memorial, something not always apparent to Englishmen unaccustomed to meeting their religion in baroque dress. Less explicitly Christian to us, though not to John Wesley, who greatly admired it, is the wonderful Nightingale tomb also in Westminster Abbey *(216)*. Lady Elizabeth Nightingale died young after the shock of a flash of lightning caused the premature birth of her child, and her husband stands holding her, trying in vain to ward off death in the form of a skeleton armed with a lance. On the Argyll monument, 1749, also in the Abbey, appear Eloquence and Minerva, and Minerva appears again, this time with Hercules, for General Fleming, 1750. But it would be superficial to dismiss these as pagan in inspiration on the strength of a few classical details; rather, they assert civilized values in the form in which the eighteenth century recognized them alongside statements of Christian belief.

Outside London two of Roubiliac's greatest works stand in the village church at Warkton, Northamptonshire. The memorial to John, Duke of Montagu, 1752, is full of rhythmic upward movement, while his Duchess's tomb, 1753, an even better composition, has three lively putti and three enchanting young female Fates *(218)*. What it lacks in drama compared with the Nightingale it makes up in beauty, and there can be few more visually attractive monuments in the whole of Britain. The two monuments together cost £2076. Unlike even the best of his rivals, Roubiliac seems to have been incapable of indifferent work, and even his most modest commissions are designed and executed with a master's touch.

Second only to Roubiliac in his day was John Michael Rysbrack, who was born in Antwerp and settled in London about 1720. Unlike Roubiliac he often executed the designs of others, and two of his best works, the Duke of Marlborough at Blenheim, 1733, and Sir Isaac Newton, 1731, in Westminster

Abbey, are among several designed by the architect William Kent. James Gibbs designed the monument to Dr Freind, 1728, in Westminster Abbey, and Robert Adam designed Sir Nathaniel Curzon's at Kedleston, Derbyshire. But whatever limitations he may have had as a designer, Rysbrack's carving, particularly of busts, is superb, as the illustration of Lord Wyndham's monument in Salisbury Cathedral shows, *(215)*.[116]

Also from Antwerp were the Scheemakers family, Peter, Henry and Thomas. Of these, Peter is generally reckoned the greatest, though all three created masterpieces, and, for that matter, all three turned out second rate work as well. Peter sometimes executed designs by James 'Athenian' Stuart, one of the pioneers of the Greek revival, like the two at Wimpole, Cambridgeshire, and his Shakespeare memorial in Westminster Abbey was designed by Kent. An excellent example of his own design is Salmon Morrice, 1740, at Betteshanger, Kent, with a bust and reliefs.

His brother Henry can be represented by Sir Francis and Lady Page, 1730, at Steeple Aston, Oxfordshire, with baroque, very relaxed effigies, plump and self-satisfied: their friends, one feels, would have recognized them more readily than they would have recognized themselves. Peter Scheemaker's son Thomas made the monument to Mrs Russell, 1786, at Powick, Worcestershire, *(219, 220)*, which has an exquisite relief of the young Mrs Russell teaching her child music, while above, reclining on one elbow, is a beautiful unselfconscious young allegory.

Roughly contemporary with Thomas Scheemakers was Peter's pupil, Joseph Nollekens. His output was vast, and, like Rysbrack, he was a particularly gifted carver of busts. In general his more modest monuments please most, but pride of place should perhaps be given to his William Weddell, 1789, in Ripon Cathedral, which consists of a bust in a sort of Corinthian garden temple.

Though his name suggests a Netherlandish ancestry, Nollekens was born in London, and the wealth of foreign names in the eighteenth century does not infer a lack of capable Englishmen at the time. Particularly from about 1770 to 1820, English sculptors could hold their own with the best in Europe, though admittedly they learned much from Dutch, French, and Italian masters.

Sir Henry Cheere, probably a pupil of John Nost, was an excellent carver who drew inspiration from Roubiliac. He used coloured stone more freely than his contemporaries, who preferred the austerity of black or grey and white. Typical of his best work is Elizabeth Drake, 1757, at Amersham, Buckinghamshire, in pink, grey and white marble, a monument which combines prettiness, elegance and poignancy. Mrs Drake died at 32, leaving six children who are shown informally with her, while she kneels in prayer. The older children kneel too, while the youngest, less aware, sits looking at a book. The frame is gay with flowers, and the inscription Christian rather than eulogistic. This feminine tomb can be contrasted with the robustly masculine Philip de Sausmarez, 1747, in Westminster Abbey, with a portrait medallion and a battle relief.

Joseph Wilton, who studied in Rome with Roubiliac, was roughly contemporary with Nollekens. His work was uneven, but a few of his tombs are of the highest quality, like Leak and Mary Okeover, c.1765, at Okeover, Staffordshire, and Charlotte St Quentin at Harpham, East Riding, both of which have portrait medallions and angels leaning on urns. The Byerleys at Goldsborough, West Riding, have a Greek-style memorial, with lovely figures of Faith and Charity, while Sir Robert Long, 1767, at Draycot Cerne, Wiltshire, is commemorated by a fine bust.

Dutch influence continued in the late eighteenth century with Peter van Gelder. His most interesting monument, with an architectural surround designed by Robert Adam, is to the Duchess of Montagu, 1775, at Warkton, Northamptonshire *(221)*. The Duchess sits in despair with two young children, flanked on one side by an old woman who offers no hope, but on the other by an angel who directs her gaze to heaven. One sympathizes with anyone faced with creating a monument designed to stand in the same modest chancel as two of the best Roubiliacs, and it is a brave attempt. Almost anywhere else it would be outstanding, but because the comparison is impossible to avoid, one notices that while Roubiliac's figures look as though they could step down from their monuments at any moment, Van Gelder's seem characterless, static, and all too obviously made of stone. Unsigned, but attributed to Van Gelder is the splendid Cornet Geary, 1776, killed in an ambush, which is depicted in relief, during the American War of Independence. Another War of Independence memorial by Van Gelder is to Major André, shot by the Americans for treason. Both these are in Westminster Abbey, and the André monument was designed by Robert Adam.

Mention of Robert Adam draws attention to the change in architectural and decorative taste towards the end of the eighteenth century, away from the baroque and rococo towards a 'chaste' – a favourite word of artistic approbation at the time – classicism.

This is already apparent in the best of Wilton's work, and, indeed, neo-classical reliefs are already to be found in Grinling Gibbons' 3rd Viscount Campden, 1686, at Exton. But it was the neo-classical period at the end of the eighteenth and the beginning of the nineteenth centuries which saw the final flowering of the long tradition of English funerary sculpture, and the names of its leading exponents are, for the first time since the end of the middle ages, almost all English.

Freestanding monuments still occur, and most sculptors used them occasionally and to good effect, as Flaxman did for Nelson, 1808–18, in St Paul's, but the hanging wall tablet, often quite modest in size, with a composition in relief, and in black or grey and white marble, was the prevailing fashion. Some could still be very cold; many were pedestrian: one thinks of the multitudinous mourning figures or angels by urns, and the ubiquitous weeping willows. Bored by these clichés, the eye tends to flicker unobservantly over them on the walls of our greater churches, and thereby much that is good is missed.

In many, emotion is shown openly, but sentiment is still dignified. John Bacon Senior's Richard Jolley, 1803, in Worcester Cathedral, shows his widow and three children weeping at his tomb. It is well done, as is his seated figure of Matthew Ridley, 1787, in Newcastle Cathedral. John Flaxman's children are particularly attractive, especially in the monument to Dr Warton, 1801, in Winchester Cathedral, and the memorial to John Lyon, the founder of Harrow School, put in the church there in 1815.

One is continually reminded of the perils of childbirth by the touching memorials to very young women, a number of which have already been mentioned. None is more poignant than Flaxman's Sarah Morley, 1784 *(224)* in Gloucester Cathedral. At 28 she was already mother of seven, and died in childbirth on her way home from Bombay. Her body was committed to the waves, and Flaxman shows her rising from the sea with her baby, greeted by angels. Since he was one of Wedgwood's designers – some of his jasperware reliefs are still current – it was fitting that Flaxman should have been chosen to commemorate Josiah Wedgwood, 1795, at Stoke-on-Trent, and equally fitting that the portrait medallion he produced should be among his finest works.

The Westmacotts, like the Scheemakers, the Bacons, the Stantons, the Marshalls, as well as many provincial men of some distinction, were a family of carvers, three generations, all called Richard, being represented in our churches. The eldest Westmacott's best work is perhaps his J.L. Dutton, 1791, at

Sherborne, Gloucestershire, where a double medallion of Mr and Mrs Dutton is revealed by a beautiful angel, while a skeleton lies below. The second Richard was knighted. At Little Gaddesden, Hertfordshire, his memorial to the 7th Earl of Bridgewater, 1823, has a tondo with a labourer and his wife and child. At Wimpole the Hon John Yorke and his wife, 1801, stand hand in hand by an urn, while their child sits below, but best of all perhaps is the 11th Earl of Pembroke at Wilton, 1827, with a gorgeous relief of the Trinity, a Grecian shepherd, and a portrait bust in relief.

Sir Richard's contemporary, Sir Francis Chantrey, was even more famous in his day. There tends to be a sameness about some of his work, since he or his clients failed to resist the temptation to repeat a successful formula. Hence if Bishop Shute Barrington in Durham, Bishop North in Winchester, Bishop Ryder at Lichfield, and Archbishop Stuart at Armagh could be shuffled while nobody was looking, few of us would be any the wiser. But Chantrey was a fine sculptor, as in the Winn monument at Wragby, West Riding, 1817, where there are two charming young mourners, and in the memorial to James Watt the engineer, 1825, at Handsworth, Birmingham.

The borderline between poignancy and sentimentality is one which people will draw in different places. All that can be briefly chronicled here are some of the steps along the road. Whether the liberation of the sense of mourning betokens a weakening of belief in eternal life is probably an unprofitable speculation, but the medieval matter-of-factness about death itself, for all the obsessional anxiety about the after life revealed by Dooms and the practice of chantries, changed gradually into a feeling that death was the last enemy whose conquest was less certain than conventional assertions of faith made out, and its reality was sometimes so unbearable that it was softened into sleep.

So Thomas Banks, in 1799, made what has become one of the most popular memorials in Britain, to Penelope Boothby at Ashbourne, Derbyshire, where the young girl is shown on a tomb chest, lying peacefully and naturally on her side, with her hands tucked up in front of her chin. 'The unfortunate parents', says the epitaph, 'ventured their all on this frail Bark, and the wreck was total.' After nearly two centuries, the heartbreak is still pathetically real. One of its successors is Chantrey's monument to the three Robinson children, who all died in 1814, and who all lie, equally naturally asleep, in Lichfield Cathedral. Britton, whose cathedral monographs are full of scorn for everything post-Reformation, and who saw it only a few years after it was made, was bowled over by it:

'As calculated to commence a new era in our national monumental sculpture, (it) must be viewed with exaltation by every real lover of art. From the demise of Henry the Eighth to the beginning of the present century, the sculpture of this country has rarely presented any thing admirable or excellent. It has either exhibited a vulgar imitation of vulgar life in monstrous costume, or tasteless copies of Greek and Roman models', but, when he gazed on the Robinson memorial, 'I must own that all my powers of criticism were subdued by the more impressive impulses of the heart.'[117]

At Hackness, North Riding, 1821, Chantrey depicts Mr Johnstone kneeling and pressing his forehead desperately against his dying wife's arm, while she holds her baby.' She was 23. Finally at Hafod church, Aberystwyth, he showed Mr and Mrs Johnes bending despairingly over the dying figure of their daughter Mariamne *(223)*. This, probably his best monument, was sadly destroyed by fire in 1932.

Westmacott expresses sentiment somewhat differently. The tomb of Mrs Warren, 1816, in Westminster Abbey, depicts a beggar girl holding her baby, doubtless with reference to Mrs Warren's charitable exercises. The girl's face is plebeian, and her expression strikes an authentic note of poverty. Less moving, though beautifully carved, is his Mrs Wilmot, 1818, at Berkswell, Warwickshire, which shows two angels embracing. Rightly or wrongly, one feels here that the sentiment is contrived rather than the outcome of natural and genuine emotion, though contemporaries clearly thought otherwise: the design is repeated, with fewer frills, for Mrs Grace Bagge, 1834, at Stradsett, Norfolk.

Two of the most spectacular monuments of this time are by M.C. Wyatt. Princess Charlotte, who died in 1817, was yet another victim of the dangers of childbirth. Her memorial in St George's Windsor was completed in 1824 *(222)*, and shows her dead, hidden by a sheet and mourned by four women. Above this scene of tragedy she rises to heaven, gazing upwards as she goes, with two angels beside her, one holding the baby who died with her. It is very artificial, and if there is sentiment, there is no real emotion; at the same time it is an arresting monument of high quality, and must have been even more dramatic originally when it was lit by yellow glass. At Belvoir Castle Mausoleum, Leicestershire, is the even more startling monument to the 5th Duchess of Rutland, c.1828. She rises to where her dead children float in the clouds, waiting to invest her with her crown of glory, an apotheosis rather than a resurrection. Wyatt creates

an artistic sensation by lighting the white marble with purple and yellow glass, and something of a theological sensation by making her monument none other than the altar of the chapel, a much closer approach to baroque continental catholicism than one would expect in late Georgian England.

By the Victorian age most monuments, even to the wealthy, were confined to churchyards and, increasingly, to cemeteries. Most of those that are in churches, however impeccable the craftsmanship, seem to lack inspiration. The latter part of the nineteenth century produced no Nicholas Stone, no Roubiliac, not even a Westmacott. The wretched urn still appeared mechanically in Grecian survival, and white marble figures of vaguely classical form even persisted into the twentieth century.

More significantly, gothic was revived. In its gothick form it had been used earlier: first in 1738 for Percyvall Hart at Lullingstone, Kent. Flaxman used it for Sarah Morley, and Chantrey quite often, in unselfconscious combination with Grecian details. Rickman, the scholar to whom we owe the classification of English gothic into Early English, Decorated and Perpendicular, went further in his monument to Robert Whitworth at Buckden, Huntingdonshire, 1831, but for all the carefully correct detail, it was still a classical composition in gothic dress. True revival began much later than in architecture, and one of the first examples must be Pugin's own tomb at Ramsgate, 1852, with its recumbent effigy on a tomb chest. But, though gothic became standard for church buildings, classical forms were often retained for monuments. Men like the youngest Westmacott, the younger Bacon, Henry Weekes and Terence Farrell produced memorials that are at the same time unmistakably Victorian and unmistakably classical.

In one respect the gothic tombs of the nineteenth century were unmedieval: the effigies were portraits. Numerous bishops in our cathedrals were the mainstay of the gothic carvers, for the most part pleasant, seemly and easily forgotten works. Few of them have any real personality, not even so stunning a piece of craftsmanship as Thomas Woolner's marble and alabaster Lord Frederick Cavendish, 1885, at Cartmel Priory.

Among the few Victorian monuments which need picking out in this survey are two outstanding works by G.F. Watts. Rev John Armitshead, 1876, at Sandbach, Cheshire, is still in the classical tradition, with an expressive three-quarter figure in relief. Much more dramatic, however, is Sir Thomas Cholmondeley, 1864, at Condover, Shropshire *(225)*. The kneeling figure is a masterpiece, without much doubt the finest High Victorian effigy to be found anywhere. The finest High Victorian architectural monument is indisputably the huge piece Alfred Stevens made to commemorate the Duke of Wellington in the nave of St Paul's. The effigy, and allegorical figures are of bronze.

At the end of the century, Alfred Gilbert used Art Nouveau forms for funerary sculpture, and here at last genuine new ground was broken. He, too, used bronze effectively, and his stature can be gauged by four monuments: to J.H. Thynne, 1887, at Longbridge Deverill, Wiltshire, in the form of an alabaster font; the Marchioness of Ailesbury, 1892, at Savernake Forest, Wiltshire, with a bronze of St Katherine; Lord Arthur Russell, 1892, at Chenies, Buckinghamshire, with figures of Love, Truth, and Courage *(226)*: and the Duke of Clarence, 1892–8, in the Albert Memorial Chapel, Windsor, with a recumbent effigy and an impressive standing angel. The statuettes of saints were not completed until the late 1920s, an example of procrastination which make Rossetti's delays at Llandaff seem trivial.

But, if the second half of the nineteenth century produced fewer memorable monuments than, say, Nicholas Stone or Chantrey alone, the twentieth century has produced even less. Memorials are now in general more modest than they have been since the eleventh century. Imagine what weight of stone Sir Winston Churchill or Field Marshal Montgomery would have had to bear had they died at any time between 1250 and 1860! In both cases there are simple inscriptions, and nothing more. If one has to single out a few twentieth century memorials, then among the best are Sir George Frampton's Mrs Wilson, 1905, at Warter, East Riding, W.B. Richmond's bronze Bishop King, 1913, in Lincoln Cathedral, Eric Gill's Mrs Foster Lodge, 1922, at Wilsford, Wiltshire, and Eric Kennington's T.E. Lawrence, 1935, at St Martin, Wareham, Dorset.

The demise of funerary sculpture is not a matter for regret, as most of our older churches already contain more than is good for them. The Victorians realized this and started the fashion of dedicating useful or edifying pieces of furniture or decoration as memorials instead. Of these, memorial windows are by far the most notable, though still the prerogative of the wealthy, and a problem nowadays if the glass is bad and the family still happens to live in the district. But the custom happily spread till in our own day comely and serviceable objects like simple font covers, altar candlesticks and cut glass flower vases are often donated to commemorate the less opulent departed. Equally sensible in these days of the church's poverty is the custom of repairing and restoring older items as a memorial, for churches exist for the benefit of the living, not of the dead.

Chapter 11
Miscellany

Acoustic Jars

Medieval pottery jars have occasionally been found embedded in interior walls, seemingly in an attempt to improve acoustics. Examples may be seen at Great Milton, Oxfordshire, Lyddington, Rutland, and Tarrant Rushton, Dorset *(229)*.

Armour

Funerary achievements often included armour, of which the Black Prince's in Canterbury Cathedral is the most famous. The room above the porch occasionally served as the village armoury, and at Mendlesham, Suffolk, the armour is still there.

Banner Staff Lockers

Long narrow recesses are sometimes found in church walls, especially in East Anglia, for the storage of the staffs which supported banners used in processions. They are of no intrinsic interest to the student of furniture except for the one at Barnby, Suffolk, which retains its traceried medieval door. Two old banner staffs preserved at Cuckfield, Sussex, show the kind of thing the lockers were provided for.

Biers

Biers, which are litters or stretchers for carrying uncoffined corpses to the grave, are still quite frequently found. A few are dated, which gives a clue to the time of origin of many of the others: West Dereham, Norfolk, 1683; Purse Caundle, Dorset, 1733; Methwold, Norfolk, 1737; Trent, Dorset, 1757.

Clocks

Clocks are generally placed on towers, but are sometimes found inside the church. Late fourteenth-century clocks can be found in the cathedrals of Salisbury and Wells. The Salisbury one, made about 1386, has its works displayed inside the cathedral. The contemporary Wells clock is still in use, and has two faces, one outside the north transept, the other inside *(231)*. The inside dial has a 24-hour face, with stars to indicate the days of the month, the hours and the minutes. It also shows the phases of the moon. When the clock strikes, figures of mounted knights rotate in mock combat, and one is struck down. The external dial has two late fifteenth-century quarter jacks, also in armour. Jacks were used for several centuries. At All Saints, Leicester, they form part of a clock dated 1620, and at Southwold, Suffolk, c.1470, and Blythburgh, 1682 *(232)* they bear witness to clocks now gone. At Wimborne Minster the clock face is dated 1740, but the quarter jacks seem to have been added early in the nineteenth century. Exeter Cathedral has a clock of about 1480 with mainly later works. The original dial covers 24 hours and shows the phases of the moon like the one at Wells. A minute hand was added by means of a separate dial in 1760. There is a similar clock at Ottery St Mary. Durham Cathedral has a fine clock case of about 1500, with a dial and works of 1632. The clock face at St Austell, Cornwall, may well belong to the sixteenth century, and the figures above the face at St Mary Steps, Exeter, certainly do, while at Rye, Sussex, the works, including an 18-foot pendulum, were made in 1562, though the face and quarter jacks belong to an eighteenth-century rebuilding.

The single-handed clock at Northill, Bedfordshire, made about 1663, has been attributed to Thomas Tompion, the 'Father of English Clockmakers', who was born at the nearby hamlet of Ickwell. Single-handed clocks were not unusual at this time, and neither were clocks with no dials at all, but simply a striking mechanism. It is possible that the late seventeenth-century clock at Long Stratton, Norfolk, was originally like this, but dials were added to the west face of the tower, and, exceptionally, to the east face of the tower inside the church, in the early eighteenth century. Both dials are single-handed. The importance of the strike is well brought out at Great Gransden, Huntingdonshire, where the carillon and chimes were probably installed in 1683. An early eighteenth-century clock of fine quality is to be found on the west gallery of St Leonard, Shoreditch. Attractive later clocks are commonplace on church towers, but among modern clocks, the one in the north transept of Gloucester Cathedral must be the most elaborate, with a rich Art Nouveau case made by Henry Wilson in 1903.

Commandment, Creed and Lord's Prayer Boards

Boards containing the Ten Commandments, the Lord's Prayer, and the Apostle's Creed were commonly set up in churches after the Reformation; often as reredoses, where they have already been mentioned (p. 125). Sometimes, however, they were placed elsewhere on the east wall or on the tympanum in the chancel arch. Survivors have now frequently been relegated to less conspicuous positions, and it is not unusual to find them lying against the tower walls among other junk, gathering dust. This is a pity, because many were good pieces of work, and some commandment boards were flanked by excellent paintings of Moses and Aaron.

Preston, Suffolk, has commandments flanking the Royal Arms in the shape of a triptych. These are Elizabethan, and must be one of the earliest sets along with those at Lanteglos-by-Camelford, Cornwall, and Badgeworth, Gloucestershire, the latter dated 1591. The set at Shipdham, Norfolk, 1630 (230) were painted on the tympanum, and are unusually pretty. At Hedgerley, Buckinghamshire, the commandments of 1664 are surrounded by rustic paintings showing from biblical examples the fate of transgressors against them.

Nearly all the texts of whatever period are painted on board. Exceptions include the brass reredos at Little Gidding already mentioned, and nineteenth-century examples in slate at Greasley, Nottinghamshire, glazed tiles at St Michael Caerhays, Cornwall, and glass (by Wailes, 1841) at Barton, North Riding.

Dole Cupboards

Gifts of bread for the poor purchased through benefactions made by well-to-do citizens out of sheer generosity or uneasy mindfulness of the parable of Dives and Lazarus were a common form of charity administered by the churches, and quite a number of dole shelves or cupboards remain, most of them made between about 1675 and 1730. Some of them are delightful pieces of carpentry, like those illustrated from Ruislip, Middlesex, 1697 (233), and St Martin-cum-Gregory, York, (234). Maid's Moreton, Buckinghamshire has a bread basket instead.

The dole cupboard at Milton Ernest, Bedfordshire, 1729, is inscribed: 'To do good And to Distribute Forget not: For with such Sacrifices God is Well Pleased. The Gift of Mrs Susanna Rolt, late of this Parish, and Tho: Rolt, in Twelve Two-Penny loaves weekly to the Poor of the Said Parish For Ever.'

These weekly distributions doubtless worked well enough. Annual ones caused problems: at East Dereham, Norfolk, Rev B.J. Armstrong records on 19 December 1854: 'The 400 loaves given annually on St Thomas's Day usually cause such confusion in the church, and in the hurry so many get them who ought not, that I determined this year to select the most deserving persons. I drove over the whole parish for this purpose.' On 21 December: 'The gifts as usual brought a large number to church, and many who had come only for the sake of them were much disgusted when told that they had previously been given to the poorest and most deserving.'[118]

Dog Tongs

Until well into the nineteenth century, dogs frequently accompanied their owners to church. The practice was accepted as long as the animals behaved themselves, but long tongs were sometimes provided so that in the event of a fight or other unseemliness, the offenders could be safely separated and ejected. They seem to be found more frequently in Wales, which may imply an aggressive or merely irreligious trait in Welsh collies. There are good examples at Bangor Cathedral and Clynnog Fawr.

Funerary Palls

Palls are cloths used to cover coffins, and one or two ancient and excellent examples survive. At Dunstable Priory, Bedfordshire, there is an early sixteenth century one made of brocaded red Florentine velvet, with a fringed satin border, and embroidered figures of John the Baptist, to whom was dedicated a religious fraternity founded at Dunstable in 1442.[119] At St Giles, Colchester, there is one belonging to the Lucas family, made of embroidered purple velvet in 1628.

Gotches

Gotches are large beer jugs provided for the refreshment of ringers, perhaps in the hope that they would no longer need to adjourn to the nearest hostelry when their work was done instead of attending divine service; more likely perhaps used during a lengthy and arduous programme of change-ringing. Among churches still possessing them are Macclesfield, Cheshire, and Hindersley, Suffolk, 1724.

Hudds

Graveside shelters for the officiating parson, known as hudds, were sometimes provided in the eighteenth and early nineteenth centuries. Few remain, though examples exist at Brookland and Ivychurch, Kent, Donington, Lincolnshire, and Wingfield, Suffolk.

Instruments of Punishment

Churches seem to have been used as storage places for instruments of punishment, and a few still survive. At other places stocks have been brought in from the churchyard or village green. Stocks are found in a number of churches like Chaceley, Gloucestershire, and Folkingham, Lincolnshire. At Rock, Worcestershire, both stocks and whipping-post are in the church, while at St Leonard, Shoreditch, they remain in the churchyard. St Martin-in-the-Fields, London, also has a whipping post, while at Walton-on-Thames there is a model of a scold's bridle, and, without a doubt the finest exhibit in this section, Leominster Priory, Herefordshire, has a ducking stool.

Lights

Candelabra and chandeliers were used in churches from the middle ages, though there are now less than a dozen pre-Reformation examples in British churches, two of which, at St Michael's Mount, Cornwall, and St John the Baptist, Norwich, were imported. Bristol Cathedral possesses an excellent fifteenth-century example from the ruined Temple Church there, *(237)* and two sixteenth-century examples in Denbighshire, at Llandeglan and Llanarmon-yn-Ial, are thought to have come from Valle Crucis Abbey.

Dutch chandeliers were introduced in the seventeenth century – there is one dated 1657 at Sherborne Abbey – and the elegance and efficiency of these pieces rapidly led to their manufacture in England. There are 12 dated seventeenth-century examples, some of which could be Dutch, but over 160 dated eighteenth-century ones, as well as many undated examples *(238)*. After 1800 the number drops sharply, and few were made after 1825. A pair at Ramsbury, Wiltshire, cost £20.10s.6d in 1751. Nearly all of them are made of brass, but there is an eighteenth-century iron one at Great Witcombe, Gloucestershire.

Candlesticks belong to plate and are not described, though no book on church furnishings could be complete without a mention of the wonderful Gloucester candlestick, made about 1110 of gilt bell-metal, and now in the Victoria and Albert Museum

(241). Candle sconces are sometimes still found on box-pews and pulpits, their gleaming brass making a delightful contrast with the polished wood. It seems that people more often brought their own candle holders, and many old pews have scorch marks where they overturned. Candles were often stuck on prickets, such as those on the grille on Queen Eleanor's tomb in Westminster Abbey, and the rood loft parapet at Patricio. Either side of the altar space on the east wall of Rowlstone, Herefordshire, there is a fifteenth century candle bracket with prickets *(240)*.

Cressets, stones with hollows for oil in which a floating wick was placed, were probably equally common in medieval churches, but few remain. There is a small one at Lower Gravenhurst, Bedfordshire, and at least three in Cornish churches, at Bodmin, Lewannick and Marhamchurch, but the largest by far is the one in Brecon Cathedral. Another alternative to candles was the rushlight, and a rushlight holder can still be seen at Warnham, Sussex.

Seemly Victorian oil lamps survive in some churches, like Barton Turf, Norfolk, but they were mostly turned out when electricity was installed. An unusual survival is a gasolier at Tetbury, Gloucestershire, in a form reminiscent of chandeliers *(239)*. Electric light fittings are in general disappointingly mundane, at best anonymous and at worst obtrusive. Perhaps the oldest, and among the nicest, are those at Ingestre, Staffordshire, installed in 1886. Another nice set, including modern reproductions, are at Great Warley, Essex, where a touch of Tiffany blends well with the rich Arts and Crafts furniture.

Miscellaneous Carvings

This rather disparaging title introduces a shockingly brief survey of over a thousand years of work, including some outstanding pieces, beginning with such Saxon masterpieces as the Angel Blessing, of c.800 at Breedon-on-the-Hill, and the early eleventh-century Christ at Barnack, *(235)*. These are beautifully expressive pieces, rounded in form, gentle and serene in expression, with that feeling of compassion which is so unexpected a feature of Saxon art, and which lasted into the twelfth century with the Lazarus reliefs at Chichester, *(101)*. Even the Daglingworth crucifixion of c.1050 *(236)*, has a similar serenity in startling contrast to the tortured crucifixes of the later middle ages.

Medieval carvings were ruthlessly violated at the Reformation, but some exquisite work has somehow survived like the fourteenth-century ivory diptych leaf *(243)*, and the alabaster of John the Baptist before

Herod, *(242)* now in the Victoria and Albert Museum. There are Nottingham alabasters in churches too, and one of the Virgin and Child, c.1470, in Worcester Cathedral, is still in its original painted wooden case. More typically, what was once a more supple and delicate fourteenth-century version of the same subject at Blunham, Bedfordshire, has had the heads knocked off both the figures by some imbecile iconoclast. There is a moving wooden Christus of 1518 in Bangor Cathedral, known as the Mostyn Christ, and it is sobering to think that such fine work in stone, alabaster, ivory and wood was once commonplace in our churches.

For some centuries after the Reformation, most British sculpture was secular, with such rare exceptions as the figures from the Inigo Jones screen at Winchester (page 28), and the Annunciation relief of 1775 by William Collins in the Beauchamp Chapel at St Mary, Warwick.

Victorian statuary was not up to the standard of other aspects of the ecclesiastical revival, and most of it, however technically accomplished, is hard and mechanical. It is perhaps stretching a point to include it here, but a much higher level is attained by Jules Destréez in his 'etched' marble scenes in the Albert Memorial Chapel, Windsor, c.1870, really enjoyable work which makes an admirable setting for Gilbert's later Duke of Clarence Memorial. Moving into the present century, Eric Gill's Stations of the Cross in Westminster Cathedral, 1913–18, *(244)* are among his finest works, and quite outstanding in their period.

Recently much good work has been done. Stylistically modern sculpture is so varied that one either has to comment at great length, or, as here, not at all. Among the best pieces are the beautiful Madonna and Child of 1944 at St Matthew, Northampton, by Henry Moore *(247)* another treatment of the same subject by Barbara Hepworth, at St Ives, Cornwall, and three notable Epsteins: Lazarus at New College, Oxford, St Michael and Lucifer at Coventry Cathedral, and Christ in Majesty on the organ case at Llandaff Cathedral, *(246)*. A striking large-scale piece, typical of the church's present sociological preoccupations, is John Hayward's Christ the Worker at Blackburn Cathedral, and there are some excellent pieces at the new Roman Catholic cathedrals at Liverpool and Clifton. In Coventry Cathedral there was also a revival of the idea of wall texts, handsomely carved in stone by Ralph Beyer *(245)*.

Musical Instruments

Organs are complex musical instruments, a description of which is alike beyond the scope of this volume and the skill of its author. Organ cases, however, have always been decorative, and there are some fine examples of all periods from the sixteenth century onwards, as well as a great many large organs which overwhelm small churches which should never have had to house them. Organ cases follow the general development of the furnishings of the various periods. The earliest survivor, made at the beginning of the sixteenth century with linenfold panelling, is at Old Radnor *(248)*. It was lucky to survive both Reformation and Commonwealth. Tewkesbury Abbey has an organ of about 1580, with embossed tin pipes, formerly at Oxford, and there is a beautiful organ of about 1600 at Stanford, Northamptonshire, probably from London. Bilton, Warwickshire, has an organ case of 1635, brought from St John's College, Cambridge. That is probably all that survive from before the Civil War.

The Restoration saw reintroductions on a considerable scale in the richer churches, and many cases of the late seventeenth and eighteenth centuries are more open to baroque and rococo fashions than most other English church furnishings. The great organ builders of the late seventeenth century were Renatus Harris and Bernard Schmidt, often anglicised as Father Smith, and quite a lot of their work can still be found in London churches, and in Schmidt's case, Cambridge too. The Tiverton organ of 1696 has a typically elegant baroque case *(249)*. A famous eighteenth-century name is Snetzler, and several of his instruments survive, especially in Norfolk.

Fashion decreed classical and gothic organ cases in turn; Chippendale, indeed, made designs for gothic chamber organs. St John, Waterloo Road, London, has a typical early nineteenth-century classical organ case, *(250)* and among Victorian gothic examples, Scott's at Chester Cathedral, 1876, *(251)* is one of his best works, though Victorian organs in general tend to be too large. Modern organs often make a great display of pipes, and there are pleasing designs in a number of places, like Coventry Cathedral, by Sir Basil Spence, *(10)* St Martin-le-Grand, York, by G.G. Pace, and Llandaff Cathedral, also by Pace, *(239)* where it spans the nave on giant arches, and is adorned not only with Epstein's Christ in Majesty, but also with some pre-Raphaelite figures from the previous organ.

Many country churches had barrel organs in the early nineteenth century, a few of which, attractively designed, still survive.

229 Right Tarrant Rushton, Dorset: acoustic jars, late medieval

230 Centre Shipdham, Norfolk: commandment board (originally tympanum) 1630

231 Below left Wells Cathedral: clock, c.1390

232 Below right Blythburgh, Suffolk: clock jack, 1682

233 Top left Ruislip,
Middlesex: dole cupboard,
1697

234 Above left St Martin-
cum-Gregory, York: dole
cupboard, early eighteenth
century

235 Far left Barnack,
Huntingdonshire: Christ in
Majesty, early eleventh
century

236 Left Daglingworth,
Gloucestershire: crucifix,
c. 1050

237 Right Bristol Cathedral:
candelabra, brass, late
fifteenth century

238 Top left Wymondham Abbey, Norfolk: chandelier, brass, 1712

239 Above left Tetbury, Gloucestershire: gasolier, Victorian

240 Left Rowlstone, Herefordshire: candle bracket, fifteenth century

241 Right Victoria and Albert Museum: the Gloucester Candlestick, gilt bell-metal, c.1110

242 Left Victoria and Albert
Museum: John the Baptist before
Herod, alabaster, fifteenth century

243 Above Victoria and Albert
Museum: leaf of a diptych, ivory,
fourteenth century

244 Right Westminster Cathedral: Stations of the Cross,
Jesus falls a second time, 1913–18, by Eric Gill

245 Below Coventry Cathedral: wall text, c.1962, by Ralph
Beyer

The widespread destruction of organs following the Order in Council of 1644 meant that after the Restoration most churches lacked the means of accompanying the singing of metrical psalms, and only the wealthier ones could afford new organs. So in many cases, amateur orchestral players were accommodated alongside the choir, often in west galleries, and their instruments sometimes still exist, for the custom survived well into the nineteenth century. The Torrington Diaries shed a contemporary light on the custom: 'At Botsford (Bottesford Leicestershire) I . . . found that the Psalmody there was on the decline, yet it was tolerably supported by 2 Bassoons, a Clarinet, and a German Flute. Nothing should be more encouraged, as drawing both Young and Old to Church, than Church Melody, tho' the Profligacy and Refinement of the age has abandon'd and ridiculed it.'[120] A painting by Thomas Webster in the Victoria and Albert Museum shows the village choir and orchestra at Bow Brickhill, Buckinghamshire, and a good collection of instruments can be seen at the St Peter Hungate Museum, Norwich, and there are others at Seagrave, Leicestershire, and Ridlington, Rutland. Barking, Suffolk, retains its serpent of about 1830; Biddenham, Bedfordshire, has the clarinet used by the parish clerk from 1821 to 1861, and Briston, Norfolk, has a metal 'cello.

Vamping Horns, acting as a sort of megaphone for the humming of the choir leader, were sometimes used as an encouragement to congregational singing in the eighteenth century where there was no organ or band, and these still exist at Braybrooke and Harrington, Northamptonshire, Haversham, Buckinghamshire, Charing, Kent, Willoughton, Lincolnshire, Ashurst, Sussex, East Leake, Nottinghamshire, and, surprisingly, at Whitby, North Riding, where there are two, attached to the pulpit. Pitchpipes were used to pitch the note for unaccompanied singing, and there is one at Burmarsh, Kent. A medieval cantor's desk, with a snatch of plainsong notation painted on it, can be seen at Ranworth, Norfolk.

Pax

The pax, a small board on which the Kiss of Peace was given, was a piece of medieval furniture which has now all but disappeared. There is a fifteenth-century example from Sandon, Essex, in the Victoria and Albert Museum; it has a crucifixion scene painted on it.

Sextons' Wheels

Sextons' wheels were used in the middle ages to determine the beginning of voluntary fasts in honour of the Virgin Mary, and consist of two disks of iron connected to a hub suspended from a handle. Only two now exist, at Long Stratton, Norfolk, and nearby at Yaxley, Suffolk. The method of use is described in a sixteenth-century poem by Thomas Kirchmeyer translated thus into contemporary English:

Besides they keepe our Lady's fast at sundrie solmne tymes
Instructed by a turning wheel, or as the lot assignes.
For every Sexton hath a wheele that hangeth for the viewe,
Markte round about with certaine dayes, unto the Virgin dewe
Which holy through ye yere are kept, from whence hangs down a thred,
Of length sufficient to be toucht, and to be handled.
Now when that any Servant of our Ladyes commeth here,
And seekes to have some certain day by lotte for to appeere,
The Sexten turnes the wheel about, and bids the stander by
To hold the thred whereby he doth the time and season try:
Wherein he ought to keep his fast, and every other thing,
That decent is or longing to our Ladies worshipping.[121]

Shrines and Reliquaries

Most shrines were destroyed at the Reformation; however, a few can still be seen, those of St Frideswide at Oxford Cathedral, and St Alban being painstaking reconstructions from fragments of Purbeck marble. At Whitchurch Canonicorum, Dorset, is the shrine of St Wite, and there are several at St Davids Cathedral, including that of St David himself. But the most beautiful without doubt is the shrine of St Thomas Cantilupe at Hereford Cathedral, made about 1287. The base, with lively carvings of Knights Templar whose Provincial Grand Master the saint was, survives practically intact.

Medieval reliquaries rarely remain in churches, most now being in museums. They are often small house-shaped objects, delicately chased or enamelled. One at Shipley, Sussex, is made of wood with copper and Limoges enamel decoration, *(252)* and the British Museum has an interesting one made of silver about 1308, *(253)*. A much plainer fourteenth-century one at Revesby, Lincolnshire, is made of pottery. A fifteenth-century cupboard in Chichester Cathedral is thought to have been for storing reliquaries. A good place to see modern shrines and reliquaries is Westminster Cathedral.

Staircases and Ladders

Stone staircases are architectural features, but wooden ones may be justifiably classed as furnishings along with ladders. Often overlooked, they can be interesting period pieces. The bell-chamber ladder at Wysall, Nottinghamshire could well be as old as the thirteenth century, and there are medieval tower stairs at North Ockenden, Essex, and Brabourne, Kent, while the cage to the tower stairs at Stratton, Dorset, has early Tudor linenfold panels. There are Jacobean tower ladders with balusters at Hogsthorpe, Lincolnshire, and Clapham, Bedfordshire. Stairs to Georgian galleries are often plain but generally beautifully constructed, and among Victorian examples, three really excellent spiral staircases can be picked out: in the towers of Harting, Sussex, 1852, and Ryton, Co Durham, 1886, and one leading from the Chapter House to the Lady Loft at Ripon Cathedral, put in during the 1860s by Sir Gilbert Scott.

Stucco

Decorative work in fine plaster known as stucco was fashionable on ceilings and occasionally on walls in important houses from Tudor times until the early nineteenth century. It is found much less commonly in churches, but some work of great beauty and interest was produced. The earliest of any importance is to be found in the ambitious nave ceilings of two Somerset churches, Axbridge, 1636, and East Brent 1637, where Jacobean motifs are combined freely with gothic ones such as lozenges cusped to form quatrefoils. A little later, in 1639, Sir Christopher Wren's father, who was rector of East Knoyle, Wiltshire, chose to decorate his chancel with plaster reliefs of biblical scenes and texts framed by strapwork, an offence which contributed to the loss of his living during the Puritan ascendancy. However, disapproval of his action did not extend to destruction of the work, which can still be enjoyed.

After the Restoration, plasterwork became much more sophisticated, as prodigious in design and execution as contemporary woodcarving, and as full of swags and garlands. Typical of the best work of the time are the ceilings of 1676 at Ingestre, of 1678 in the Chapel of Arbury Hall, Warwickshire, of 1690 at King Charles the Martyr, Tunbridge Wells, and of c.1694

at Trinity College Chapel, Oxford (*1*). Two simpler ceilings of high quality are at Willen, Buckinghamshire, 1680, and in the Arlington Pew at Euston, Suffolk, 1676. In a totally different style, Wren used plaster for the ambitious fan vault of his gothic church of St Mary Aldermary, London, in 1682, and another prettily detailed plaster fan vault was designed by Henry Keene for his church at Hartwell, Buckinghamshire, c.1753.

Most eighteenth century stucco work is more refined than its predecessors, perhaps losing some of its character in the process. An early example is the ceiling of the perfect early Georgian village church at Gayhurst, Buckinghamshire, which is transitional in spirit between Stuart exuberance and late eighteenth century delicacy. The domical vault of 1751 at Berkley, Somerset, has a complicated design of acanthus and scrolly foliage, but the fruit and flowers of the previous century have gone. More typical of the change of mood, though, is St James, Whitehaven, of c.1753, where a largely plain ceiling is relieved by two charming roundels, one of the Virgin, the other of the Ascension. Binley, Warwickshire, of 1771–3, is in the late Adam manner, though the architect is unknown. As well as a very restrained plaster ceiling, there is stucco decoration on the walls with medallions and draped cords, exquisite in the 'chaste' style just coming into fashion in country houses.

Plaster rib vaults occur occasionally as at Tetbury, Gloucestershire, by Francis Hiorn, 1781, and Chilworth, Hampshire, 1812, and a ceiling of 1821 by Francis Goodwin, decorated to look like a late medieval pendant vault, is to be found in the nave of St Matthew, Walsall.

Sword and Mace Rests

Town churches, attended by civic dignitaries in their official capacities, often provided rests for ceremonial swords and maces. Dated examples begin in 1610 with the sword rest at St Philip and St Jacob, Bristol, and they were used into the nineteenth century. The two eighteenth century examples illustrated, (*255, 256*) from St Stephen, Bristol, and All Saints, Worcester, show how good the craftsmanship could be, and men of the calibre of William Edney were sometimes employed to make them. The best places to see them are in the churches of London, Bristol, Norwich, Worcester and Gloucester, though there are others elsewhere.

Tiles

Many parish churches had plain stone or earth floors in the Middle Ages and often much later. The Hon. John Byng complains in the Torrington Diaries about the 'dirt floor' at Kyme, Lincolnshire[122] in the eighteenth century. Tiles, however, were commonly used in the sanctuary, and for other parts of richer churches. There are a few outstanding examples of tile mosaic. In the Trinity Chapel at Canterbury Cathedral is the Opus Alexandrinum pavement laid down about 1220 before the shrine of Becket. It consists of a complicated geometrical pattern executed in small marble tesserae, mostly red, white and purple, the abstract design giving a superficially almost Islamic impression. Near it are some large oolitic limestone discs with designs cut out and filled in with red mastic. Perhaps about the same time or a little earlier is the mosaic tiling at Byland Abbey, North Riding, mostly in yellow and green, with tesserae in a variety of shapes – square, round, lozenge, triangular, elliptical and petal, but combined to make clear, simple geometrical designs *(257)*. Similar tiling of a later date has been excavated at Warden Abbey, Bedfordshire. About 1330, Prior Crauden's Chapel at Ely was given a tile mosaic pavement with geometrical designs, but also plants and animals, and, in the middle, Adam and Eve with the Serpent. The colours are brown, yellow and green, and some of the figure tiles are also line-impressed. The Feretory and Presbytery pavements at Westminster Abbey are the most spectacular examples, however, made about 1268 by Italian craftsmen in Cosmati work with red and green porphyry and glass mosaic. Again the patterns are geometrical. The presbytery pavement was originally signed in bronze by 'Odericus Romanus'.

More often, rectangular pottery tiles were laid, and patterns on them were contrived in three ways. One was inlay, a method particularly associated with Chertsey, where the pattern was stamped on the tile, and the depressions then filled with a pale clay that fired white or yellow. The second method, particularly associated with Penn, Buckinghamshire, is

248 Below left Old Radnor: organ case, early sixteenth century

249 Below right Tiverton, Devon: organ, 1696, by Bernard Schmidt (Father Smith)

250 Above right St John, Waterloo Road,
London: organ c. 1825

251 Right Chester Cathedral: organ screen and
case, 1876, by Sir Gilbert Scott

252 Left Shipley, Sussex: reliquary, wood, copper and Limoges enamel, thirteenth century

253 Below left British Museum: reliquary, silver, c.1308

254 Right Highnam, Gloucestershire: heater case, c.1850, by Henry Woodyer

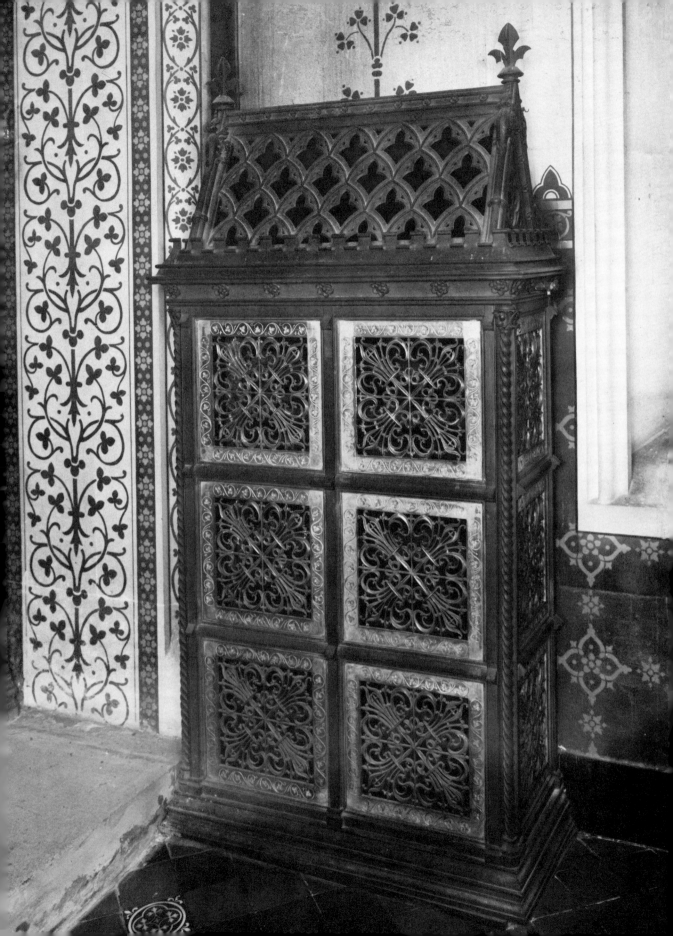

255 Left St Stephen, Bristol: sword rest, wrought iron, early eighteenth century
256 Above All Saints, Worcester: sword rest, wrought iron, eighteenth century

257 Right Byland Abbey, Yorkshire: mosaic tile pavement, early thirteenth century

258 Centre right Gloucester Cathedral: floor tile, c.1350

259 Bottom right Westminster Abbey: Chapter House, floor tiles, 1253–58

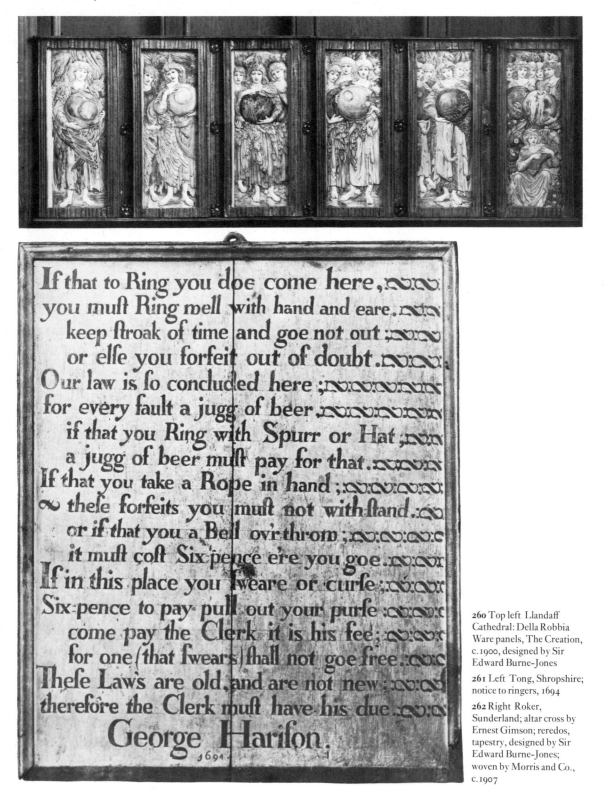

If that to Ring you doe come here,
you muſt Ring well with hand and eare.
keep ſtroak of time and goe not out;
or elſe you forfeit out of doubt.
Our law is ſo concluded here;
for every fault a jugg of beer.
if that you Ring with Spurr or Hat;
a jugg of beer muſt pay for that.
If that you take a Rope in hand;
theſe forfeits you muſt not withſtand.
or if that you a Bell ovr throw;
it muſt coſt Six pence ere you goe.
If in this place you ſweare or curſe;
Six pence to pay pull out your purſe
come pay the Clerk it is his fee;
for one that ſwears ſhall not goe free.
Theſe Laws are old, and are not new;
therefore the Clerk muſt have his due.
George Hariſon.
1694.

260 Top left Llandaff
Cathedral: Della Robbia
Ware panels, The Creation,
c. 1900, designed by Sir
Edward Burne-Jones

261 Left Tong, Shropshire;
notice to ringers, 1694

262 Right Roker,
Sunderland; altar cross by
Ernest Gimson; reredos,
tapestry, designed by Sir
Edward Burne-Jones;
woven by Morris and Co.,
c. 1907

printing, where the tiles were stamped with a die dipped in white slip. The third method was to make designs in relief; the Bawsey tilery is thought to have been the most important source of these tiles. All three types can be found in a wide variety of locations. The best places to see medieval tiles in quantity are Westminster Abbey *(259)*, Gloucester Cathedral *(258)* and Bangor Cathedral, but some smaller churches like Besselsleigh, Berkshire, Brook, Kent, and Acton Burnell, Shropshire, also have extensive displays. At Great Malvern Priory there are fifteenth-century floor tiles and wall tiles in red with yellow inlay, a revival of a technique by then regarded as old-fashioned.

Between the Reformation and the Gothic Revival there is little to report, only the tiles of 1622 in the Willoughby Chapel at Wilne, Derbyshire. Most floors of importance laid in that period were not of tiles, but of black and white marble, and where they have been spared they are still a pleasing feature of several cathedrals and a number of Stuart and Georgian churches.

The revival of encaustic tiles in Victorian times is particularly associated with the firms of Minton and Maw. They occur very widely, and have been severely criticized for their harshness and shininess which can destroy the atmosphere of a simple village church. Nevertheless, they are gradually mellowing with wear, and may come to be more kindly regarded in time. In some cases, like Ingham, Norfolk, tiles have designs in medieval fashion, and these are already very pleasing and not in the least glaring. Such tiles, however, are usually best seen in Victorian churches where their strong contrasts of red and black or red and yellow are not obtrusive. The tiles at Lilley, Hertfordshire, c.1871, are unusual in consisting mostly of a gentle green colour.

Outstanding among Victorian tiles are the wall panels of Della Robbia Ware depicting the six days of creation from designs by Burne-Jones originally intended for glass, and given to Llandaff Cathedral about 1900 *(260)*.

The use of mosaic for floors was effectively revived by Einar Forseth in the Chapel of Unity, Coventry Cathedral.

Treadwheels

Though not items of furniture in the normally accepted sense, treadwheels were essential pieces of builders' equipment in any medieval church where stone had to be raised to a considerable height. Two medieval ones still exist, in the tower of Salisbury Cathedral, and at Beverley Minster.

Watching Lofts

Watching lofts were provided at popular shrines in the Middle Ages to keep an eye on the flow of pilgrims, and to prevent the theft of relics or precious offerings. Two examples of c.1500 survive, at Oxford Cathedral for the shrine of St Frideswide, and at St Albans Cathedral. Both are excellent pieces of carpentry bearing a close likeness to the screens of the same period.

Wigstands

Wigstands are occasionally found as pulpit accessories, and there is one at Stowmarket, Suffolk, dated 1675. The problem arose when a surplice needed to be donned over a full-bottomed wig, and at first the only convenient way to do it was to remove the wig first. Archbishop Tillotson, however, solved the problem towards the end of the century by wearing his surplice open at the front, a practice soon followed by a number of his clergy, and amazingly still employed in some Oxford and Cambridge Colleges today.[123]

Notes

Chapter 1 – Introduction

1 Quoted by Pevsner, The Buildings of England, *Buckinghamshire*, p.288

2 Trollope, writing in 1860, described the church at Framley, where his hero, Rev. Mark Robarts was incumbent, as 'but a mean, ugly building, having been erected about a hundred years since, when all churches then built were made to be mean and ugly.' (*Framley Parsonage*, The World's Classics edition, p.11.) Though Trollope's tongue is always to some extent in his cheek, he has nevertheless summed up accurately enough how ecclesiastical 1860 felt about ecclesiastical 1760. It was a view that persisted remarkably late: 'The eighteenth century produced little that was edifying in ecclesiology' (J.C. Wall, *Porches and Fonts*, p. 335, 1912.)

Chapter 2 – The Porch

3 The purpose of the rare stone benches on the exteriors of some churches, like Patricio, Brecon, is uncertain, though they could be connected with open-air preaching.

4 Among early porches are twelfth-century ones at Malmesbury Abbey, Sherborne Abbey and Southwell Minster. Even in the thirteenth century, parochial porches, like the ones at West Walton, Norfolk, Great Massingham, Norfolk, and Barnack, Huntingdonshire, are rare.

5 Now belonging to St Peter Hungate Museum, but, at the time of writing, displayed in Norwich Castle Museum. It is said that it is to be returned in due course to St Gregory.

Chapter 3 – Fonts

6 J.M. Slader, *The Churches of Devon*, p. 29.

7 Attributed to the eleventh century or earlier are fonts of some interest at Little Maplestead, Essex; Alfold and Thursley, Surrey; All Saints, Bingley, West Riding; Llanfilo, Brecon; Llantarnam, Gwent; Potterne, Wiltshire; and Little Billing, Northamptonshire. Other adaptations of Roman stones of various sorts are at Great Salkeld and Over Denton, Cumberland; Hexham Priory, Northumberland; Kenchester, Herefordshire; Wroxeter, Shropshire; and West Mersea, Essex.

8 Proctor and Frere, *A New History of the Book of Common Prayer*, p. 143.

9 At Tangmere, Sussex, the font is said to have ridges like the joins in a wooden barrel font.

10 Could such metal strips have been an alternative to the clumsier cables on wooden fonts? Or are the prototypes all-metal fonts now vanished?

11 The other five are at Oxenhall, Sandhurst, Siston, Tidenham, and Gloucester Cathedral (originally at Lancaut). A few much simpler lead fonts were made at about the same time, like the ones at Long Wittenham, Berkshire, and Barnetby, Lincolnshire.

12 The font at Dearham, Cumberland, is so explicitly like a capital that it could be an arcade capital put to a new use.

13 Among the best examples of traceried fonts are those at All Saints, Long Stanton, Cambridgeshire; Little Totham, Essex; Marwood, Leicestershire; St Martin, Stamford, Lincolnshire; and Bintree, Norfolk.

14 The Seven Sacraments are Baptism, the Mass, Confirmation, Marriage, Ordination, Penance, and Extreme Unction.

15 J.C. Wall; *Porches and Fonts*, p. 210.

16 Other excellent spired font covers are at Worlingworth, Suffolk; North Walsham, Norfolk; Takeley, Essex; Ewelme, Oxfordshire; Bradford Cathedral, Selby Abbey and Halifax, West Riding; St Andrew, Newcastle, and, a seventeenth-century example, St John, Newcastle.

17 The font at St Peter Mancroft has plain panels, originally with *paintings* of the Seven Sacraments, of which traces remain.

18 'Very characteristic of the period, but recently removed by someone with lack of knowledge' – W.G. Hoskins, in Collins *Guide to English Parish Churches*, p. 314. The author of the church guide hopes 'that antiquarians who have been hurt by its removal to its present position, will try to think kindly of the fact that this is primarily a place of worship, and a font fixed to the Altar rails is convenient neither for Baptism nor Communion.'

Chapter 4 – Congregational Seating

19 All the church guides tell us that this is the origin of the otherwise inexplicable expression, 'the weakest go to the wall'. If so, the proverb has certainly changed its meaning, for there is no obvious connection between providing seats for the infirm in church and the idea of abandoning them in time of danger.

20 Some bench ends at St Mary Haverfordwest, Pembrokeshire, are carved in a very similar style to those at East Budleigh, though they have poppy-heads.

21 Tintinhull 1511, Kingston 1522, Hartland 1530, Barwick 1533, Crowcombe 1534, Spaxton 1536, North Molton 1537, North Cadbury 1538, Thorn Falcon 1542, Affpuddle 1547, Chedzoy 1557, Milverton 1557, Trull 1560, Braunton 1560, Spaxton 1561, Braunton 1568, 1578, 1583, 1593, North Petherton 1596.

22 M.D. Anderson; *History and Imagery in British Churches*, p. 159. She cites the text of the Chester Plays as proof, and a misericord at Lincoln as an example. Other examples are the altarpiece in St Luke's Chapel, Norwich Cathedral, and an alabaster panel at Ripon Cathedral.

23 Flitwick, Marston Moreteaine, Streatley, Studham, Totternhoe, all Bedfordshire, and Great Hampden, Buckinghamshire.

24 Ecclesfield, West Riding, 1564, Otley, Yorkshire, 1582, Kirkburton, Yorkshire 1584, Hope, Derbyshire, now made into stall backs, 1587, Hockerton, Nottinghamshire 1599.

25 Charcoal braziers are illustrated in *English Church Furniture*, by Cox and Harvey; a few footwarmers survive; the Octagon Chapel at Bath was perhaps the first in which warmth was taken seriously. Parson Woodforde remarks in 1769: 'a handsome building, but not like a place of worship, there being fire-places, especially on each side of the altar, which I cannot think at all decent.' Most churchgoers in the winter continued to shiver, many still do.

26 Prejudice survived later than this. The box pews at Dennington, Suffolk, are fortunate to survive. In the late 1950s the then incumbent, a jovial, rotund figure, told me that he leaned hard on them at intervals in the hope of breaking them so that they could be removed. Alternatively, he felt it might be possible to make them presentable by painting them duck-egg blue and gold.

27 Even that model squire Sir Roger de Coverley permitted himself to doze occasionally, though the privilege was forbidden to everyone else. *Spectator*, 1711, quoted Carpenter, *Eighteenth Century Church and People*, p. 172.

28 J. Newman, *The Buildings of England: West Kent and the Weald*, p. 478.

29 Compare the screen at St Margaret Lothbury, London.

30 Sir N. Pevsner; *The Buildings of England: South Lancashire* pp. 90–1.

Chapter 5 – Other Nave Furniture

31 Previous writers on this subject are irritatingly coy. Francis Bond, in *Screens and Galleries*, p. 121 asserts the evidence for preaching from the rood-loft 'in at least two Devonshire parishes . . . till a comparatively recent date.' He gives no details. J.C. Cox, *Pulpits, Lecterns and Organs*, p. 28 says that there is evidence that the sermon was occasionally preached from the pulpitum: again no details given. An alternative theory, sometimes put forward, that the loft was used for gospel reading, is demolished by Cox and Harvey, *English Church Furniture*, pp. 94–96.

32 Pulpits which can be tentatively ascribed to this period are at Upper Winchendon, Buckinghamshire, Mellor, Cheshire (carved out of a single block of wood), Chivelstone, Devon (also carved out of a single block of wood), Weobley, Herefordshire (fragments), Higham, Kent, possibly Castle Acre, Norfolk, though it may have been made up from early screen panels, and Combe, Oxfordshire, probably 1395.

33 Proctor and Frere, *A New History of the Book of Common Prayer*, p. 39.

34 Cox and Harvey; *English Church Furniture*, p. 151.

35 A list, even of the finest Jacobean pulpits, would be tediously long. Here is a selection from among them of those whose dates are completely or almost certain: Rotherham 1604; Stoke d'Abernon 1620, Dinder (of stone, very exceptionally) 1621, Bishop's Waltham 1626, Wylye 1628, Clyffe Pypard 1629, Little Hadham 1633 (later made into a three-decker), Petton 1635, St Cuthbert, Wells, 1636, St Helen, Abingdon 1636, Shrivenham 1638, Great Baddow 1639.

36 Proctor and Frere; *A New History of the Book of Common Prayer*, p. 360.

37 J.C. Cox; *Pulpits. Lecterns and Organs* p. 92. Examples are, or were, at Magdalen College, Oxford 1617; Hollingbourne Kent, c.1650; Shalden, Hampshire, 1655, Portsmouth Cathedral 1693, Dunstable Priory 1732.

38 Henry Cobbe; *History of Luton Church*, 1899, p. 643.

39 Cox and Harvey, *English Church Furniture*, p. 159. For length of sermons in general, see J.C. Cox; *Pulpits, Lecterns and Organs*, p. 152. He also quotes an instance in Cornwall where the pulpit hour glass was removed to the parson's kitchen for use as an oven timer (p. 158).

40 They are at Chaddesden, Crich, Spondon and Taddington, Derbyshire, Walsall, Staffordshire, Ottringham and Paull, East Riding.

41 No distinction is made in this book between the two very similar alloys, brass and latten. Both are made primarily of copper and zinc, but latten has small quantities of other metals as well, and was a rather higher quality alloy.

42 Dated examples are St Gregory, Norwich 1496, Lowestoft 1504, Wiggenhall St Mary the Virgin 1518, Wrexham 1524. These enable approximate dates to be suggested for others of the same type.

43 W.G. Hoskins, *Midland England*, p. 27.

44 According to the bestiaries the pelican fed her young with blood from her own breast, which she is shown pecking. Hence she was a symbol of Christ's sacrifice.

Chapter 6 – Screens

45 There is a very similar screen in Trondheim Cathedral, which may have inspired the restorations.

46 They appear to be *in situ*. There is apparently documentary evidence, which I cannot trace, of a rood loft at Furneaux Pelham, Hertfordshire, in 1297.

47 Attleborough, Norfolk; Avebury and Hullavington, Wiltshire; Charlton-on-Otmoor, Oxfordshire; Marwood, Devon; Strensham, Worcestershire; Upper Sheringham, Norfolk and a number of other places like Kenton, Devon, and Edington, Wiltshire, where they have been restored from existing fragments. At Oakley, Bedfordshire, and Dennington, Suffolk, chapel screens retain their lofts. Others retain the loft floor, but not the parapet.

48 They include Llaneilian, Anglesey; Derwen and Llanrwst, Denbighshire; Llanderfel and Llanegryn, Merionethshire; Conwy, Clynnog Fawr, and Llanengan, Caernarvonshire; Llanelieu, Llanfilo, Merthyr Cynog and Patricio, Brecon; Cascob and Llananno, Radnorshire; Llangynog, Montgomery and (a fragment) Trelystan, Montgomeryshire; Bettws Newydd and Llangwm, Gwent.

49 For example Clynnog Fawr, Conwy, Gresford, Montgomery, Old Radnor, and Usk.

50 Vallance, *English Church Screens*, p. 54; Sir N. Pevsner; *The Buildings of England:South Devon*, pp. 27, 86; J.M. Slader; *The Churches of Devon*, p. 83.

51 C.f. the retables in Norwich Cathedral. The screen at Catfield, at present undergoing restoration, seems to be earlier than most of the others, unless the Castle Acre pulpit was originally part of a screen. At any rate, there is enough evidence to follow the tradition from the St Luke's Chapel retable of c.1380 through to the latter part of the fifteenth century.

52 A. Vallance; *English Church Screens*, p. 34. C.f. F. Bond; *Screens and Galleries*, p. 165, but most of the references he gives to fence screens seem in fact to refer to rood screens in churches which also had a pulpitum. The evidence seems to me to be far less than conclusive.

53 Sir N. Pevsner; *The Buildings of England: Cambridgeshire*, p. 108.

54 How can the removal of a medieval screen from a medieval church to make a vista be called restoration? Restoration of what? from what? to what? How sad that the protests of men of the sense and sensibility of Pugin and Morris were so often ignored!

55 Among undated screens of Elizabethan type may be cited Clophill, Bedfordshire, Clipston, Northamptonshire, and Mitton, West Riding. The striking screen at Holdenby, Northamptonshire came from Holdenby Hall.

56 Other fine screens of the first half of the seventeenth century are found at Hunsdon, Hertfordshire, Yarnton, Oxfordshire, Thurloxton, Somerset, and Slaidburn and Wakefield Cathedral, 1635, West Riding.

57 A. Vallance; *English Church Screens*, p.90, describes these screens as reflecting the days of Nell Gwynne and her sister courtesans 'with a riot of misapplied architectural details . . . and dexterous greengroceries in the manner of Grinling Gibbons'.

58 Significantly, Hawksmoor's Corinthian high altar reredos at Beverley has not survived.

59 John Harvey; *Mediaeval Craftsmen*, p. 181.

60 Obviously, as the rector would have held the key, abuse was still possible, but the gates were a strong hint that if people really had to indulge in cock-fighting in church, they could at least confine it to the nave. Such incidents help one to understand the fussiness of Archbishop Laud.

61 St Mary Redcliffe also has some good later iron gates and screens, possibly made by John Jones in 1756.

62 Sir N. Pevsner and I. Nairn; *The Buildings of England: Sussex*, p. 374.

63 Among the arms of Elizabeth I, those at Beckington, Somerset, of stone, are outstanding; others are at Tivetshall and Ludham, Norfolk, on tympana, Green's Norton, Northamptonshire 1592, Basingstoke, Hampshire, 1576.

Chapter 7 – Chancel Seating

64 Much Hadham, Hertfordshire, has two chairs of about 1400, but it is uncertain whether they are of ecclesiastical or secular origin. The Dunmow Flitch chair at Little Dunmow, Essex, is made up from fragments of thirteenth-century stalls.

65 One set, perhaps from Jervaulx Abbey, seems to have been divided among the churches of Leake, Aysgarth, Over Silton and Wensley. The dates 1519 and 1528 appear on them.

66 Interested readers should consult G.L. Remnant; *Catalogue of Misericords in Great Britain*; J.C.D. Smith, *A Guide to Church Woodcarvings*; and M.D. Anderson, *History and Imagery in British Churches*. This paragraph is based on Chapter 9 of Miss Anderson's book.

67 Quoted in Proctor and Frere; *A New History of the Book of Common Prayer*, p. 160. At Disserth, Radnorshire, there are post-Restoration box pews to the north and south of the altar, presumably for communicants, which suggests that Puritan customs sometimes died hard.

Chapter 8 – Eucharistic Furniture

68 At Duvillaun, an islet in Co Mayo, there is a tiny

oratory with what seems to be an outdoor congregational space attached to it. See Françoise Henry; *Irish Art*, pages 24ff.

69 At Llanpumpsaint, Carmarthenshire, there is a mensa with nine crosses.

70 Proctor and Frere, *A New History of the Book of Common Prayer*, p. 69.

71 A mid-eighteenth century table at Holy Trinity, Hull, has a carved retable as part of the composition, with reliefs of the communion vessels symmetrically displayed.

72 Gloucester Cathedral has two fine processional crosses on display, one by Omar Ramsden, 1922; the other by Leslie Durbin, 1959.

73 A latèr reredos at St Cuthbert, Wells, also depicts the Tree of Jesse.

74 The National Gallery of Scotland has a splendid example from Trinity Church, Edinburgh.

75 This paragraph is deeply indebted to Benedict Read: 'The Work of Rossetti and the Pre-Raphaelites at Llandaff' 1975, lecture printed in the 43rd Annual Report, 1975–6, of the Friends of Llandaff Cathedral.

76 Since cloth fabrics in general are not covered in this volume, a brief note here may not be out of place. Winchester College Chapel has a Flemish tapestry of c.1500. There is a seventeenth-century tapestry dorsal at All Saints, Wigan, and a dorsal with matching frontal of the same period at Coltishall, Norfolk. Among a number of surviving tapestries by Morris and Burne-Jones may be cited those at Eton College Chapel, Brockhampton-by-Ross, Herefordshire, and Exeter College, Oxford. Wormington, Gloucestershire has curtains designed by Morris. Lancing College Chapel, Sussex, has three large tapestries of the 1930s, by Lady Chilston, and Manchester Cathedral has tapestries of 1957 by Austin Wright and Theo Moorman. Hereford Cathedral has large tapestries of 1979, designed by John Piper and woven in Africa, hanging in the transept.

77 Quoted by Cox and Harvey, *English Church Furniture*, p. 18.

78 For example Thorpe, Tissington and West Hallam, Derbyshire, Pilton, Devon, and Patricio, Brecon.

79 Classical fashions in the late eighteenth and early nineteenth centuries are rarely reflected in communion rails, but there are Roman Doric balusters at St James, Whitehaven, c.1753, and an iron rail in the Grecian style at St Matthew, Brixton, 1822.

80 So did Salvin, 1848–9, but the communion rail can hardly be so early.

81 Parson Cole, in the mid-eighteenth century ordered the table at Waterbeach 'to be set under the Middle East Window, it being before in the middle of the chancel.' (Quoted by S.C. Carpenter, *Eighteenth Century Church and People*, p. 181.)

82 Sir N. Pevsner, *The Buildings of England: York & the East Riding*, p. 176.

83 Francis Bond; *The Chancel of English Churches*, pp. 233f. The quotation from the St Mary Redcliffe archives below comes from the same source, and the first three paragraphs of this section are greatly indebted to Chapter IX of Bond's book.

84 Wardour Castle Chapel has a number of pieces which are unusual in England to say the least, including two censers, an altar vase, sanctuary lamp and holy water bucket, all of the eighteenth century. See Sir N. Pevsner, *The Buildings of England: Wiltshire*, p. 553.

Chapter 9 – Wall-Painting, Glass and Mosaics

85 Quoted by Jean Hubert, *Romanesque Art*, in the *Larousse Encyclopaedia of Byzantine and Medieval Art*, p. 261.

86 For an impression of what a medieval nave looked like complete with its paintings, one should see Little Kimble, Buckinghamshire, c.1300, and Pickering, North Riding, c.1450, the first a small village church, the other a sizeable town church.

87 See A. Caiger-Smith, *English Medieval Mural Paintings*, p. 57.

88 See especially St Matthew 24:29–31; 25:31,34,41,46.

89 A. Caiger-Smith, *English Medieval Mural Paintings*, p. 38.

90 This method is still used in Eastern Orthodoxy, and there are recent examples in the Serbian Orthodox Church in London.

91 *The Buildings of England: Sussex*, pp. 158–9, where it also stands in quotation marks.

92 Imagery had in fact tentatively reappeared as early as about 1600 in the poorly-preserved Last Supper in the sedilia at Maids Moreton, Buckinghamshire.

93 Hans Feibusch has done some interesting work; for example at Goring-by-Sea, Sussex, in 1954, at All Hallows, Wellingborough, 1952, and at St John, Preston, 1956.

94 Quoted by John Harries, *Discovering Stained Glass*, p. 16; source not given. Culmer's precarious position must have been sorely tempting to any bystander who did not share his iconoclastic inclinations.

95 Examples of grisaille glass can be seen, *inter alia*, at Ashbourne, Derbyshire, Hereford Cathedral, North Canon, Herefordshire, Salisbury Cathedral, Selling, Kent, and Stanton Harcourt, Oxfordshire.

96 Other good figure glass of c.1300 or earlier can be seen at Beverley Minster (east window); Chetwode, Buckinghamshire; Dewsbury, West Riding; East Harling, Norfolk; Madley, Herefordshire; Saxlingham, Norfolk; West Horsley, Surrey; and White Notley, Essex. There is some very fine glass from French churches at

Twycross, Leicestershire, and Rivenhall, Essex.

97 John Harvey, *The Perpendicular Style*, p. 90.

98 The most interesting medieval glass in the parish churches of York is to be found at All Saints, Pavement, c.1370; St Denys, Walmgate, c.1370; All Saints, North Street, c.1420; St Michael Spurriergate, c.1430; St Martin-le-Grand, c.1440, and Holy Trinity Goodramgate, c.1470.

99 For this paragraph see Ben Johnson's article on stained glass on pp. 58–67 of *The Buildings of England: York & the East Riding*. The St William window in York Minster has 105 scenes, the Apocalypse window has 81. The south chancel aisle windows at Great Malvern Priory originally had 72 scenes.

100 Not everyone would agree. E. Liddell Armitage, *Stained Glass*, p. 51, describes the Mary and Martha window at University College as follows: 'In the top centre tracery the Arms are those of Dudley and in the two smaller, rather rectangular traceries are what appear to be extracts from some family photograph album. This three light window is the apotheosis of vulgarity. If it were not for the halo round Christ's head it would be impossible to tell that this was a religious picture at all, and as it is the right-hand light would be very appropriate in a wayside hostel.'

101 As Liddell Armitage is when he describes the use of enamel as 'an artistic poison . . . which killed practically every aesthetic faculty the craftsmen of the period might inherently have possessed.' (*Stained Glass*, p.53.)

102 For example Nantwich, Cheshire, 1876; Youlgreave, Derbyshire, 1893; North Petherton, Somerset, 1896; Stockton-on-Teme, Shropshire, 1876; Leighton Buzzard, Bedfordshire; Wakefield Cathedral, and above all Hucknall Torkard, Nottinghamshire, where there are 25 of his windows.

103 Good representative selections of Victorian glass can be seen in many churches, like Alnwick, Northumberland (Clayton & Bell, Bagulay, Lavers Barraud & Westlake, Burlisson and Grylls, Atkinson, Powell, Ward & Hughes); Cranbourne, Berkshire (Morris, Kempe, Powell, Clayton & Bell, Hardman, O'Connor); Tavistock (Morris, Kempe, Fouracre, Dixon, Wailes, Ward and Hughes, Powell, Mayer of Munich, Bacon, Clayton & Bell); Doncaster (Hardman, Ward and Hughes, Wailes, Capronnier of Brussels, O'Connor, Clayton & Bell); Ecclesfield, West Riding (Hedgeland, Wailes, Hardman, Heaton Butler & Bayne, Kempe, Dixon). Art Nouveau glass tends to be disappointing, and the only important contributions seem to be Walter Crane's of 1891 at Christ Church, Streatham, and a window by Rosencrantz, 1896, at Wickhambreux, Kent.

104 Where is it now? Tyneham church is in the military area and is boarded up. Names to look for in the period c.1910–1950 include Nuttgens, Douglas Strachan, A.K. Nicholson and Louis Davis.

105 John Piper, Margaret Traherne, Lawrence Lee, Geoffrey Clarke, Keith New, Einar Forseth.

106 Excellent modern glass occurs in many places; among the best is the following: Tudeley, Kent, by Chagall, 1967; St Peter, Hall Green, Birmingham, by Tristan Ruhlmann, 1964; St Mark, Sheffield, by H.J. Stammers, c.1963. The best of Evie Hone's glass outside Eton is perhaps at St Luke, Wallsend, Northumberland, 1922 and All Hallows, Wellingborough, 1955. There is a good deal of Piper-Reyntiens glass including Totternhoe, Bedfordshire; All Hallows, Wellingborough; Eton College Chapel; Marden, Kent, (designed by Reyntiens); Nutfield, Oxfordshire; St Mark, Sheffield, and Llandaff Cathedral.

Chapter 10 – Memorials to the Dead

107 Readers interested in pursuing this subject are referred to the full bibliography in Lloyd Laing, *The Archaeology of Late Celtic Britain and Ireland* (Methuen, 1975).

108 The effigy is supposed to date from c.1100, and so not to be Losinga's. But if it is not his, whose can it be? He became bishop in 1091, and transferred the see from Thetford in 1094. Did he also transfer the bones of his predecessor? Or did he commission the effigy during his lifetime? Or was it merely a bit old-fashioned when it was made?

109 The contract for the Green tomb, dated 1419, survives, giving the names of the carvers, Thomas Prentys and Robert Sutton, and the price, £40.

110 For example, Colonel Rudhall, 1651, at Ross-on-Wye, Herefordshire; Sir Hatton and Lady Fermor, 1662, possibly by Pierre Besnier, at Easton Neston, Northamptonshire; Sir Thomas Wendy, 1673, at Haslingfield, Cambridgeshire; Sir John Poley at Boxted, Suffolk. He died in 1638, but his monument must be about 25 years later at least.

111 Others of this rare kind are at Burford, Shropshire, 1588, by Melchior Salabuss, Besford, Worcestershire, 1605, and Appleby Castle, 1646. See the appropriate volumes of the *Buildings of England* for details.

112 The best collection of medieval brasses is at Cobham, Kent, where there are 17, ranging in date from c.1310 to 1529. For very late brasses, one should go to Llanrwst, Denbighshire, where there are six of between 1620 and 1671.

113 Sir N. Pevsner, *The Buildings of England: Sussex*, p. 638.

114 Outstanding, too, are Sir William and Lady Villiers, 1711, at Brooksby, Leicestershire, by Thomas Green of Camberwell; Richard Ladbroke, 1730, at Reigate, Surrey, by Joseph Rose the Elder; and 1st Earl Fitzwilliam, 1719, by James Fisher, at Maulden, Bedfordshire.

115 Pevsner (*Buildings of England: Buckinghamshire*, p. 228) questions the attribution to Roubiliac on the grounds that he was not in England at the time it was made, but pertinently asks who can have made it.

116 See also his monuments to Edward Eliot, 1722, at St Germans, Cornwall; the Duke of Kent, 1740, at Flitton, Bedfordshire; Sir William Foley, 1743, at Great Witley, Worcestershire; 1st Earl of Harborough, 1732, at Stapleford, Leicestershire, and 2nd and 3rd Dukes of Beaufort, 1754, at Badminton, Gloucestershire.

117 Britton's *Cathedral Antiquities*; Lichfield, p. 51.

Chapter 11 – Miscellany

118 Rev B.J. Armstrong, *A Norfolk Diary*, edited by his grandson, Rev H.B.J. Armstrong, pp. 27–8.

119 Joyce Godber; *History of Bedfordshire*, p. 158.

120 Quoted by S.C. Carpenter, *Eighteenth Century Church and People*, p. 177. Two excellent articles on this subject by F.C. Hamlyn, were published in the *Bedfordshire Magazine*: Vol.1, p. 257 (1948) 'Psalm-Singing in Bedfordshire'; Vol.III, p. 99 (1951) 'In Quires and Places where they Sing – The Gallery Musicians of Bedfordshire.'

121 I am indebted to the article by Rev W. Cummings in the Long Stratton church guide for this information, taken in turn from an article of 1884 in the *Norfolk Journal of Archaeology* by Rev W.H. Sewell, then Vicar of Yaxley.

122 I am not certain whether this refers to North Kyme or South Kyme.

123 See S.C. Carpenter, *Eighteenth Century Church and People*, p. 29, note.

Select Bibliography

The Buildings of England (Penguin, 46 volumes, 1951–74; revised editions appearing at intervals) edited and largely written by Sir Nikolaus Pevsner, though uneven in quality, are in a class of their own: such indispensable guides to the traveller and works of reference to the student that it is amazing how people coped without them. At the time of going to press the Buildings of Wales have only just begun to appear. The publications of the Royal Commission on Ancient and Historic Monuments (Wales) (and the RCHM England) are limited in their terms of reference. Ten Welsh volumes have so far been published (1911–64). The earlier publications are now seriously inadequate. Within their period the later volumes are better, and the most recent, three volumes devoted to Caernarvonshire, are excellent. Breconshire, Cardiganshire, Glamorgan and Gwent are still unpublished.

Other excellent general works of reference include the following:

Oxford Dictionary of the Christian Church (2nd edn., 1974)
Oxford History of English Art (9 volumes published 1949–78; 2 forthcoming)
Oxford Companion to Art (1970)
Oxford Companion to the Decorative Arts (1975)
A Dictionary of Liturgy and Worship, ed. J.G. Davies, 1972

More specific works, some concerned more with the background than with furniture and decoration directly, include the following:

Addleshaw, G.W.O. and Etchell, The Architectural Setting of Anglican Worship, 1948
Anderson, M.D., History and Imagery in British Churches (1971)
Anson, Peter F., Fashions in Church Furnishing, 1840–1940 (2nd edn., 1965)
Armitage, E. Liddell, Stained Glass (1959)
Baker, John, English Stained Glass (1960)
Baker, John, and Lammer, H, English Stained Glass of the Medieval Period (1978)
Batsford, H. and Fry, C., The Greater English Church (1940)
Batsford, H. and Fry, C., The Cathedrals of England, (7th edn., 1948)

Beasley, E.A., Burrow's Glossary of Church Architecture, Furniture and Fittings (1937)
Beckwith, J., Early Medieval Art (1964)
Betjeman, J. (ed), Collins Guide to English Parish Churches (1958)
Binney M, and Burman, P, Change and Decay, the Future of our Churches (1977)
Blatch, Mervyn, A Guide to London Churches, (1978)
Bond, F., Screens and Galleries (1908)
Bond, F., The Chancel of English Churches (1916)
Bouquet, A.C., Church Brasses, British and Continental (1956)
Bottomley, F., The Church Explorer's Guide (1978)
Caiger-Smith, A., English Medieval Mural Paintings (1963)
Carpenter, S.C., Eighteenth Century Church and People (1959)
Chatfield, Mark, Churches the Victorians Forgot, (1979)
Clarke, B.F.L., Church Builders of the Nineteenth Century (1938)
Clifton-Taylor, A., English Parish Churches as Works of Art (1974)
Cook, M., Brasses (3rd edn., 1968)
Cox, J.C., Pulpits, Lecterns and Organs (1915)
Cox, J.C., English Church Fittings, Furniture and Accessories (1923)
Cox, J.C. and Ford, C.B., The Parish Churches of England (5th edn., 1947)
Cox, J.C. and Harvey, A., English Church Furniture (1907)
Croft-Murray, E., Decorative Painting in England, 1537–1870 (2 vols, 1962 & 1970)
Crossley, F., an important article on Welsh Screens in (1921)
Crossley, F., English Church Craftsmanship (2nd edn., 1947)
Crossley, F.: an important article on Welsh Screens in Archaeologia Cambrensis, Vol. XCVII, Part II, 1943, pp. 135ff.
Crossley, F. and Howard, F.E., English Church Woodwork (1942)
Delderfield, E.R., A Guide to Church Furniture (1966)
Eames, E.C., Medieval Tiles (1968)
Esdaile, K.A., English Monumental Sculpture since the Renaissance (1927)
Esdaile, K.A., English Church Monuments 1530–1840 (1946)

Gardner, A., *Minor English Wood Sculpture 1400–1550* (1958)

Gunnis, R., *Dictionary of British Sculptors 1660–1851* (1951)

Harries, J., *Discovering Stained Glass* (1968)

Harvey, J., *Mediaeval Craftsmen* (1975)

Henderson, G., *Early Medieval* (1972)

Henderson, G., *Gothic* (1967)

Henderson, P., *William Morris: his life, work and friends* (1967)

Kemp, B., *English Church Monuments* (in preparation)

Little, B., *Catholic Churches since 1623* (1966)

Macklin, H.W., *Monumental Brasses*, revised by J. Page-Phillips (1969)

Mann, Sir J.G., *Monumental Brasses* (1957)

Martindale, A., *Gothic Art*, (1967)

Norris, M., *Monumental Brasses* (2 vols. 1977 & 1978)

Oughton, Frederick, *Grinling Gibbons and the English Woodcarving Tradition*

Penny, Nicholas, *Church Monuments in Romantic England*, (1977)

Petersen, J.M., *Altar Frontals: their history and construction* (1962)

Pocknee, C.E., *The Christian Altar* (1963)

Prior, E.S. & Gardner, A., *An Account of Medieval Figure Sculpture in England* (1912)

Procter, F. and Frere, W.H., *A New History of the Book of Common Prayer* (1902)

Read, H., *English Stained Glass* (1926)

Reyntiens, P., *The Technique of Stained Glass* (2nd edn., 1977)

Rickert, M., *Painting in Britain: the Middle Ages* (2nd edn., 1965)

Rouse, E.C., *Discovering Wall Paintings* (revised edn., 1971)

Smith, E., Cook, O. & Hutton, G., *English Parish Churches* (1976)

Smith, J.C.D., *A Guide to Church Woodcarvings* (1974)

Stone, L., *Sculpture in Britain: The Middle Ages* (2nd edn., 1972)

Tate, W.E., *The Parish Chest* (3rd Edn., 1969)

Vallance, A., *English Church Screens* (1936)

Vallance, A., *Greater English Church Screens* (1947)

Victoria and Albert Museum, *Victorian Church Art* (Exhibition Catalogue) (1971)

Wall, J.C., *Porches and Fonts* (1912)

Whiffen, M., *Stuart and Georgian Churches* (1947–48)

Whinney, M., *Sculpture in Britain 1530–1830* (1964)

Woodforde, C., *English Stained and Painted Glass* (1954)

Zarnecki, G., *English Romanesque Sculpture, 1066–1140* (1951)

Zarnecki, G., *English Romanesque Lead Sculpture: Lead Fonts of the Twelfth Century* (1957)

Zarnecki, G., *Later English Romanesque Sculpture, 1140–1210*, (1953)

Finally, many counties and regions have their own church guides. Among them are: Cautley, H.M., *Norfolk Churches* (1949); Cautley, H.M., *Suffolk Churches and their Treasures* (3rd edn., 1952); Cobb, G., *London City Churches* (revised edn., 1977); Slader, J.M., *The Churches of Devon* (1968), Wickham, A.K., *Churches of Somerset* (1965), Richards, R., *Old Cheshire Churches* (1947); and Verey, D., *Cotswold Churches* (1976).

Index

Architects, Artists & Craftsmen